BASIC

COVER

⁞ BASIC ⁞
COVER

INDEX BOOK, SL
Aragó 174, 16º 3ª
08011 Barcelona
T +34 93 454 55 47
F +34 93 454 84 38
ib@indexbook.com
www.indexbook.com

Publisher: Sylvie Estrada
Design: Anna Blanco
Text: Maureen Cooley
ISBN: 978-84-15308-37-9

Printed in Spain.

BASIC

COVER

PAGES

008-079

BOOKS

Woody van Amen
Deep Space
Signaal
Switch
2006/
Good Vibrations
Glow
2005/
De kunst van TL
Design in Dialoog
Geregistreerd Museum
Regine Schumann
2004/
Open/Closed
Paul Critchley
10.000e bezoeker
2003/
Old materials/blacklight/new art
2002/
Opening

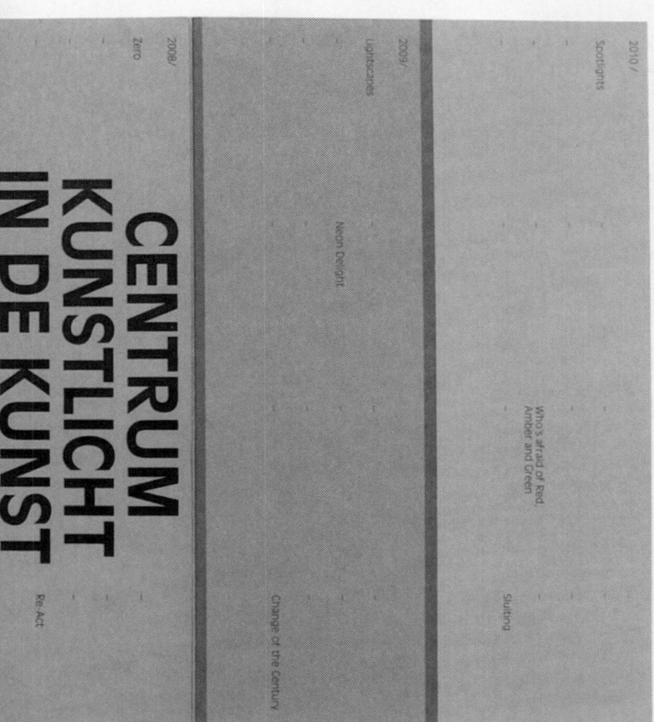

001

RAW COLOR

CLIENT I Centrum Kunstlicht in de Kunst

The Light Art Museum in Eindhoven focuses on contemporary art dealing in one way or another with light. This can mean that the medium of artificial light sources is used. Besides the museum's own collection, the main focus is on group- and solo exhibitions. Nationally and internationally renowned artists presented their work in Eindhoven, including Dan Flavin, Bruce Nauman, Nan Hoover, and Zero among others. For several years we have been working as graphic designers for the museum, doing all their external communication.

In the 2011 the museum stopped its activities. For this reason a book was commissioned to give an overview of the museum's activities from 2002 – 2011.

The cover is an 8-page unfoldable timeline that is structured by year and colour. The inside is Japanese bound, allowing the years and images to blend into each other. The photos are threaded in a way that the reader gets the impression of browsing through one long timeline, resulting in one big gradient. All colours are created from the CMYK palette and a specific shade is assigned to each year.

INES BARNER UND
GÜNTER BLAMBERGER (HRSG.)
LITERATOR 2010
Dozentur für Weltliteratur
DANIEL KEHLMANN
1
MORPHOMATA
LECTURES COLOGNE

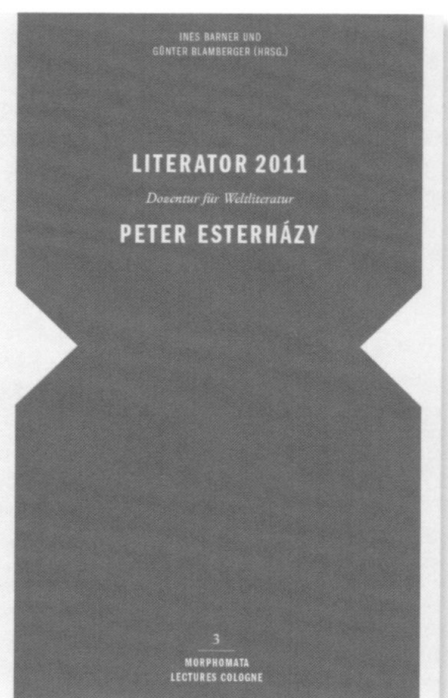
INES BARNER UND
GÜNTER BLAMBERGER (HRSG.)
LITERATOR 2011
Dozentur für Weltliteratur
PETER ESTERHÁZY
3
MORPHOMATA
LECTURES COLOGNE

INES BARNER UND
GÜNTER BLAMBERGER (HRSG.)
LITERATOR 2012
Dozentur für Weltliteratur
CHRISTIAN KRACHT
4
MORPHOMATA
LECTURES COLOGNE

ALAN SHAPIRO
RE-FASHIONING
ANAKREON IN
CLASSICAL ATHENS
2
MORPHOMATA
LECTURES COLOGNE

STEFAN HORST
ÄSTHETISCHE
MÖGLICHKEITEN DES
NOTWENDIGEN
Eine Figuration der Dimensionen
5
MORPHOMATA
LECTURES COLOGNE

OLIVER FUNKE
REFIGURATIONEN IM
POLITISCHEN
Dynamische Kulturen im Wandel
der Zeit
6
MORPHOMATA
LECTURES COLOGNE

002

SICHTVERMERK

CLIENT | Morphomata Centre for Advanced Studies, University of Cologne

The Morphomata Centre for Advanced Studies is publishing this series of books, which is in fact two series. The first is the so-called "Literator" series which is about one author, holding the two-week "Chair of World Literature". The second series is comprised of monographs of the centre's fellows. The aim of the design was to distinguish the two topics from each other while making it clear that they both belong to the same series. This goal is reached by rotating the graphic elements by 90 degrees and giving the series different coloured-atmospheres, reddish for the monographs and blueish for the "Literator" volumes.

003

SICHTVERMERK

CLIENT | Aesthetic Figurations of the Political, Centre for Advanced Studies at the University of Luxemburg

Politics have aesthetic aspects that are to be researched. So does *Aesthetic Figurations of the Political*, a Centre for Advanced Studies at the University of Luxemburg. This design of the book series reflects the "imaginary dimension of politics". Only the beholder will be able to interpret the abstract six-cornered forms as perspectivically stretched rectangles. The forms change from volume to volume as well as the colours.

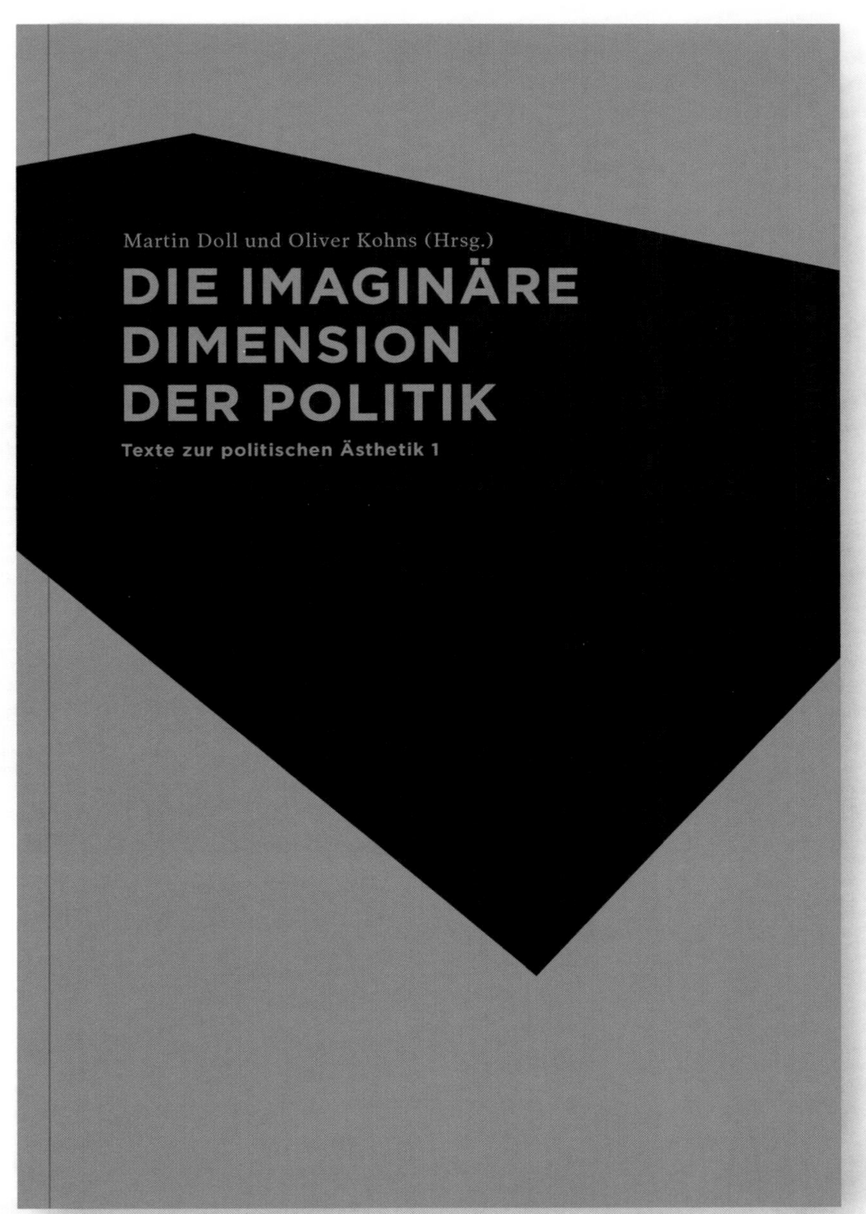
Martin Doll und Oliver Kohns (Hrsg.)
DIE IMAGINÄRE
DIMENSION
DER POLITIK
Texte zur politischen Ästhetik 1

004

RUN DESIGN

CLIENT | Random House Mondadori

Collection of covers for the trade paperback edition of the complete works of Borges. Time, the infinite, mirrors, labyrinths, reality, identity and fantastic elements. Impossible, unclassifiable covers.

Contemporánea
JORGE LUIS
BORGES
Historia
de la
eternidad
DEBOLSILLO
Contemporánea
JORGE LUIS
BORGES
El libro
de arena
DEBOLSILLO
Contemporánea
JORGE LUIS
BORGES
Textos
recobrados
(1956-1986)
DEBOLSILLO
Contemporánea
JORGE LUIS
BORGES
El Aleph
DEBOLSILLO
Contemporánea
JORGE LUIS
BORGES
El hacedor
DEBOLSILLO
DEBOLSILLO
DEBOLSILLO

Madame Bovary
Gustave Flaubert
Madame Bovary Gustave Flaubert
1

Great Expectations
Charles Dickens
Great Expectations Charles Dickens
2

Wuthering Heights
Emily Brontë
Wuthering Heights Emily Brontë
3

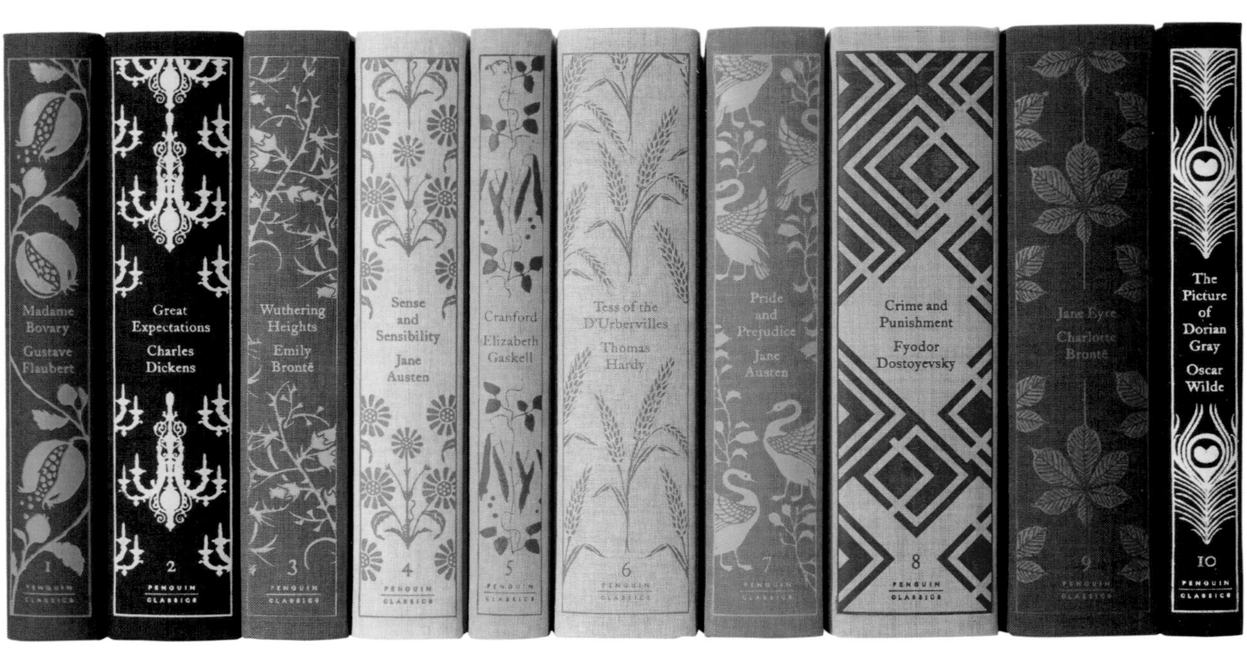

Madame Bovary Gustave Flaubert 1
Great Expectations Charles Dickens 2
Wuthering Heights Emily Brontë 3
Sense and Sensibility Jane Austen 4
Cranford Elizabeth Gaskell 5
Tess of the D'Urbervilles Thomas Hardy 6
Pride and Prejudice Jane Austen 7
Crime and Punishment Fyodor Dostoyevsky 8
Jane Eyre Charlotte Brontë 9
The Picture of Dorian Gray Oscar Wilde 10

005

CORALIE BICKFORD-SMITH

CLIENT | Penguin Classics UK

These titles explore my obsession with creating beautiful, timeless artifacts for people to enjoy, cherish and pass on. Sumptuous, tactile books that evoke a rich heritage of bookbinding while retaining fresh appeal to modern readers, that both stand out in bookshops and have a longevity appropriate to the contents.

Titles:
Crime and Punishment – Fyodor Dostoyevsky
Madame Bovary – Gustave Flaubert
Great Expectations – Charles Dickens
Wuthering Heights – Emily Brontë
Sense and Sensibility – Jane Austen
Cranford – Elizabeth Gaskell
Tess of the d'Urbervilles – Thomas Hardy
Pride and Prejudice – Jane Austen
Jane Eyre – Charlotte Brontë
The Picture of Dorian Gray – Oscar Wilde

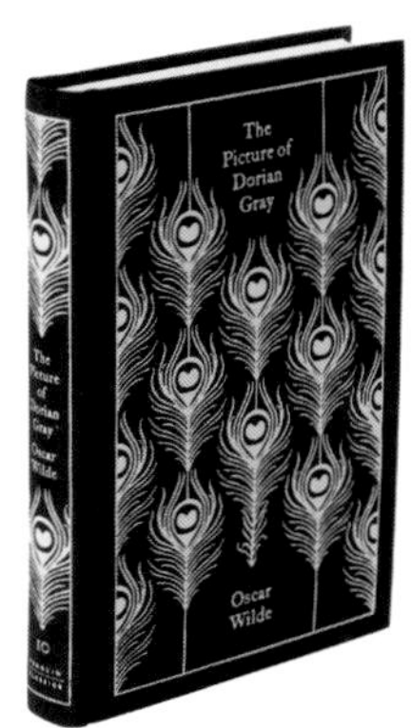

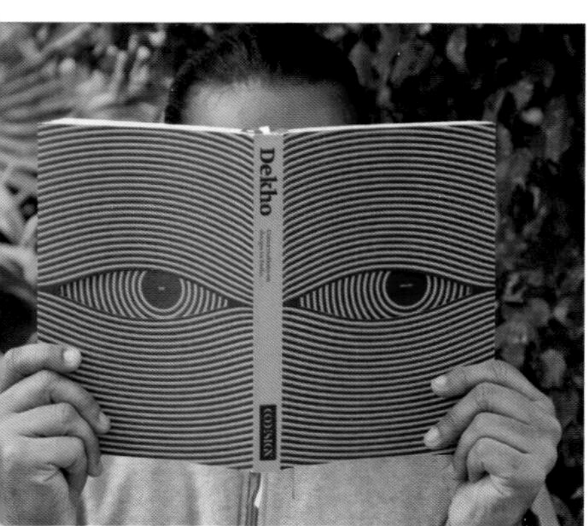

006

CODESIGN

CLIENT | Codesign / Self-initiated

Dekho is an anthology of inspirational conversations with designers in India, probing their stories for cues to the development of design in India and highlighting approaches that are unique to designing for India.

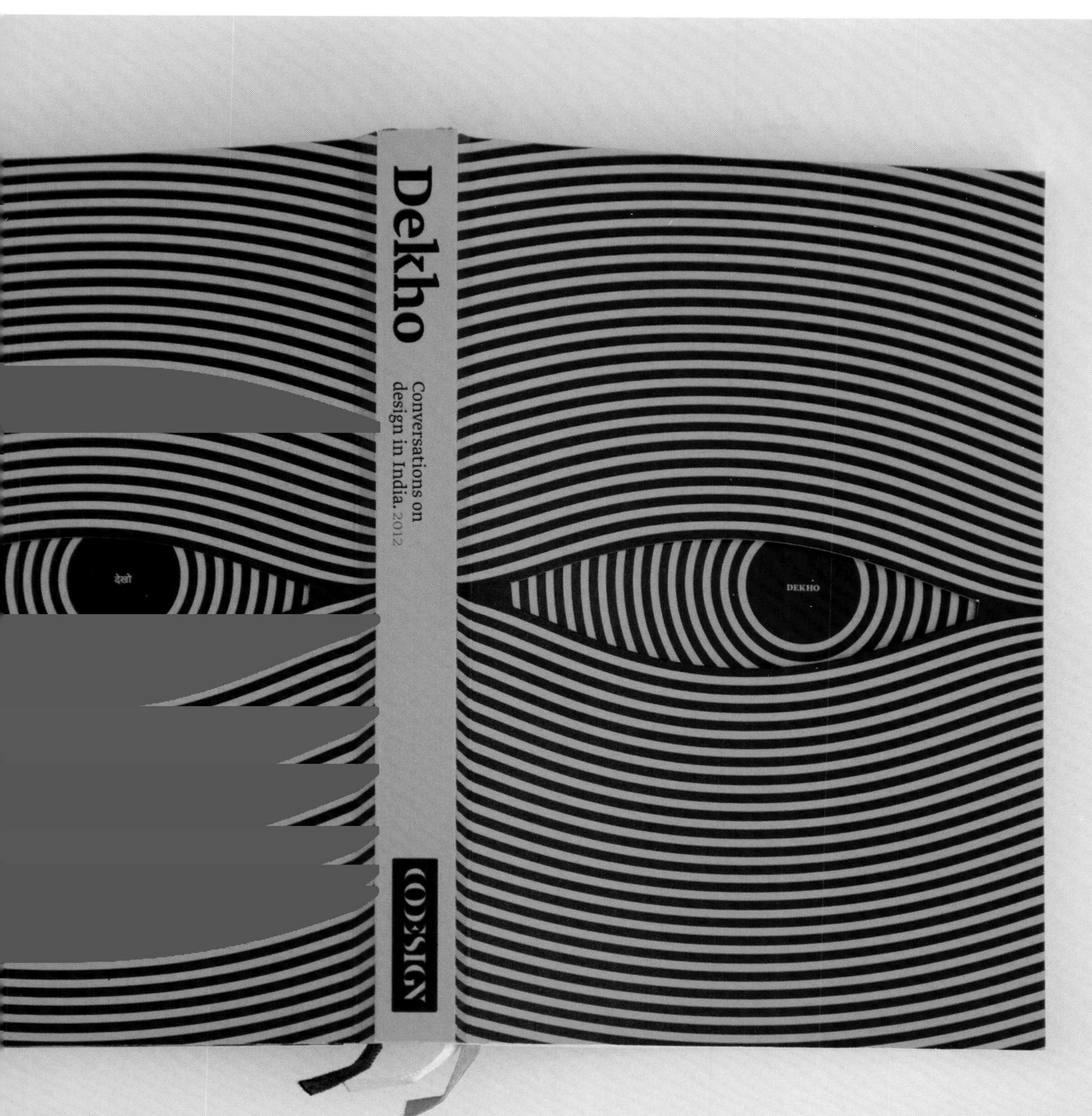
Dekho
Conversations on
design in India. 2012
CODESIGN
देखो
DEKHO

007

RUN DESIGN

CLIENT | Grupo Tragaluz

"A journey of a thousand miles begins with a single step." -Laozi (579 - 490 A.C.).

4,997 km Pekin - Lhasa is a book that collects the experiences of an intense journey and is edited to celebrate the inauguration of the new Chinese restaurant from Grupo Tragaluz, La Xina.

All the materials were chosen with great care, trying to respect the Eastern sensibility. It was developed over several months in order to create a complete work that perfectly integrates shape and content, conceiving the book as a work of art, looking for the balance between the contemporaneity of Paula Ospina's photos, the delicacy of the Chinese culture and the freshness of a country in constant evolution.

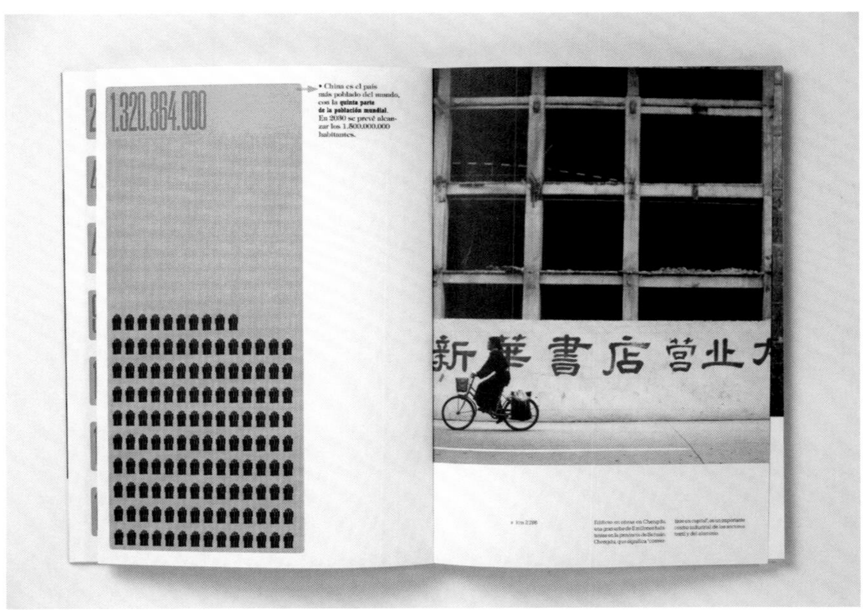

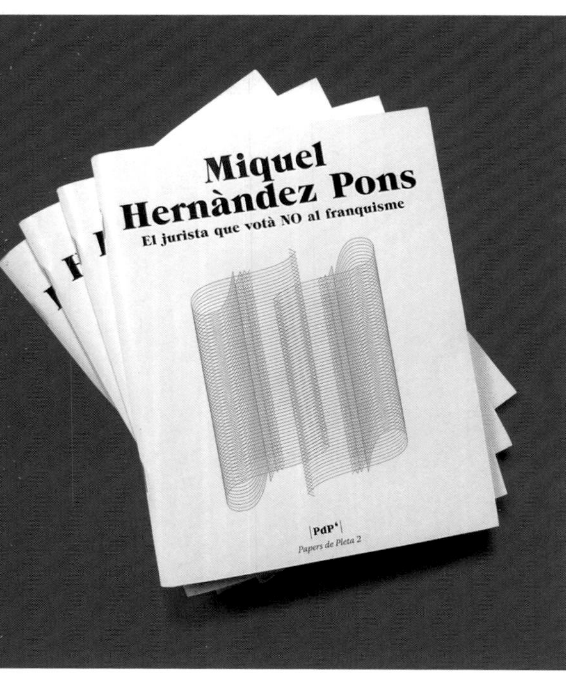

008

DÚCTIL

CLIENT | Llibres de la Terra

Design of these new editorial collections.

"Llibres de la Terra" (Earth Books) brings together studies, investigative work and outreach projects, etc. It is defined as a new brand of editing books, preferably unpublished ones. At the same time, it delimits families by homogeneous content (history, anthropology, folklore, biography, science, nature, etc.).

"Papers de Pleta" (Pleta Papers). If a "pleta" is an agricultural term for a small valley, then this collection is a true "pleta" of texts, as it collects original texts that are proportionally smaller than the other collection, "Llibres de la Terra".

Dos mil anys d'Església,
quatre bisbes menorquins
Guillem Gonyalons Coll, Antoni Vila Camps
Manuel Moll Salord, Sebastià Taltavull Anglada
| LLdT* |
Llibres de la Terra Història Biografia

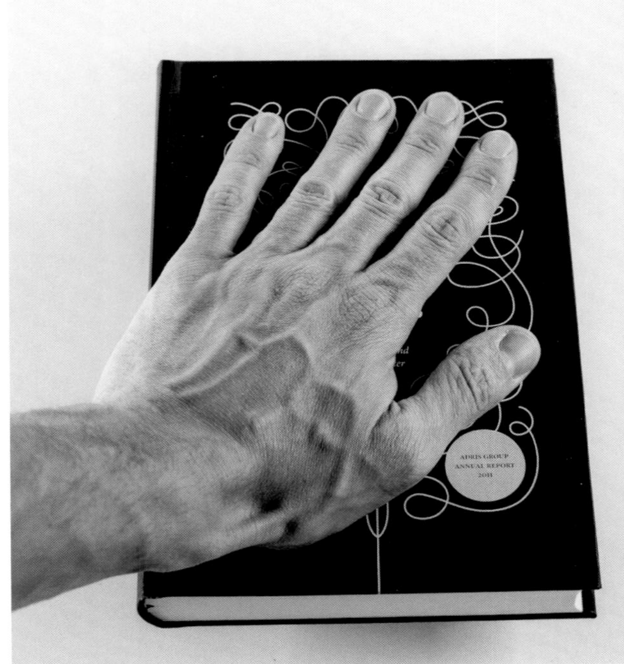

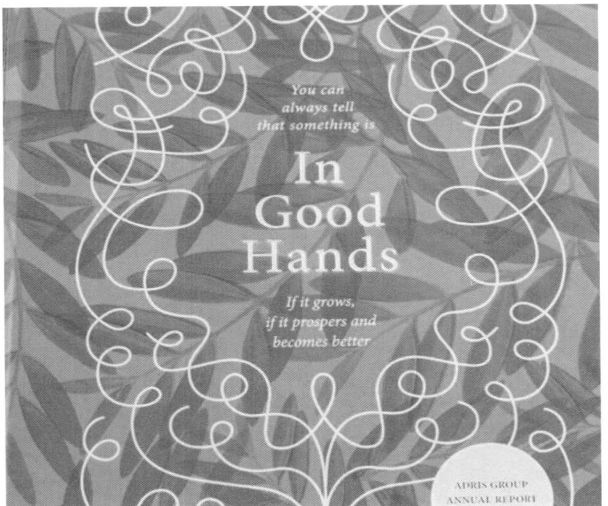

009

BRUKETA&ZINIC OM

CLIENT | Adris Group

Good things grow in good hands. Adris Group is a company owned by its employees which is why it has grown in the past year, despite the crisis. Adris Group's annual report entitled *In good hands* reveals floral details when heated by the palms of the hands, metaphorically illustrating how hands can achieve anything.

The same specially-calibrated thermo colour used on the covers was also used for the inside illustrations, and the concept of the annual report is also evoked by the short stories from workers-stockholders.

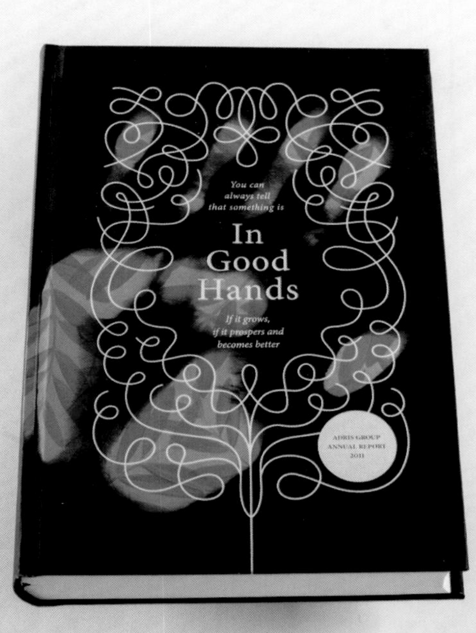
You can
always tell
that something is
In
Good
Hands
If it grows,
if it prospers and
becomes better
ADRIS GROUP
ANNUAL REPORT
2011

You can
always tell
that something is
In
Good
Hands
If it grows,
if it prospers and
becomes better

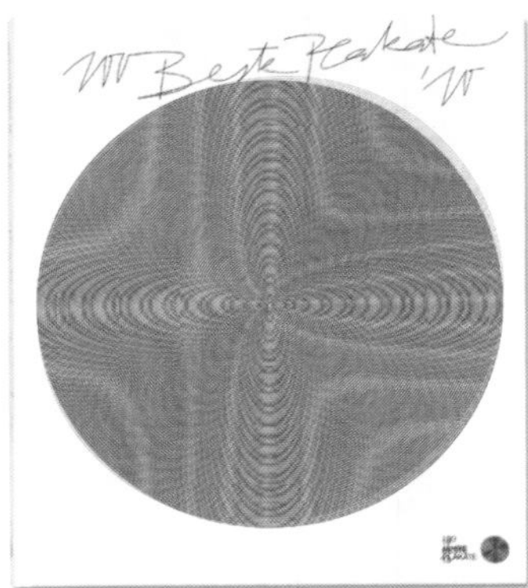
100 Beste Plakate '10

100 Beste Plakate '10
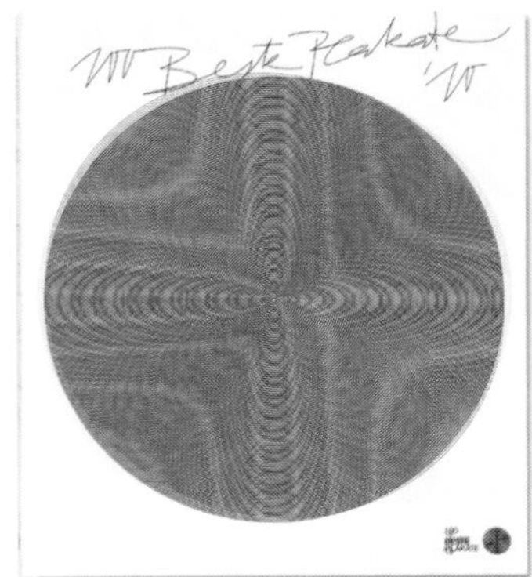
100 Beste Plakate '10
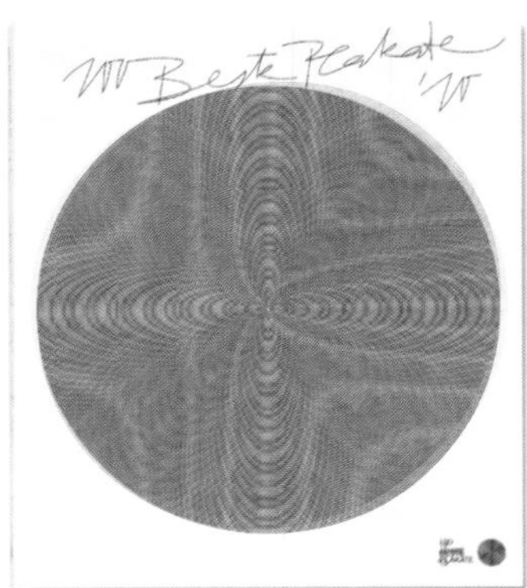
100 Beste Plakate '10
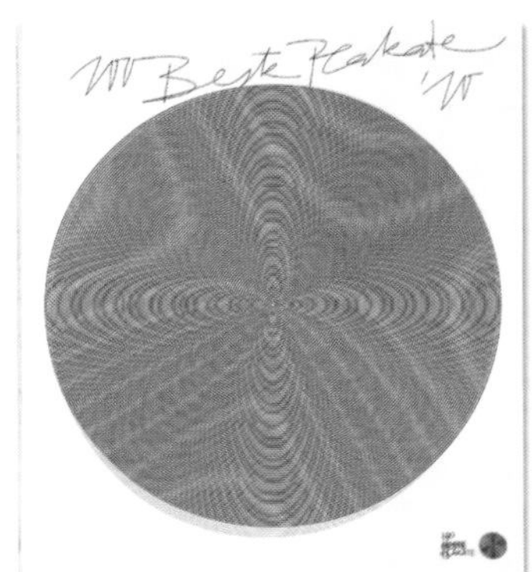
100 Beste Plakate '10

100 Beste Plakate '10

100 Beste Plakate '10
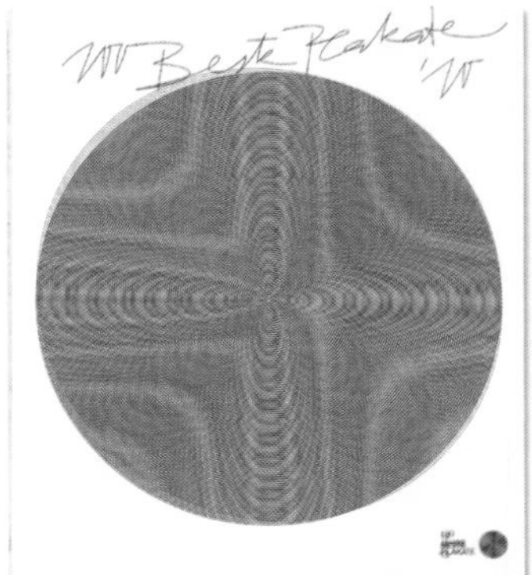
100 Beste Plakate '10

100 Beste Plakate '10

010

L2M3 KOMMUNIKATIONSDESIGN GMBH

CLIENT I 100 beste Plakate e.V.

One hundred circles stand for the *100 Best Posters* in the logo, with the overlapping circles creating a moiré pattern. By means of shifts and changes of colours, a hundred different poster designs are created in the printing process.

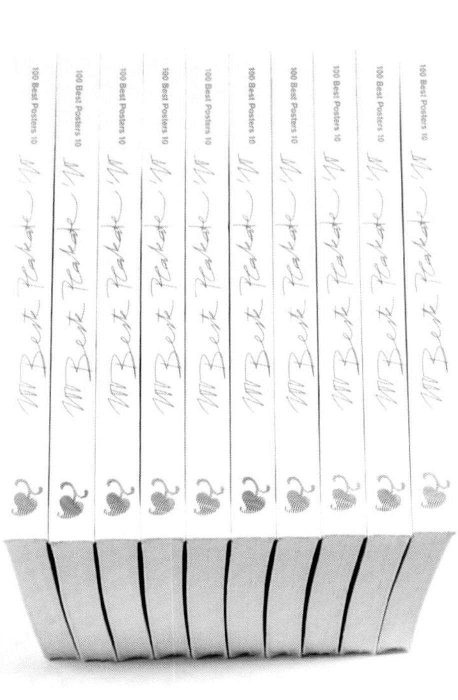

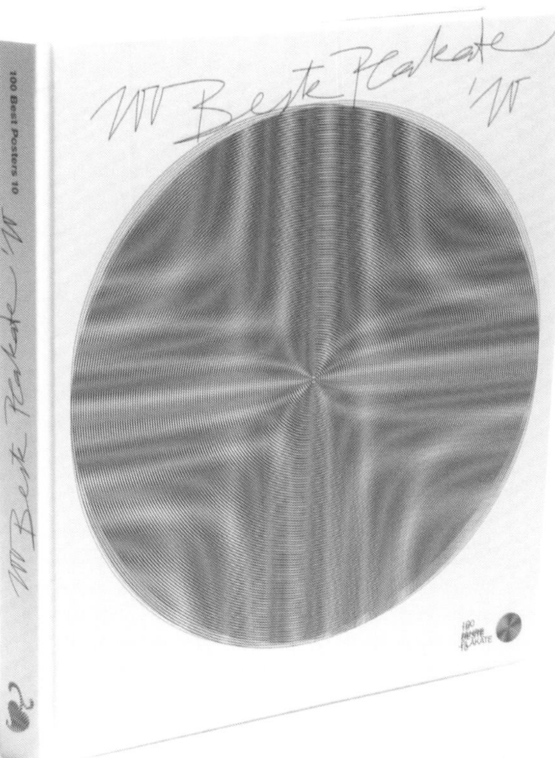

MY OBSESSION
YOUR IMPRESSION

011

PONTO

CLIENT | Self-initiated

MOYI is a self-initiated project that was born out of the day-to-day contact with old and new visual collections. It first started as a book, but it's an ongoing project, that will soon be transported into other formats, such as the website. The book is the house of the first discussion where we analysed the relations between personal collections and haunted obsessions with the values of appropriation in art, while looking specifically into internet art, since it has also become part of our day-to-day visual collection.

012

PONTO

CLIENT | Self-initiated

This book is an exploration of new ways of reading by using different optical patterns. Inspired by the composition of the song "Williams Mix", by John Cage, there are six different patterns that interact with the Western culture reading format. These patterns were inspired by the golden-section rule of geometry and work as tools to determine new reading interpretations. The book records the process.

S
EC
T
IO
N

013

ARIS ZENONE STUDIO

CLIENT | Département de Pédiatrie - CHUV

This is a summary book of a 3-day congress that questions and speaks about childhood dangers in everyday life. We designed a simple and useful typographic layout with the focus on readability. To illustrate every chapter we used basic and simple children's safety games that we turned into monsters.

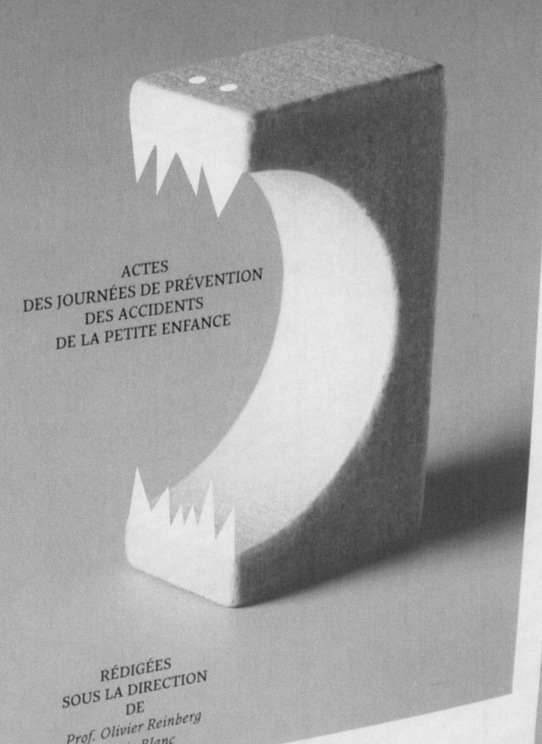
LAUSANNE
27
et
28
MAI
2009
Un accident
est si vite... évité!
ACTES
DES JOURNÉES DE PRÉVENTION
DES ACCIDENTS
DE LA PETITE ENFANCE
RÉDIGÉES
SOUS LA DIRECTION
DE
Prof. Olivier Reinberg
Valérie Blanc
UN ACCIDENT
EST
SI VITE...
ÉVITÉ!
LAUSANNE
27 ET 28
MAI
2009
ACTES DES JOURNÉES
DE PRÉVENTION
DES ACCIDENTS
DE LA PETITE ENFANCE
RÉDIGÉES
SOUS LA DIRECTION DE
Prof. Olivier Reinberg
Valérie Blanc

32 - 33▲

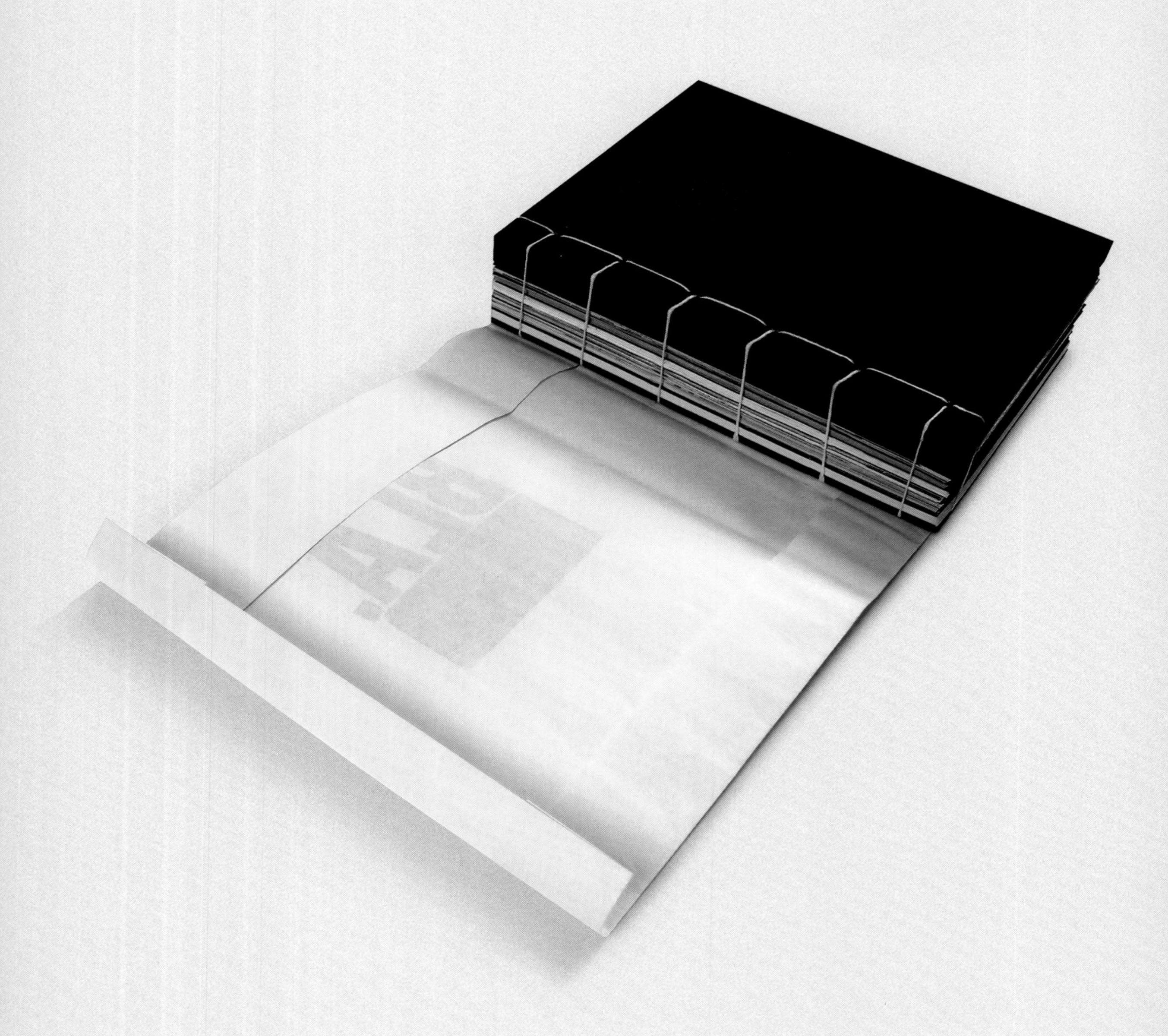

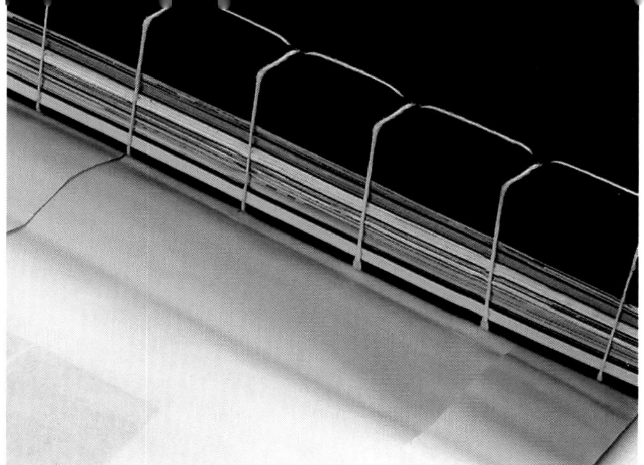

014

ALBERTO HERNÁNDEZ

CLIENT | Self-initiated

Visual exploration about narration documenting 24 moments from my day over a week. In order to tell the story of each of these 7 days, onomatopoeias, colours, Google images, emoticons, signs, security camera images and logotypes were used.

015

WILLIAM HALL

CLIENT | London College of Fashion

Commissioned by London College of Fashion in its centenary year and edited and conceived by Louise Clarke, contributors to *The Measure* include Jimmy Choo, Giles Deacon, Zandra Rhodes, Paul Smith, Mario Testino and Vivienne Westwood.

Canvassing a cross section of fashion and design practitioners, academics and historians, *The Measure* asks each contributor to reflect on the effect London has had on contemporary culture – and specifically fashion – over the last century.

The images (right hand page) and text (left hand page) are strictly separated allowing an already image-rich book to be read purely as a visual essay. This demarcation is exaggerated by placing the image page at right angles.

The index and contents page are combined in a fold-out back cover. The position of each entry relates both to the page number and the eponymous tape measure positioned alongside.

Tim Gutt's Tall Fashion image envelopes the outside, playfully interpreting the book title, and making an unexpected and engaging cover.

For the book launch a limited edition poster dustjacket was made featuring Nick Knight's 3D Naomi Campbell image. This lustrous, black and gold wrapping gave the book great visual impact at a party attended by many of the contributors.

William Hall contributed an essay on Terry Jones, the founder and creative director of i-D magazine.

The Measure
The Measure

016

BELIEVE IN®

CLIENT | Bernadette Jiwa

You are the Map Maker features inspirational insights from 13 international, creative and resourceful entrepreneurs.

The book uses a structured grid and graphic system based around the key contributors from the book. Each contributor is symbolised by a cross-hair within a circle, locating their mark or place within the book's own map system. These marks form part of the system or theme of the book, and become the navigational device throughout, highlighting the sections and featured contributors. They also act as a playful graphical element throughout, evolving and sympathetic from page to page, dictating and changing the pace of the book.

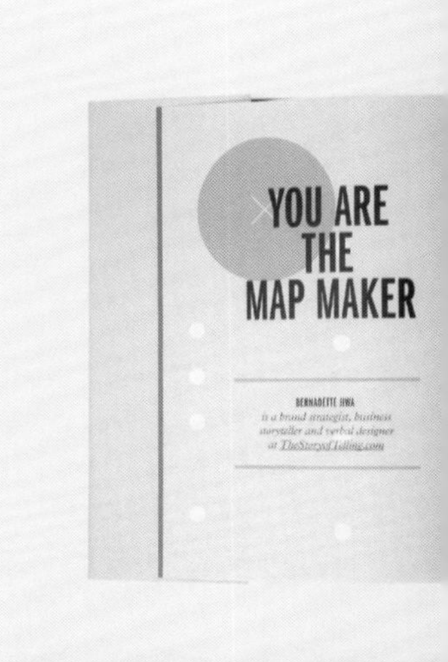

With contributions from
ERIC KARJALUTO
NUBBY TWIGLET
CHRIS GUILLEBEAU
DAVID AIREY
LEE NEWHAM
MARK BLOOM
REESE SPYKERMAN
JESSICA HISCHE

Credits
DESIGN & ART DIRECTION
Believe in™
www.believein.co.uk
WRITTEN AND PRODUCED BY
Bernadette Jiwa
www.thestoryoftelling.com
THANKS TO
Eric Karjaluto
Nubby Twiglet
Chris Guillebeau
David Airey
Lee Newham
Mark Bloom
Reese Spykerman
Jessica Hische
Derek Sivers
Jonathan Woodward
Blair Thomson
Lea Woodward
Tara Gentile
VISIT
www.youarethemapmaker.com

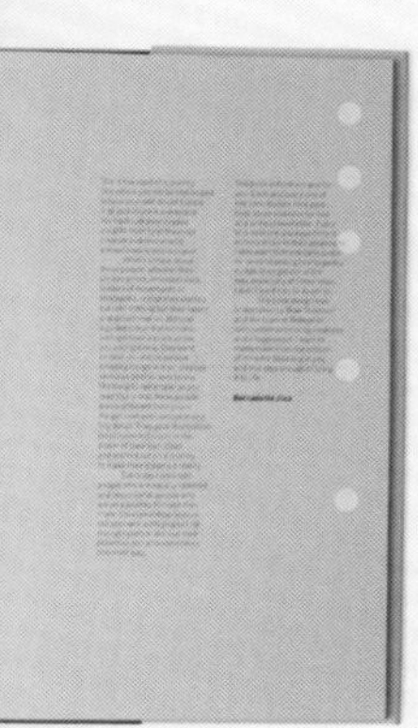

017

CORALIE BICKFORD-SMITH

CLIENT | Penguin Classics UK

I designed the patterns in an attempt to give these books something of the elegance and glamour of the Art Deco period, with the sense of ornate detail fused with the modernist aesthetic of mechanical repetition. The combination of metallic foil and matte paper is designed to feel good in the hand as well as look good on the shelf; by evoking the Jazz Age of Fitzgerald's stories, I hope these books will give a little tactile enhancement to the reading experience.

There are a couple of subtle nods to specific incidents: for instance, there's a suggestion of car wheels in the circular pattern on *The Great Gatsby*, with the vertical distortion hinting at a crash. Mainly though, the function of the patterns is to evoke the world of the books.

Titles:
The Beautiful and Damned
This Side of Paradise
The Last Tycoon
Flappers and Philosophers
The Great Gatsby
Tender is the Night

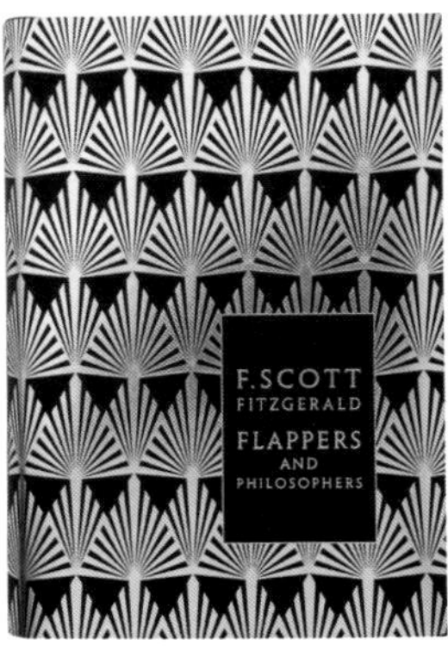
F.SCOTT
FITZGERALD
FLAPPERS
AND
PHILOSOPHERS

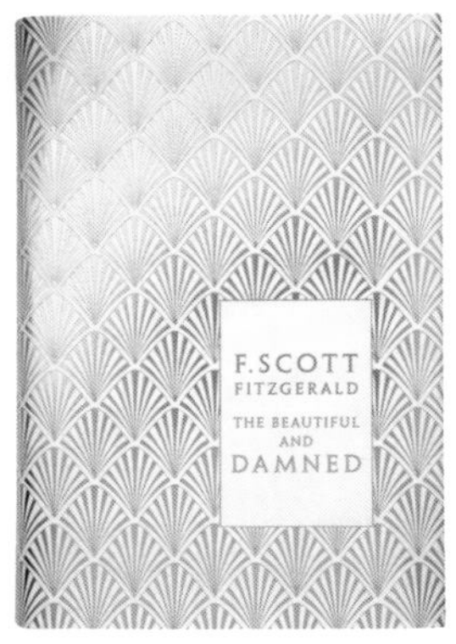
F.SCOTT
FITZGERALD
THE BEAUTIFUL
AND
DAMNED

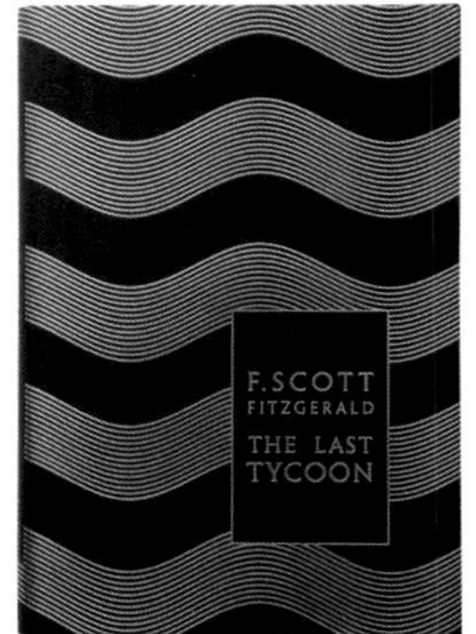
F.SCOTT
FITZGERALD
THE LAST
TYCOON

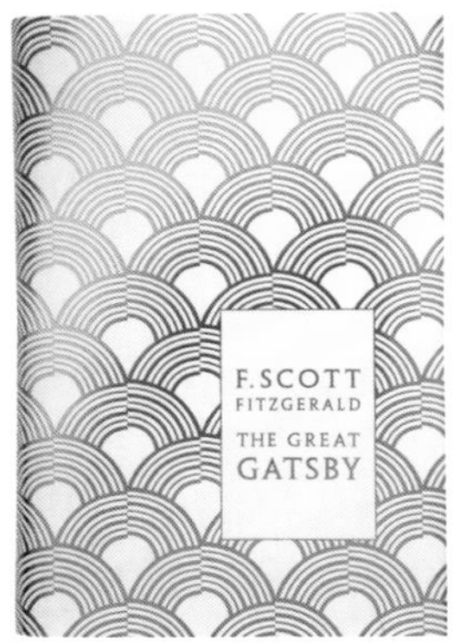
F.SCOTT
FITZGERALD
THE GREAT
GATSBY

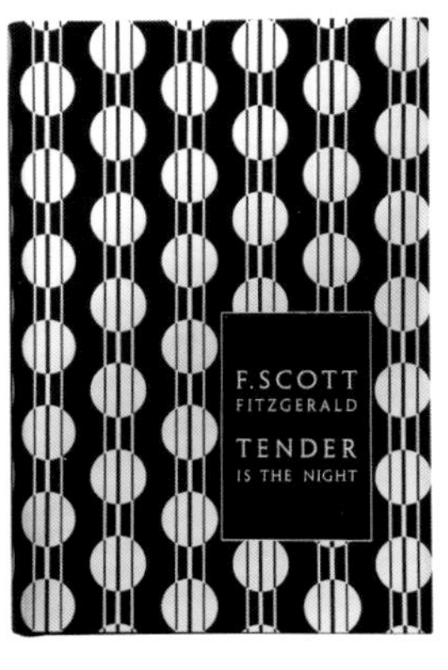
F.SCOTT
FITZGERALD
TENDER
IS THE NIGHT

F.SCOTT
FITZGERALD
THIS SIDE OF
PARADISE

F.SCOTT
FITZGERALD
TENDER
IS THE NIGHT

F.SCOTT
FITZGERALD
THE LAST
TYCOON

F.SCOTT
FITZGERALD
THE GREAT
GATSBY

F.SCOTT
FITZGERALD
THE BEAUTIFUL
AND
DAMNED

SO·WE·BEAT·ON,
BOATS·AGAINST
THE·CURRENT,
BORNE·BACK
CEASELESSLY
INTO·THE·PAST
BOOKMARK

L & F

018

THE RAINY MONDAY®

CLIENT I Luis & Fina

"All life deserves to be told."
These were the words that Luis and Fina used to define this autobiographical limited-edition piece. A large-format book, with artisan details and protected by a special container designed to protect embellish. A story and a look at the past, present and future that this couple decided to make to share with their loved ones.

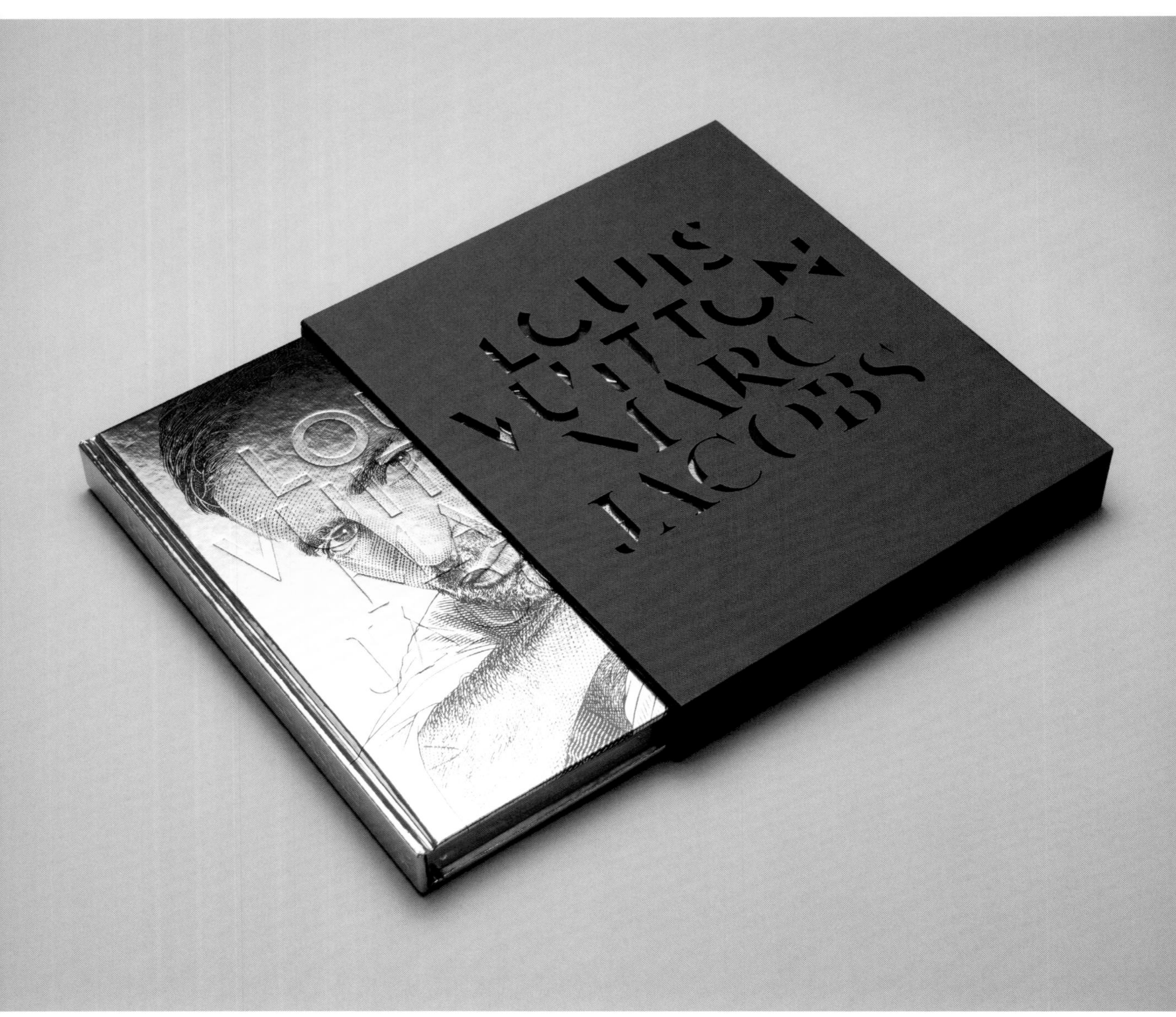
LOUIS
VUITTON
MARC
JACOBS

019

NR2154

CLIENT | Rizzoli/Louis Vuitton

Published to coincide with an exhibition of the same name at the Musée des Arts Décoratifs in Paris, *Louis Vuitton/Marc Jacobs* celebrates the roles that the two men played in the evolution of the brand, 100 years apart. With a limited edition and trade edition, the book also features two custom typefaces.

020

NAKANO DESIGN OFFICE

CLIENT | Musashino Art University Museum & Library

The exhibition introduced book designs of Japanese literary books which were published from the Meiji period to the early Showa period.

However, while we represented typography and materiality which were often seen in book design around that time, we tried to design a book that can give the today's reader another fresh impression.

＊近現代
のブック
デザイン
考I＊書
物にとっ
ての美＊

造本の美

浦島
いとし可愛子に旅させ親よ。
辛苦いも旅で知る。

DET
SER
SORT
UD
MEN DET ER DET IKKE!

021

HVASS&HANNIBAL

CLIENT | Hyggefactory

This is a book cover for a project called Ordskælv, initiated by Hyggefactory's Karen Siercke. The book is a collection of essays written by 13-21 year-olds who have all experienced the loss of a parent. Through weekly workshops since September 2011 the young writers have received guidance from professional authors and journalists, and the result is a handful of beautiful and touching stories. The essays are all illustrated by artists, including names like Michael Kvium, Bjørn Nørgaard and HuskMitNavn.

022

A BEAUTIFUL DESIGN

CLIENT | The Browsing Copy Project

The Browsing Copy project focuses on unloved books, those that remained on the shelves unsold. These books are collected from bookstores and designers are invited to use them as canvasses to express their creativity. The 'before & after' results are documented.

This catalogue features both series one & two of the project and the 45 designers' contributions. Only 300 copies were printed and circulated around the world's best bookstores, shops and design studios, just for people to browse. It's not for sale. The catalogues will be collected back after a period of time and passed on to the next line of shops. The condition of the catalogues and the places they've been are documented on the website www.browsingcopy.com.

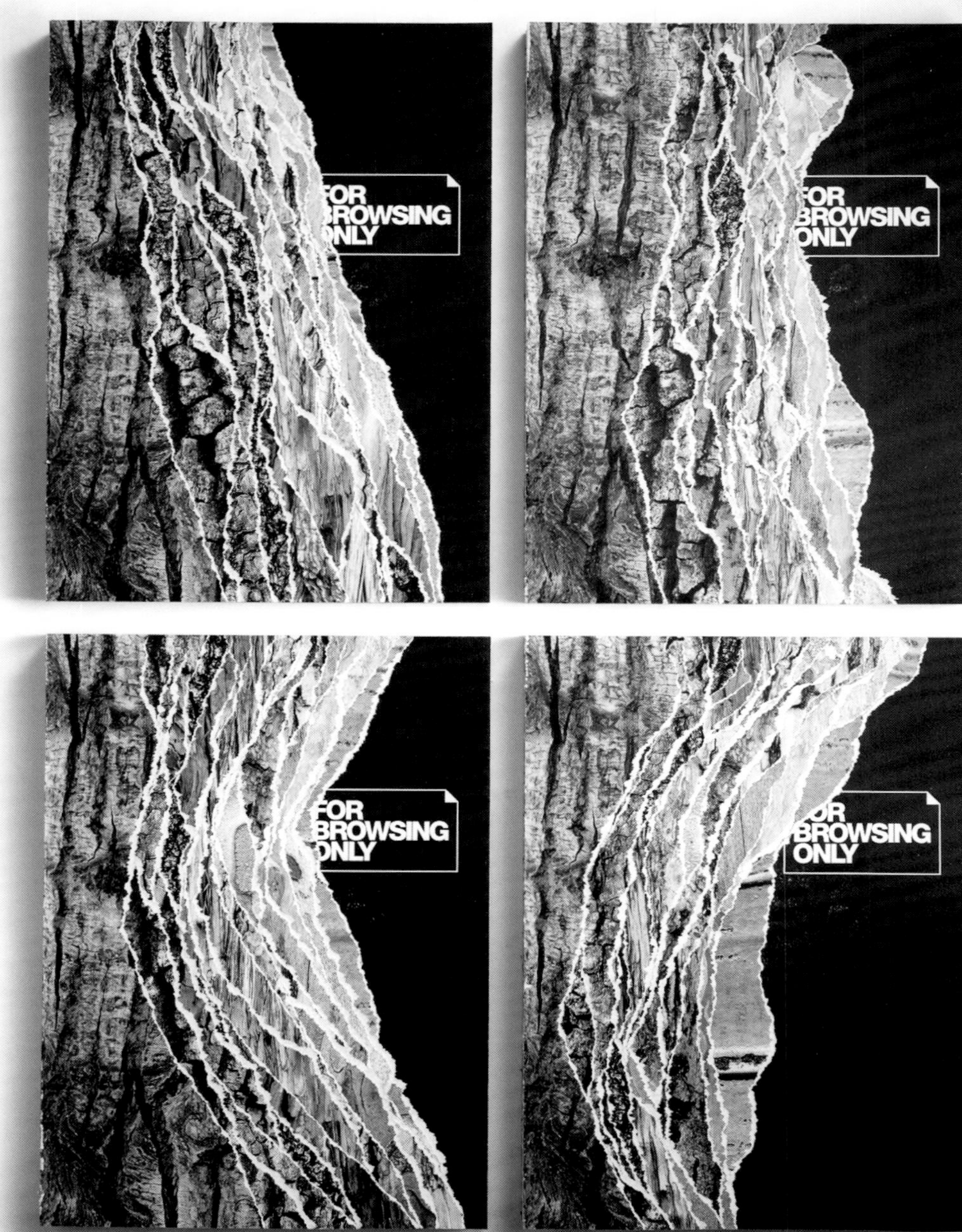
FOR
BROWSING
ONLY
FOR
BROWSING
ONLY
FOR
BROWSING
ONLY
FOR
BROWSING
ONLY

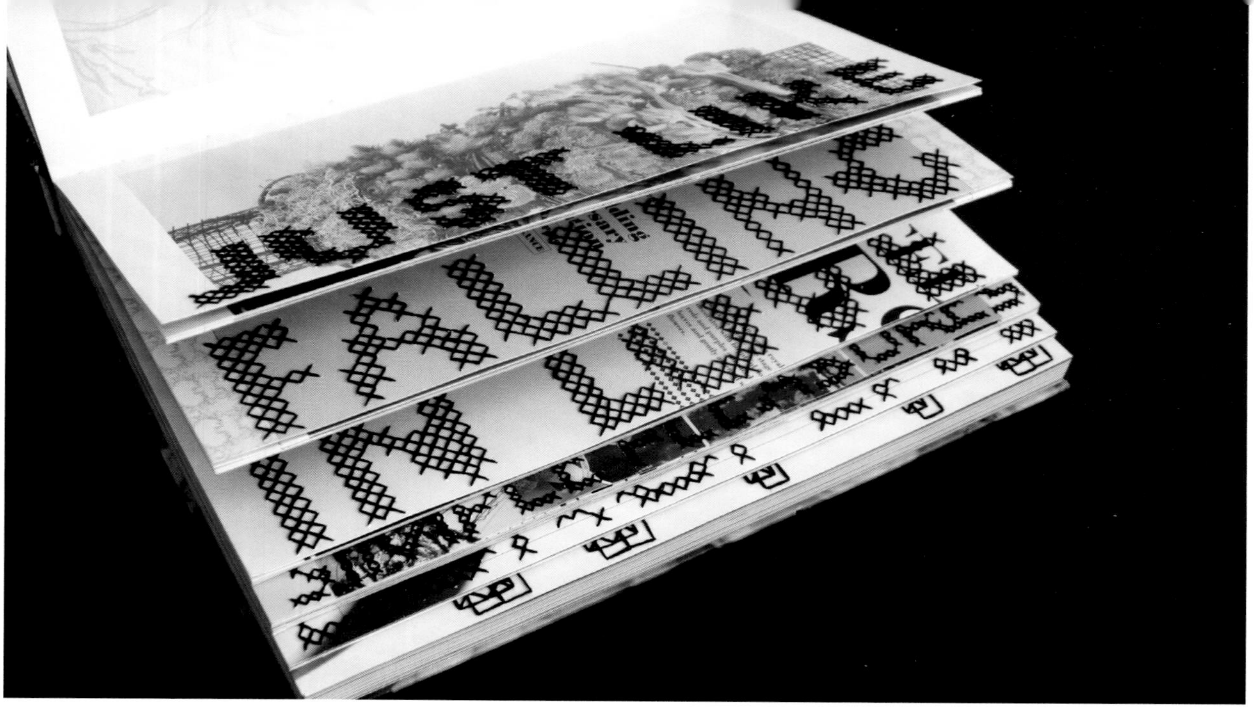

023

EVELIN KASIKOV

CLIENT | A Beautiful Design

Browsing Copy is a project by Singapore design studio A Beautiful Design, aiming to make better use of unsold books. Designers from all over the world were invited to give them new life as works of art. I received the following title to work with: *Flowers Never Last. The Impression Will. Exquisite flowers by Fiore Dorato.* Ignoring all the visuals I took fragments of author's text and stitched back into spreads in black cotton thread. I divided the book (consisting of 272 pages = 17 signatures/16 pages each) in half and applied stitched elements to the first half leaving the second half as it was.

Sensibilities

TIPOGRAFÍA. UNA EXPERIENCIA DOCENTE.
TYPEX
TYPE
HERNÁN ORDOÑEZ
¿QUÉ ES LO PROYECTUAL?
LIFE IN TYPE
DISEÑO DE LA COMUNICACIÓN
DE LO general A LO particular
Diseñar ES INNOVAR Y CUESTIONAR
PROCESOS DE CREACIÓN Y REALIZACIÓN
SSA
SABON
COMPRENSIÓN IDEOLÓGICA, TÉCNICA, ESTÉTICA.
IS Frutiger THE NEW SANS?
I AM Goudy and you?
EL CONCEPTO MANDA
La AVANT GARDE nos habla
EQUIVOCARSE Y SEGUIR BUSCANDO!
CASLON OLD FACE
me
Bodoni → POSTER? Ó BOLD?
TYPE IS ART?
ENSEÑAR Y REPRODUCIR
IDEAS
EL MEDIO ES EL MENSAJE
para el Times New Roman
gill?
GOD SAVE THE TYPE
CUT & PASTE IS TYPE TOO!
garamond
Troy Golden ¿PARA QUÉ?

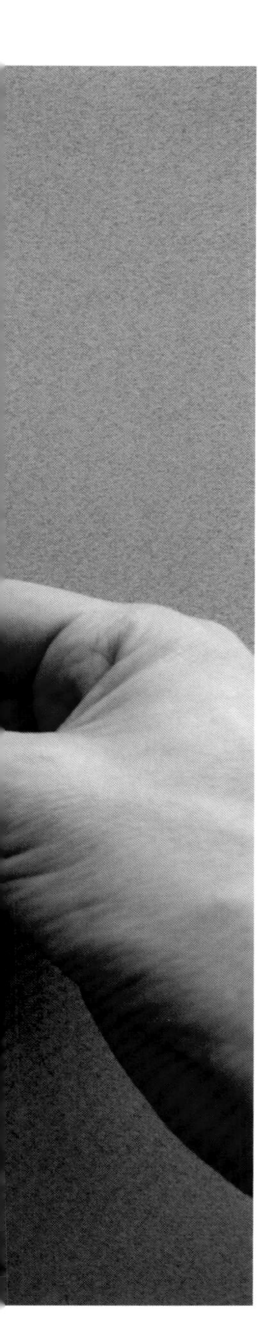

024

MAX-O-MATIC

CLIENT | Hernán Ordoñez / Index Book

Design and illustration for the book *Typex, A Teaching Experience*. The book, which is about the teaching of typography, proposes a cover where the "classics" of typography strike up an open dialogue about the possibilities of typography as a form of communication.

025

JIM WONG@ GOOD MORNING

CLIENT | Roundtable Community

Published by Roundtable Community, *Vision of Civil Society* is a publication of collected articles written by Dr Chan Kin Mun about the development and happenings of Hong Kong Civil Societies.

We were commissioned to design the cover of the book. A calm, peaceful aqua colour was used to emphasis the character of Dr Chan's critiques toward politics, which are objective and temperate. The custom-made title was used to reflect the message of the chaotic situation in Hong Kong.

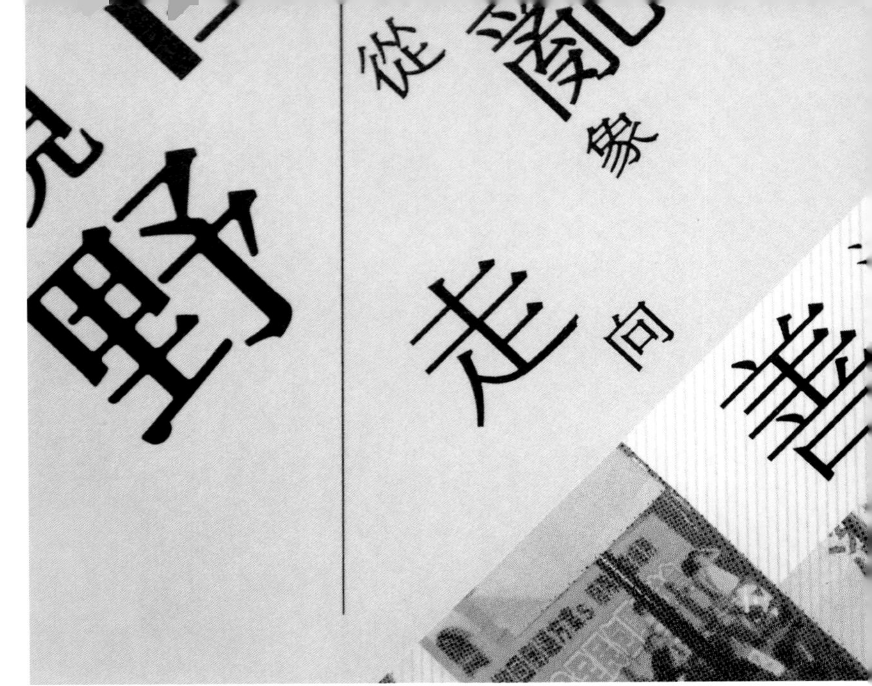

Drift 010 公民社會視野 從亂象走向善治

Drift 010 公民社會視野 從亂象走向善治

Drift 010 公民社會視野 從亂象走向善治

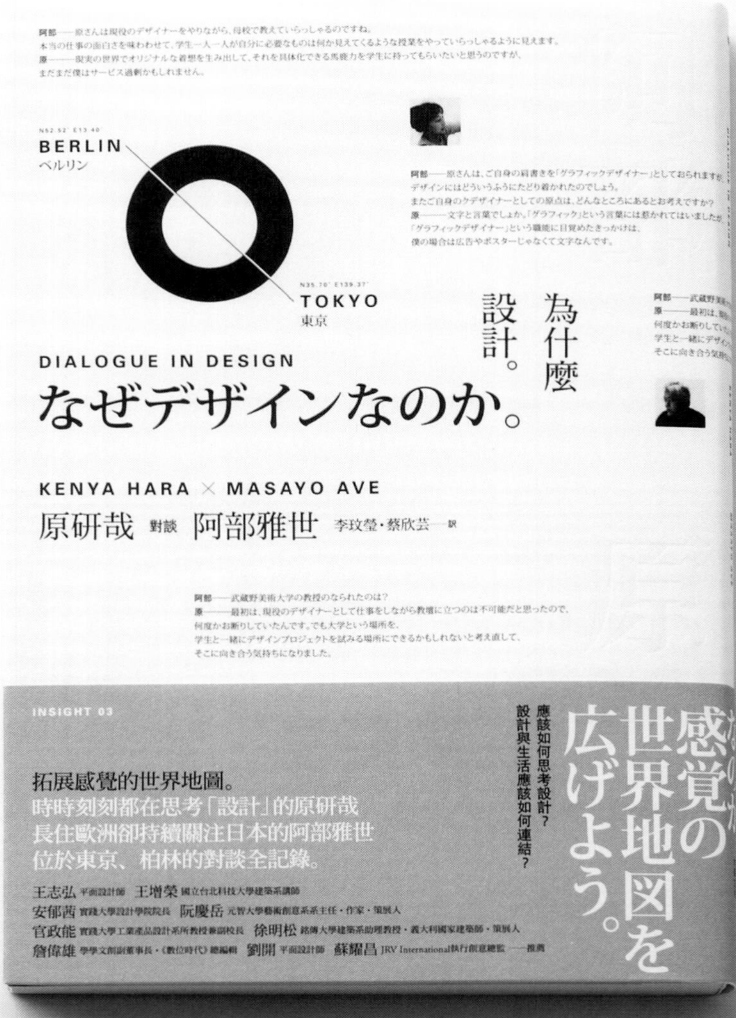

阿部——原さんは現役のデザイナーをやりながら、母校で教えていらっしゃるのですね。
本当の仕事の面白さを味わわせて、学生一人一人が自分に必要なものは何か見えてくるような授業をやっていらっしゃるように見えます。
原——現実の世界でオリジナルな着想を生み出して、それを具体化できる馬鹿力を学生に持ってもらいたいと思うのですが、
まだまだ僕はサービス過剰かもしれません。

N52.52' E13.40'
BERLIN
ベルリン

N35.70' E139.37'
TOKYO
東京

阿部——原さんは、ご自身の肩書きを「グラフィックデザイナー」としておられますが、
デザインにはどういうふうにたどり着かれたのでしょう。
またご自身のケデザイナーとしての原点は、どんなところにあるとお考えですか？
原——文字と言葉でしょか。「グラフィック」という言葉には惹かれてはいましたが、
「グラフィックデザイナー」という職能に目覚めたきっかけは、
僕の場合は広告やポスターじゃなくて文字なんです。

為什麼設計。

DIALOGUE IN DESIGN

なぜデザインなのか。

KENYA HARA × MASAYO AVE

原研哉 對談 阿部雅世 李玟瑩・蔡欣芸——譯

阿部——武蔵野美術大学の教授のなられたのは？
原——最初は、現役のデザイナーとして仕事をしながら教壇に立つのは不可能だと思ったので、
何度かお断りしていたんです。でも大学という場所を、
学生と一緒にデザインプロジェクトを試みる場所にできるかもしれないと考え直して、
そこに向き合う気持ちになりました。

INSIGHT 03

應該如何思考設計？
設計與生活應該如何連結？

感覚の世界地図を広げよう。

拓展感覺的世界地圖。
時時刻刻都在思考「設計」的原研哉
長住歐洲卻持續關注日本的阿部雅世
位於東京、柏林的對談全記錄。

王志弘 平面設計師　王增榮 國立台北科技大學建築系講師
安郁茜 實踐大學設計學院院長　阮慶岳 元智大學藝術創意系系主任・作家・策展人
官政能 實踐大學工業產品設計系所教授兼副校長　徐明松 銘傳大學建築系助理教授・義大利國家建築師・策展人
詹偉雄 學學文創副董事長・《數位時代》總編輯　劉開 平面設計師　蘇耀昌 JRV International執行創意總監 ——推薦

026

WANG ZHI HONG

CLIENT | Ecus Publishing

This book is a collection of dialogues between two renowned Japanese designers: Tokyo-based Kenya HARA and Berlin-based Masayo AVE. Through their conversations, they exchange views on design in Japan and Germany. I used a round symbol to respond to their geographical difference. Their portrait photos and conversations are arranged in a cascading way, echoing the dialogues in motion.

FROM POLAND WITH SHORTS
FROM POLAND WITH SHORTS
FROM POLAND WITH SHORTS
FROM POLAND WITH SHORTS

027

EDGAR BAK

CLIENT | Munk Studio

Studio Munka's project, organised as a part of the cultural program of the Polish presidency in the UE, covers a presentation of young Polish cinema in 4 chosen cities: Berlin, Paris, London and Moscow in autumn of 2011. The programme was comprised of short fims by young filmmakers that have been successful in recent years and who are currently working on their debut features. It has been a trend in recent years that the most interesting and bold Polish films are made by young filmmakers. It's also young filmmakers that shape the short film scene in Poland. Every year more names appear and one can even start talking about a wave of youth entering the market. It's time to present this phenomenon abroad.

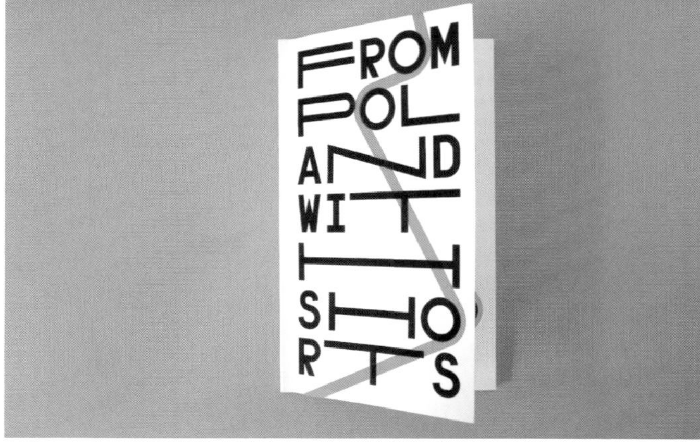

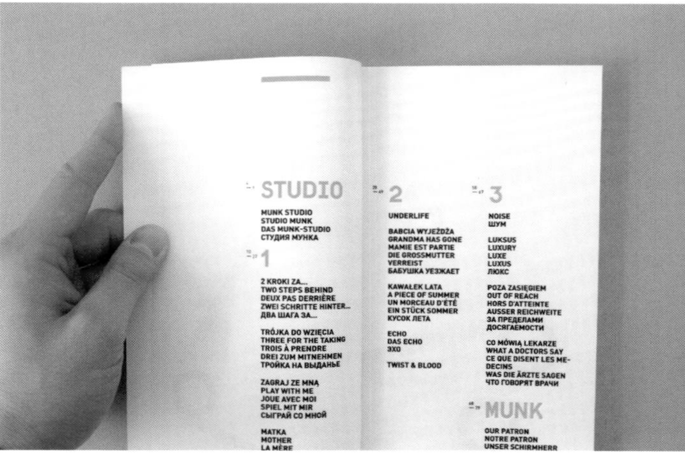

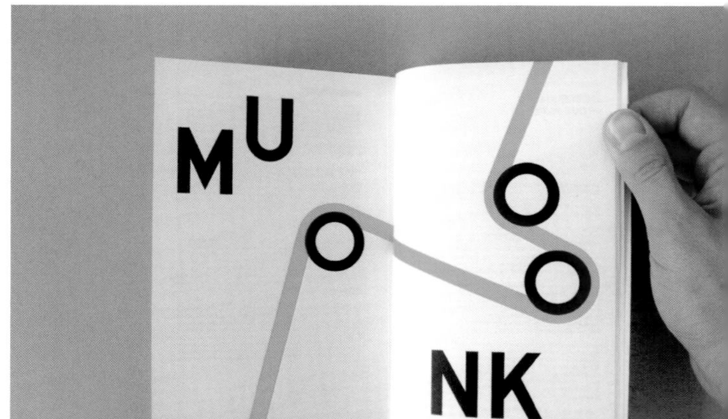

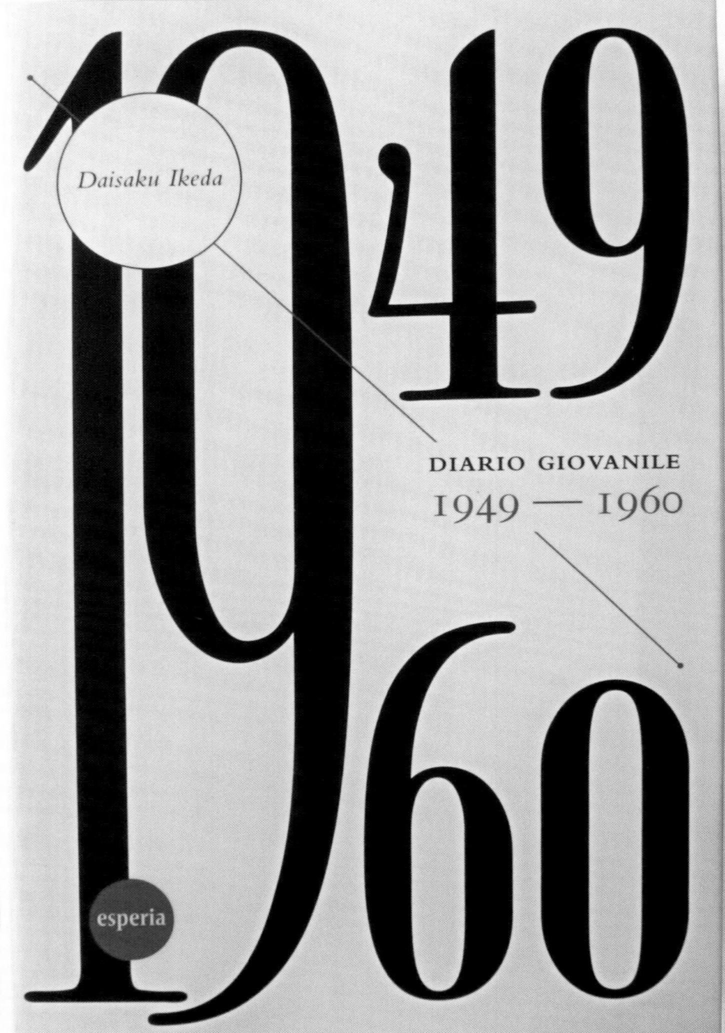
Daisaku Ikeda
1949
1960
DIARIO GIOVANILE
1949 — 1960
esperia

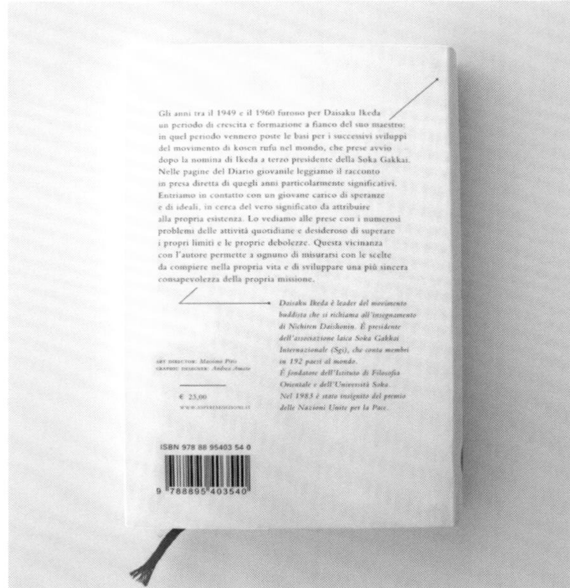

028

PITIS

CLIENT I Esperia Edizioni

Diario Giovanile (A Youthful Diary):
In 1949, a 21-year-old Daisaku Ikeda began a private diary that would continue for 11 years, until May 1960, shortly after he became the third president of the Soka Gakkai. *A Youthful Diary* records the day-to-day reflections of this young man struggling with day-by-day problems and develop his own worldview under the tutelage of his mentor in life, Josei Toda, during what became the formative years of the lay Buddhist Soka Gakkai organisation in Japan.

The dates being the focus of the subject, the studio designed the numbers in a very condensed and quirky serif shape, so they can fit perfectly into the space of the cover, with a stylish black/white and red composition.

029

THE RAINY MONDAY®

CLIENT | Fundació Taller de Guionistes

For nearly two decades Taller de Guionistes (Screenwriters Workshop) have been dedicated to training screenwriting professionals. The objective of these pieces was to create a collection of reference within the sector. They wanted to encourage future screenwriters starting with the cover. A piece created from basic materials combined with an attractive design facilitates the reading of both copies.

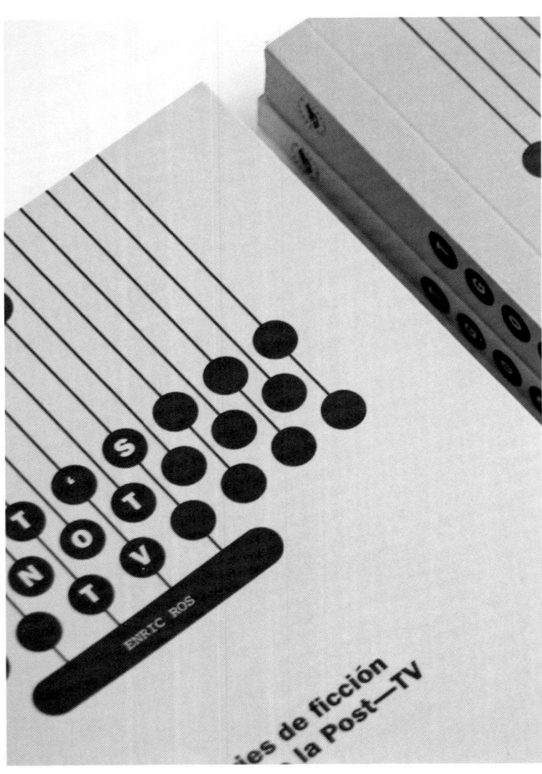

TG02
IT'S NOT TV
ENRIC ROS
Las series de ficción en la era de la Post—TV
Editado por
Fundación Taller de Guionistas
TG01
EL GUION HABLADO
Conversaciones con guionistas y directores del s.XXI
Editado por
Fundación Taller de Guionistas
Con la colaboración de Jordi Picatoste Verdejo

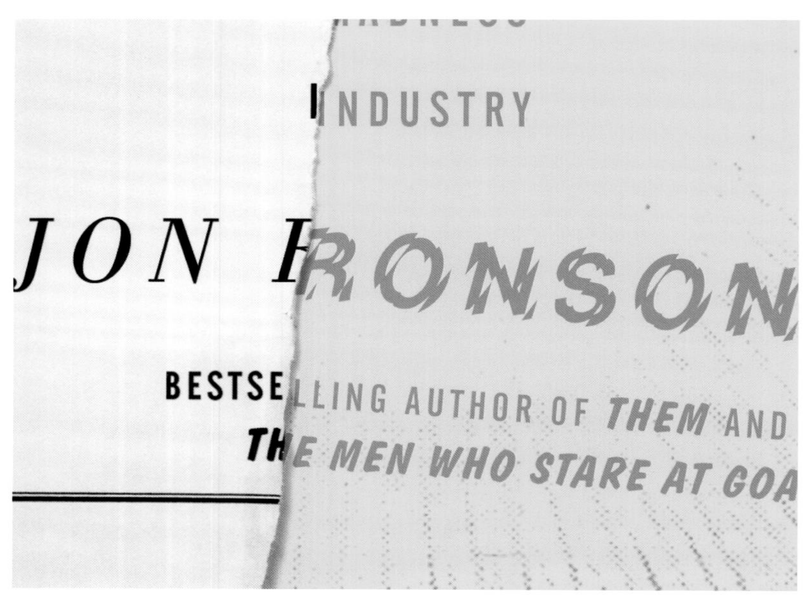

030

MATT DORFMAN

CLIENT | Riverhead Books

This book is a tour of modern psychopathy in which the author profiles an imprisoned leader of a former foreign death squad, a patient in an asylum for the criminally insane and a wealthy power lusting CEO, and arrives at some uncomfortable parallels with regards to how a psychopath (and psychopathy) is defined and applied in contemporary society. There is an unsettling suspicion that psychopathic behavior is more present among people outside of prisons than not.

Author: Jon Ronson.

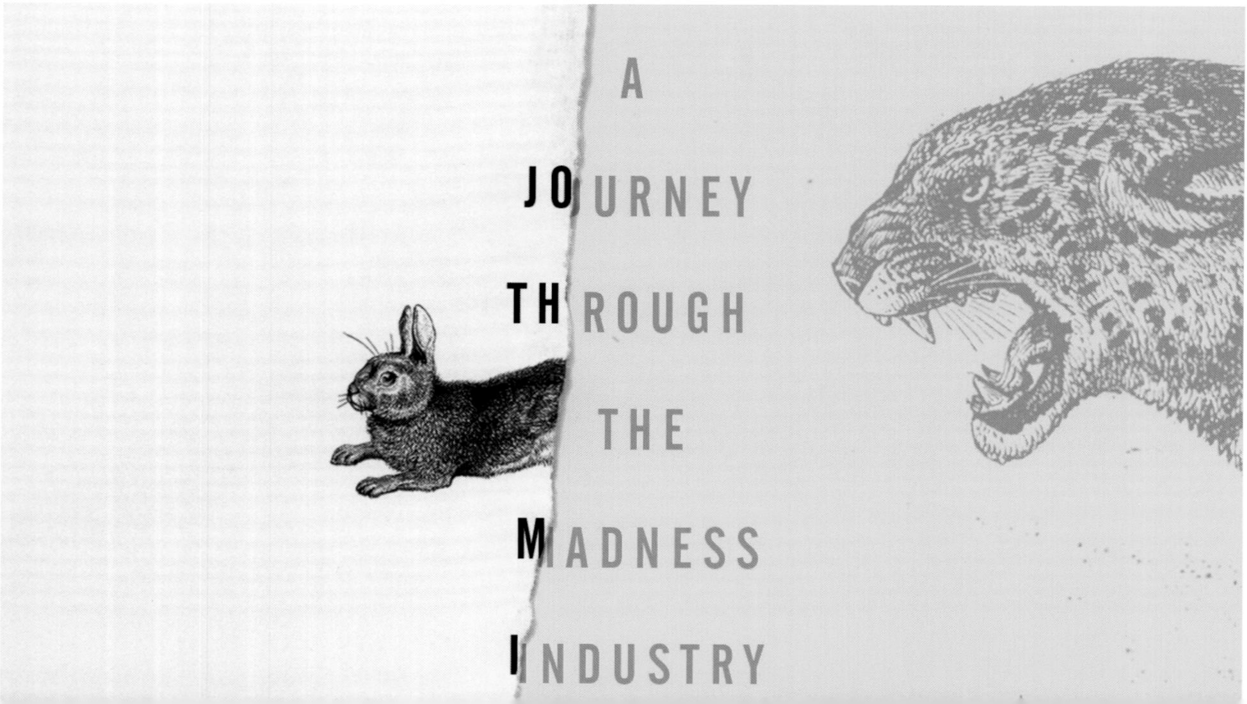

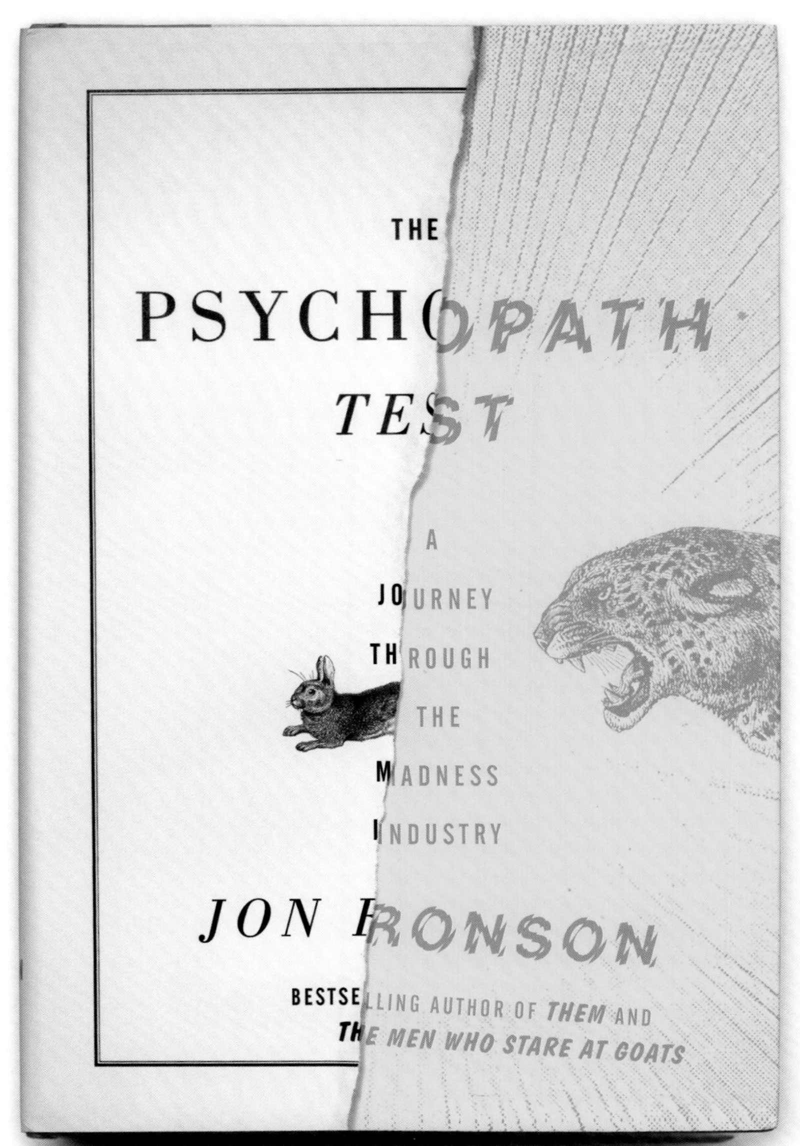
THE
PSYCHOPATH
TEST
A
JOURNEY
THROUGH
THE
MADNESS
INDUSTRY
JON RONSON
BESTSELLING AUTHOR OF THEM AND
THE MEN WHO STARE AT GOATS

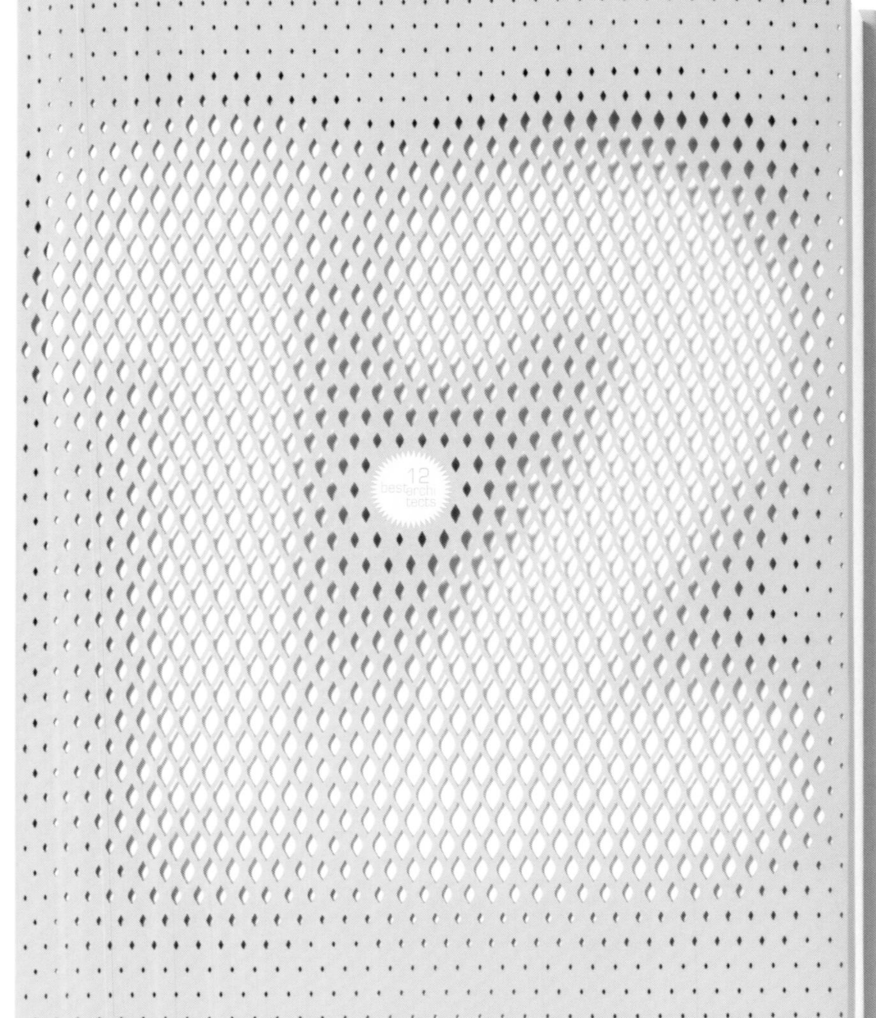
12
best archi
tects

031

ZINNOBERGRUEN GMBH

CLIENT | best architects Award

The book *best architects 12* is the official publication of the architecture award of the same name. All award-winning projects are presented in the book. Particular attention was paid to producing the elaborate cover, which features hundreds of small diamond shapes in different sizes laser-cut into the paper to form the title motif "12". The small star (the award's logo) was screen-printed in white onto the book jacket (Curious Skin paper).

032

BILDI GRAFIKS

CLIENT I DHUB - Disseny Hub Barcelona

For the cover of the book Fabvolution, it was decided to do some augmented reality models, each one of which would explain a process of digital production. So for the cover, the letters FAB explain the three principal processes of digital production: substractive production (F, eliminating material), additive production (A, adding material, including from different owners) or transformative production (B, mechanically doubling).

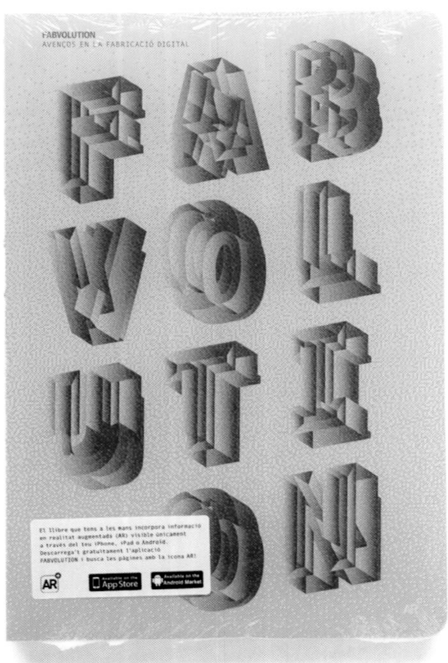

FABVOLUTION
AVENÇOS EN LA FABRICACIÓ DIGITAL
Available on the
App Store
AR

LOST AT SEA

THE JON RONSON MYSTERIES

BESTSELLING AUTHOR OF *THE PSYCHOPATH TEST*

JON RONSON

033

MATT DORFMAN

CLIENT | Riverhead Books

This followed up *The Psychopath Test* in which the author profiles people and groups whose belief systems are either leading them dangerously astray or enabling them to create their own moral and existential certainties. As is Ronson's talent, he's able to tease out the gray area between the two.

Author: Jon Ronson.

number

STUDIO

Client

Country

Descriptive text.

001
RAW COLOR
Centrum Kunstlicht in de Kunst
The Netherlands

The Light Art Museum in Eindhoven focuses on contemporary art dealing in one way or another with light. This can mean that the medium of artificial light sources is used. Besides the museum's own collection, the main focus is on group- and solo exhibitions. Nationally and internationally renowned artists presented their work in Eindhoven, including Dan Flavin, Bruce Nauman, Nan Hoover, and Zero among others. For several years we have been working as graphic designers for the museum, doing all their external communication. In the 2011 the museum stopped its activities. For this reason a book was commissioned to give an overview of the museum's activities from 2002 – 2011. The cover is an 8-page unfoldable timeline that is structured by year and colour. The inside is Japanese bound, allowing the years and images to blend into each other. The photos are threaded in a way that the reader gets the impression of browsing through one long timeline, resulting in one big gradient. All colours are created from the CMYK palette and a specific shade is assigned to each year.

002
SICHTVERMERK
Morphomata Centre for Advanced Studies, University of Cologne
Germany

The Morphomata Centre for Advanced Studies is publishing this series of books, which is in fact two series. The first is the so-called "Literator" series which is about one author, holding the two-week "Chair of World Literature". The second series is comprised of monographs of the centre's fellows. The aim of the design was to distinguish the two topics from each other while making it clear that they both belong to the same series. This goal is reached by rotating the graphic elements by 90 degrees and giving the series different coloured-atmospheres, reddish for the monographs and blueish for the "Literator" volumes.
Designer: Kathrin Roussel.

003
SICHTVERMERK
Aesthetic Figurations of the Political, Centre for Advanced Studies at the University of Luxemburg
Germany

Politics have aesthetic aspects that are to be researched. So does *Aesthetic Figurations of the Political*, a Centre for Advanced Studies at the University of Luxemburg. This design of the book series reflects the "imaginary dimension of politics". Only the beholder will be able to interpret the abstract sixcornered forms as perspectivically stretched rectangles. The forms change from volume to volume as well as the colours.
Designers: Kathrin Roussel, Stefan Claudius.

004
RUN DESIGN
Random House Mondadori
Spain

Collection of covers for the trade paperback edition of the complete works of Borges. Time, the infinite, mirrors, labyrinths, reality, identity and fantastic elements. Impossible, unclassifiable covers.

005
CORALIE BICKFORD-SMITH
Penguin Classics UK
United Kingdom

These titles explore my obsession with creating beautiful, timeless artifacts for people to enjoy, cherish and pass on. Sumptuous, tactile books that evoke a rich heritage of bookbinding while retaining fresh appeal to modern readers, that both stand out in bookshops and have a longevity appropriate to the contents.

Credits:
Crime and Punishment – Fyodor Dostoyevsky
(Illustration: Coralie Bickford-Smith)
Madame Bovary – Gustave Flaubert
(Illustration: Coralie Bickford-Smith)
Great Expectations – Charles Dickens
(Illustration: Coralie Bickford-Smith)
Wuthering Heights – Emily Brontë
(Illustration: Coralie Bickford-Smith)
Sense and Sensibility – Jane Austen
(Illustration: Coralie Bickford-Smith)
Cranford – Elizabeth Gaskell
(Illustration: Coralie Bickford-Smith)
*Tess of the d'Urberville*s – Thomas Hardy
(Illustration: Coralie Bickford-Smith)
Pride and Prejudice – Jane Austen
(Illustration: Stapleton Collection/Corbis)
Jane Eyre – Charlotte Brontë
(Illustration: Coralie Bickford-Smith)
The Picture of Dorian Gray – Oscar Wilde
(Illustration: Coralie Bickford-Smith)

Designer: Coralie Bickford-Smith, Senior Cover Designer Penguin UK / Art Director: Jim Stoddart

006
CODESIGN
Codesign / Self-initiated
India

Dekho is an anthology of inspirational conversations with designers in India, probing their stories for cues to the development of design in India and highlighting approaches that are unique to designing for India.

007

RUN DESIGN

Grupo Tragaluz
Spain

"A journey of a thousand miles begins with a single step." -Laozi (579 - 490 A.C.). 4,997 km Pekin - Lhasa is a book that collects the experiences of an intense journey and is edited to celebrate the inauguration of the new Chinese restaurant from Grupo Tragaluz, La Xina. All the materials were chosen with great care, trying to respect the Eastern sensibility. It was developed over several months in order to create a complete work that perfectly integrates shape and content, conceiving the book as a work of art, looking for the balance between the contemporaneity of Paula Ospina's photos, the delicacy of the Chinese culture and the freshness of a country in constant evolution.

008

DÚCTIL

Llibres de la Terra
Spain

Design of these new editorial collections. "Llibres de la Terra" (Earth Books) brings together studies, investigative work and outreach projects, etc. It is defined as a new brand of editing books, preferably unpublished ones. At the same time, it delimits families by homogeneous content (history, anthropology, folklore, biography, science, nature, etc.). "Papers de Pleta" (Pleta Papers). If a "pleta" is an agricultural term for a small valley, then this collection is a true "pleta" of texts, as it collects original texts that are proportionally smaller than the other collection, "Llibres de la Terra".

009

BRUKETA&ZINIC OM

Adris Group
Croatia / Serbia / Azerbaijan / Austria

Good things grow in good hands. Adris Group is a company owned by its employees which is why it has grown in the past year, despite the crisis. Adris Group's annual report entitled *In good hands* reveals floral details when heated by the palms of the hands, metaphorically illustrating how hands can achieve anything. The same specially-calibrated thermo colour used on the covers was also used for the inside illustrations, and the concept of the annual report is also evoked by the short stories from workers-stockholders.
Creative Directors: Davor Bruketa, Nikola Zinic / Art Directors: Nebojsa Cvetkovic, Neven Crljenak / Senior Copywriter: Ivan Cadez / Copywriter, Production Manager: Vesna Durasin / DTP: Radovan Radicevic / Account Director: Zrinka Jugec / Account Executive Senior: Ivana Drvar / Illustrator: Vedran Klemens / Editor: Predrag D. Grubic / Executive editor: Kristina Miljavac / Text: Hrvoje Patajac / Print: Cerovski print boutique, Stegatisak / Thermo color printing: Knepsen / Binding and blind folding: Knjigoveznica First / Photographer: Domagoj Kunic.

010

L2M3 KOMMUNIKATIONSDESIGN GMBH

100 beste Plakate e.V.
Germany

One hundred circles stand for the *100 Best Posters* in the logo, with the overlapping circles creating a moiré pattern. By means of shifts and changes of colours, a hundred different poster designs are created in the printing process.

011

PONTO

Self-initiated
United Kingdom

MOYI is a self-initiated project that was born out of the day-to-day contact with old and new visual collections. It first started as a book, but it's an ongoing project, that will soon be transported into other formats, such as the website. The book is the house of the first discussion where we analysed the relations between personal collections and haunted obsessions with the values of appropriation in art, while looking specifically into internet art, since it has also become part of our day-to-day visual collection.

012

PONTO

Self-initiated
United Kingdom

This book is an exploration of new ways of reading by using different optical patterns. Inspired by the composition of the song "Williams Mix", by John Cage, there are six different patterns that interact with the Western culture reading format. These patterns were inspired by the golden-section rule of geometry and work as tools to determine new reading interpretations. The book records the process.

013

ARIS ZENONE STUDIO

Département de Pédiatrie - CHUV
Switzerland

This is a summary book of a 3-day congress that questions and speaks about childhood dangers in everyday life. We designed a simple and useful typographic layout with the focus on readability. To illustrate every chapter we used basic and simple children's safety games that we turned into monsters.

014

ALBERTO HERNÁNDEZ

Self-initiated
Spain / United Kingdom

Visual exploration about narration documenting 24 moments from my day over a week. In order to tell the story of each of these 7 days, onomatopoeias, colours, Google images, emoticons, signs, security camera images and logotypes were used.

015

WILLIAM HALL

London College of Fashion
United Kingdom

Commissioned by London College of Fashion in its centenary year and edited and conceived by Louise Clarke, contributors to *The Measure* include Jimmy Choo, Giles Deacon, Zandra Rhodes, Paul Smith, Mario Testino and Vivienne Westwood.
Canvassing a cross section of fashion and design practitioners, academics and historians, *The Measure* asks each contributor to reflect on the effect London has had on contemporary culture – and specifically fashion – over the last century.
The images (right hand page) and text (left hand page) are strictly separated allowing an already image-rich book to be read purely as a visual essay. This demarcation is exaggerated by placing the image page at right angles.
The index and contents page are combined in a fold-out back cover. The position of each entry relates both to the page number and the eponymous tape measure positioned alongside.
Tim Gutt's Tall Fashion image envelopes the outside, playfully interpreting the book title, and making an unexpected and engaging cover.
For the book launch a limited edition poster dustjacket was made featuring Nick Knight's 3D Naomi Campbell image. This lustrous, black and gold wrapping gave the book great visual impact at a party attended by many of the contributors.
William Hall contributed an essay on Terry Jones, the founder and creative director of i-D magazine.
Designers: William Hall, Nicholas Barba.

016

BELIEVE IN®

Bernadette Jiwa
Australia / United Kingdom

You are the Map Maker features inspirational insights from 13 international, creative and resourceful entrepreneurs.
The book uses a structured grid and graphic system based around the key contributors from the book. Each contributor is symbolised by a cross–hair within a circle, locating their mark or place within the book's own map system. These marks form part of the system or theme of the book, and become the navigational device throughout, highlighting the sections and featured contributors. They also act as a playful graphical element throughout, evolving and sympathetic from page to page, dictating and changing the pace of the book.
Author: Bernadette Jiwa.

017

CORALIE BICKFORD-SMITH

Penguin Classics UK
United Kingdom

I designed the patterns in an attempt to give these books something of the elegance and glamour of the Art Deco period, with the sense of ornate detail fused with the modernist aesthetic of mechanical repetition. The combination of metallic foil and matte paper is designed to feel good in the hand as well as look good on the shelf; by evoking the Jazz Age of Fitzgerald's stories, I hope these books will give a little tactile enhancement to the reading experience.
There are a couple of subtle nods to specific incidents: for instance, there's a suggestion of car wheels in the circular pattern on *The Great Gatsby*, with the vertical distortion hinting at a crash. Mainly though, the function of the patterns is to evoke the world of the books.

Titles:
The Beautiful and Damned
This Side of Paradise
The Last Tycoon
Flappers and Philosophers
The Great Gatsby
Tender is the Night

Designer: Coralie Bickford-Smith, Senior Cover Designer Penguin UK / Art Director: Jim Stoddart

018

THE RAINY MONDAY®

Luis & Fina
Spain

"All life deserves to be told."
These were the words that Luís and Fina used to define this autobiographical limited-edition piece. A large-format book, with artisan details and protected by a special container designed to protect embellish. A story and a look at the past, present and future that this couple decided to make to share with their loved ones.

019

NR2154

Rizzoli/Louis Vuitton
Denmark / United States of America

Published to coincide with an exhibition of the same name at the Musée des Arts Décoratifs in Paris, *Louis Vuitton/Marc Jacobs* celebrates the roles that the two men played in the evolution of the brand, 100 years apart. With a limited edition and trade edition, the book also features two custom typefaces.

020

NAKANO DESIGN OFFICE

Musashino Art University Museum & Library
Japan

The exhibition introduced book designs of Japanese literary books which were published from the Meiji period to the early Showa period. However, while we represented typography and materiality which were often seen in book design around that time, we tried to design a book that can give the today's reader another fresh impression.
Art Director and Designer: Takeo Nakano / Edit: Musashino Art University Museum & Library.

021

HVASS&HANNIBAL

Hyggefactory
Denmark

This is a book cover for a project called Ordskælv, initiated by Hyggefactory's Karen Siercke. The book is a collection of essays written by 13-21 year-olds who have all experienced the loss of a parent. Through weekly workshops since September 2011 the young writers have received guidance from professional authors and journalists, and the result is a handful of beautiful and touching stories. The essays are all illustrated by artists, including names like Michael Kvium, Bjørn Nørgaard and HuskMitNavn.

022

A BEAUTIFUL DESIGN

The Browsing Copy Project
Singapore

The Browsing Copy project focuses on unloved books, those that remained on the shelves unsold. These books are collected from bookstores and designers are invited to use them as canvasses to express their creativity. The 'before & after' results are documented. This catalogue features both series one & two of the project and the 45 designers' contributions. Only 300 copies were printed and circulated around the world's best bookstores, shops and design studios, just for people to browse. It's not for sale. The catalogues will be collected back after a period of time and passed on to the next line of shops. The condition of the catalogues and the places they've been are documented on the website www.browsingcopy.com.
Creative Director - Designer: Roy Poh / Photographer: John Nursalim.

023

EVELIN KASIKOV

A Beautiful Design
United Kingdom

Browsing Copy is a project by Singapore design studio A Beautiful Design, aiming to make better use of unsold books. Designers from all over the world were invited to give them new life as works of art. I received the following title to work with: *Flowers Never Last. The Impression Will. Exquisite flowers by Fiore Dorato.* Ignoring all the visuals I took fragments of author's text and stitched back into spreads in black cotton thread. I divided the book (consisting of 272 pages = 17 signatures/16 pages each) in half and applied stitched elements to the first half leaving the second half as it was.

024

MAX-O-MATIC

Hernán Ordoñez / Index Book
Spain

Design and illustration for the book *Typex, A Teaching Experience*. The book, which is about the teaching of typography, proposes a cover where the "classics" of typography strike up an open dialogue about the possibilities of typography as a form of communication.

025

JIM WONG@ GOOD MORNING

Roundtable Community
Hong Kong

Published by Roundtable Community, *Vision of Civil Society* is a publication of collected articles written by Dr Chan Kin Mun about the development and happenings of Hong Kong Civil Societies.
We were commissioned to design the cover of the book. A calm, peaceful aqua colour was used to emphasis the character of Dr Chan's critiques toward politics, which are objective and temperate. The custom-made title was used to reflect the message of the chaotic situation in Hong Kong.

026

WANG ZHI HONG

Ecus Publishing
Taiwan

This book is a collection of dialogues between two renowned Japanese designers: Tokyo-based Kenya HARA and Berlin-based Masayo AVE. Through their conversations, they exchange views on design in Japan and Germany. I used a round symbol to respond to their geographical difference. Their portrait photos and conversations are arranged in a cascading way, echoing the dialogues in motion.

027
EDGAR BAK
Munk Studio
Poland

Studio Munka's project, organised as a part of the cultural program of the Polish presidency in the UE, covers a presentation of young Polish cinema in 4 chosen cities: Berlin, Paris, London and Moscow in autumn of 2011. The programme was comprised of short fims by young filmmakers that have been successful in recent years and who are currently working on their debut features. It has been a trend in recent years that the most interesting and bold Polish films are made by young filmmakers. It's also young filmmakers that shape the short film scene in Poland. Every year more names appear and one can even start talking about a wave of youth entering the market. It's time to present this phenomenon abroad.

028
PITIS
Esperia Edizioni
Italy

Diario Giovanile (A Youthful Diary):
In 1949, a 21-year-old Daisaku Ikeda began a private diary that would continue for 11 years, until May 1960, shortly after he became the third president of the Soka Gakkai. *A Youthful Diary* records the day-to-day reflections of this young man struggling with day-by-day problems and develop his own worldview under the tutelage of his mentor in life, Josei Toda, during what became the formative years of the lay Buddhist Soka Gakkai organisation in Japan. The dates being the focus of the subject, the studio designed the numbers in a very condensed and quirky serif shape, so they can fit perfectly into the space of the cover, with a stylish black/white and red composition.
Designers: Massimo Pitis, Andrea Amato.

029
THE RAINY MONDAY®
Fundació Taller de Guionistes
Spain

For nearly two decades Taller de Guionistes (Screenwriters Workshop) have been dedicated to training screenwriting professionals. The objective of these pieces was to create a collection of reference within the sector. They wanted to encourage future screenwriters starting with the cover. A piece created from basic materials combined with an attractive design facilitates the reading of both copies.

030
MATT DORFMAN
Riverhead Books
United States of America

This book is a tour of modern psychopathy in which the author profiles an imprisoned leader of a former foreign death squad, a patient in an asylum for the criminally insane and a wealthy power lusting CEO, and arrives at some uncomfortable parallels with regards to how a psychopath (and psychopathy) is defined and applied in contemporary society. There is an unsettling suspicion that psychopathic behavior is more present among people outside of prisons than not.
Author: Jon Ronson / Jacket Design: Matt Dorfman / Art Director: Helen Yentus / Publisher: Riverhead Books.

031
ZINNOBERGRUEN GMBH
| best architects Award
Germany

The book *best architects 12* is the official publication of the architecture award of the same name. All award-winning projects are presented in the book. Particular attention was paid to producing the elaborate cover, which features hundreds of small diamond shapes in different sizes laser-cut into the paper to form the title motif "12". The small star (the award's logo) was screen-printed in white onto the book jacket (Curious Skin paper).

032
BILDI GRAFIKS
DHUB - Disseny Hub Barcelona
Spain

For the cover of the book Fabvolution, it was decided to do some augmented reality models, each one of which would explain a process of digital production. So for the cover, the letters FAB explain the three principal processes of digital production: substractive production (F, eliminating material), additive production (A, adding material, including from different owners) or transformative production (B, mechanically doubling).

033
MATT DORFMAN
Riverhead Books
United States of America

This followed up *The Psychopath Test* in which the author profiles people and groups whose belief systems are either leading them dangerously astray or enabling them to create their own moral and existential certainties. As is Ronson's talent, he's able to tease out the gray area between the two.
Author: Jon Ronson / Jacket Design: Matt Dorfman / Art Director: Helen Yentus / Publisher: Riverhead Books.

082-185

MAGAZINES

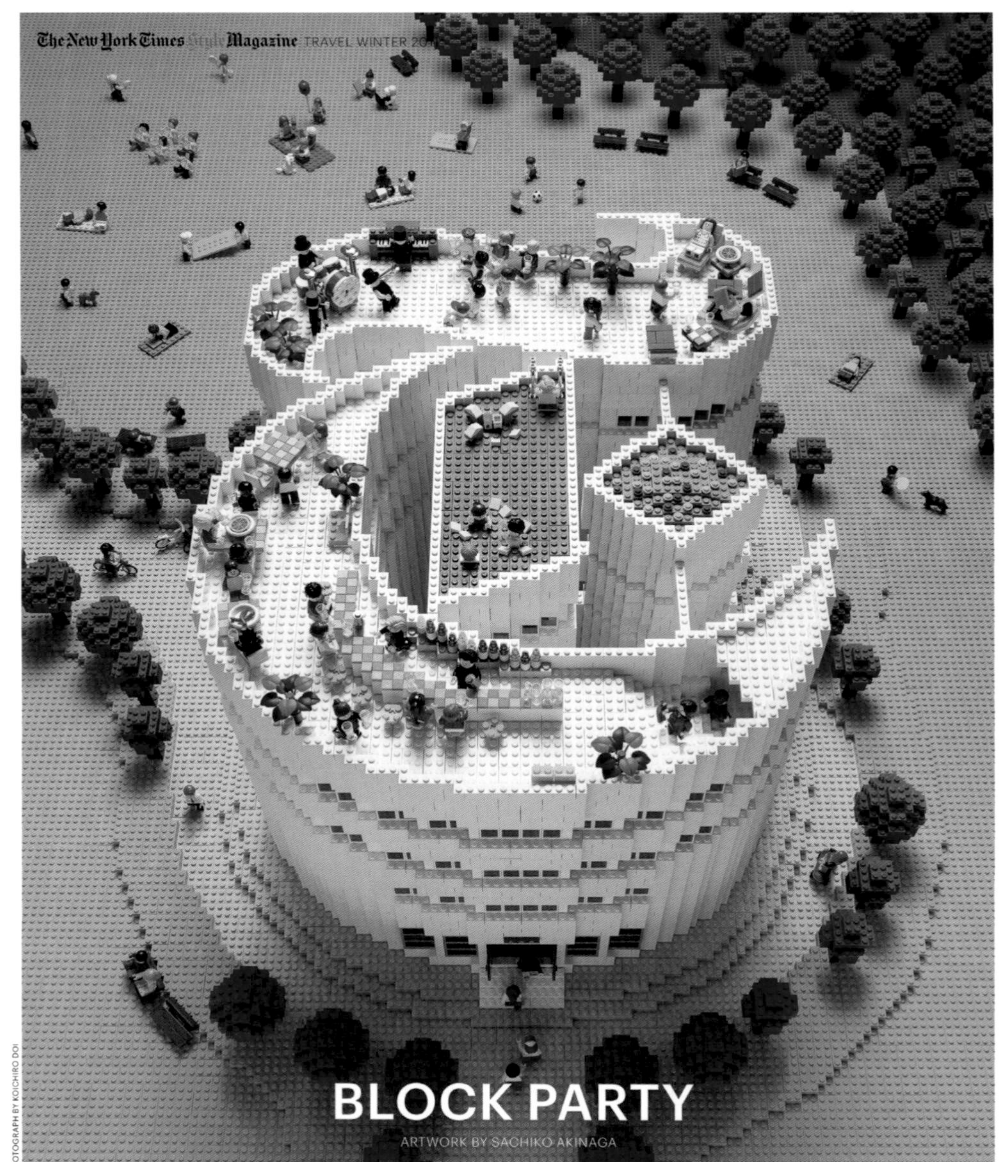

BLOCK PARTY

ARTWORK BY SACHIKO AKINAGA

PHOTOGRAPH BY KOICHIRO DOI

034

SACHIKO AKINAGA

CLIENT | New York Times Style Magazine

Who doesn't like a party? Especially a rooftop pool party on a sunny day where the jazz quartet sounds out harmony to a perfect lego land jubilee. Travel in the winter? Yes, please. This beloved Akinaga well opener, entices the reader to saddle up to a luxurious hotel bar, catch the rays, and tell the bartenders, "I'll have what they're having".

035

JUDY KAMEON & ERIK OTSEA

CLIENT | New York Times Style Magazine

We have all the seasons colours here. A whole year's worth of them in fact. Violets fall into sylvan mosses over a pebbled backdrop. The Fall Travel 2011 T logo articulately prompts the reader to expect change throughout the season. Plant textures juxtaposed by the chilly Autumn colour flux give the ensuing fall travel features an exotic, yet comforting opening remark.

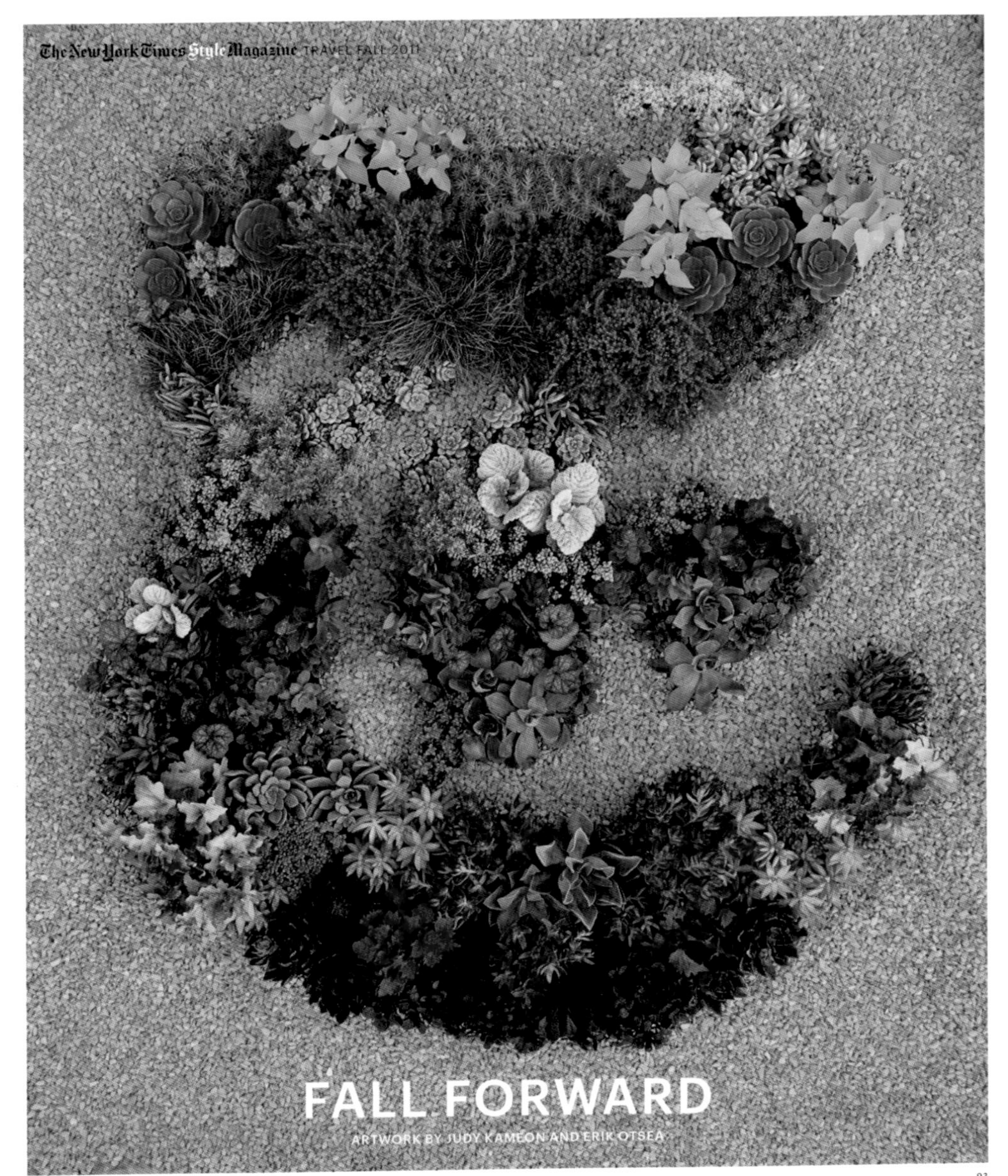
The New York Times Style Magazine TRAVEL FALL 2011
FALL FORWARD
ARTWORK BY JUDY KAMEON AND ERIK OTSEA
93

昭和22年9月18日第三種郵便物承認
2012年10月20日発行(毎月1回20日発行)
第127集・第1637号

建築雑誌
JABS
Journal of Architecture and Building Science

10 2012
vol.127
No.1637

特集：

耐震の今：成熟から拡張へ

Earthquake Resistance Now: From Maturity to Expansion

この図は東北地方太平洋沖地震の際に、防災科学技術研究所の強震観測網(K-NET及びKiK-net)で観測された地震動加速度波形(東西動)のうち、太平洋岸に沿った直線に近い地点の波形を北から並べたものである。最初の大きな揺れは宮城県沖で発生し、それが北側と南側へと伝播している様子が見られる(❶の帯)。その数十秒後には宮城県沖で再び強い揺れが発生し、最初の強い揺れと同じように各地へ伝わっている(❷の帯)。3番目の大きな揺れは茨城県北部の陸に近い沖合で発生し、北側と南側へ強い揺れが伝播している(❸の帯)。今回の大地震では3つの大きな揺れが次々に発生し、重なりあいながら各地に伝播していった。この地震により、津波による未曾有の大災害に加え、東北地方の沿岸・内陸部や関東北部など各地での強い揺れによる建物の構造被害や地盤災害、建物の非構造部材の被害、液状化被害、首都圏や関西圏までの超高層建物の長周期地震動による被害等、全国各地で様々な被害を生じた。

今回の特集では、非常な広範囲に影響を及ぼす大地震という、明治以降の近代化の歴史の中で初めての出来事を受け、これまでに培ってきた建築物の耐震について改めて見直すとともに、今後のさらに強い揺れが大都市を襲う場合を想定して、建物・都市・社会の対地震設計としての「耐震」を、より広い視点から考える契機にしたいと考えている。なお、図の素材は東京大学地震研究所のEP(野口科子・古村孝志、http://outreach.eri.u-tokyo.ac.jp/eqvolc/201103_tohoku/#gmsource)からご提供いただいた。

日本建築学会 Architectural Institute of Japan

036

NAKANO DESIGN OFFICE

CLIENT | Architectural Institute of Japan

The October edition of the magazine published by the Architectural Institute of Japan.

We visualised the Japanese intensity scale of the Great East Japan Earthquake that hit on March 11, 2011.

In this image, a vertical line indicates passage of time, and waveforms of intensity, scale of the area from Tohoku region to Kanto region, are spaced along the time-shift.

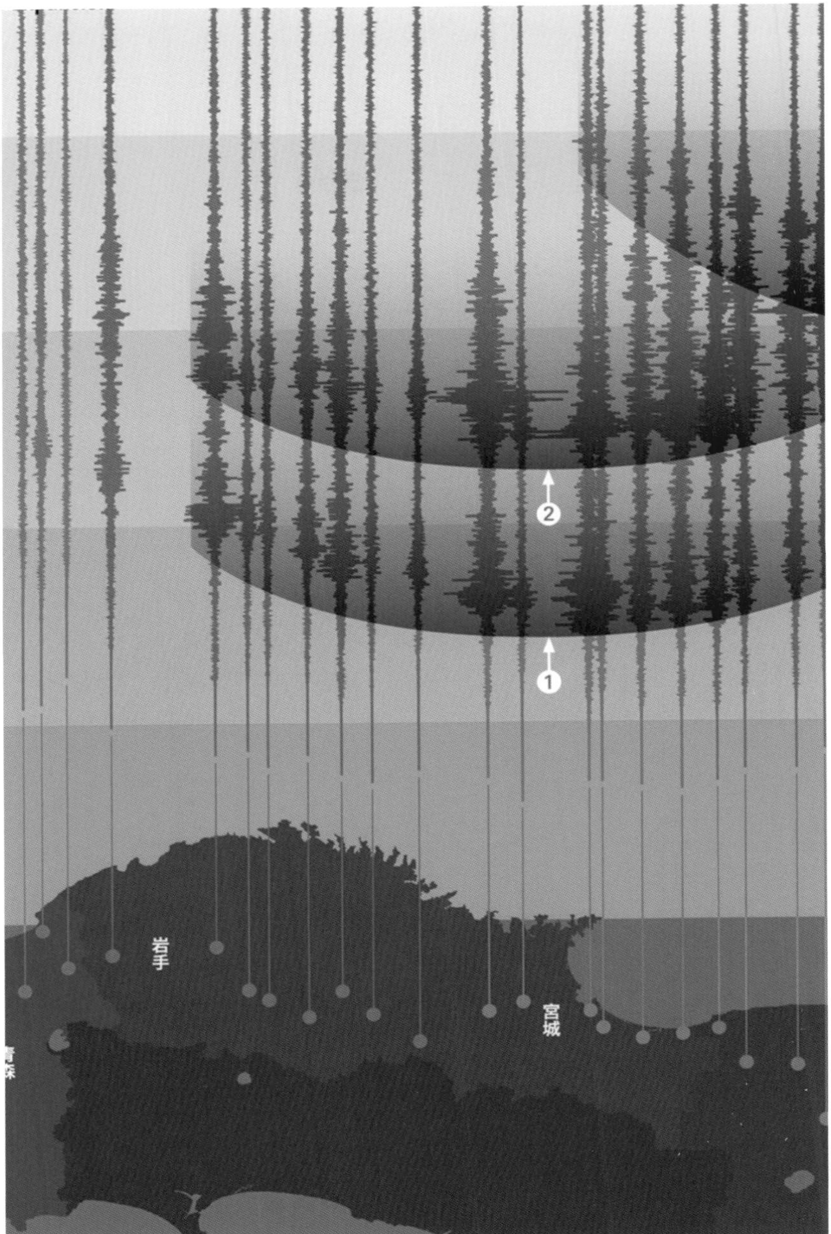

037

SANTOS HENAREJOS & ROC CANALS

CLIENT | Brands & Roses

Ling is the onboard magazine from Vueling. It's a monthly publication centered around the cities that the airline flies to. It's a bilingual magazine and is organised in four sections: living, inspiration, now and good.

LING
LIVING p.7
Los clérigos asistirán a clases de canto para no desentonar en la llamada a la oración.
Istanbul's clerics take singing lessons to stay in tune during call to prayer.
INSPIRATION p.21
Las fotos dentro de fotos del francés Jean François Rauzier.
Jean François Rauzier creates images which contain images inside more images.
NOW

ling
GOOD
NOW
INSPIRATION
LIVING
APOLO
WOK

ling
SEPTIEMBRE 2010
GOOD
NOW
INSPIRATION
LIVING

ling
HERE, THERE & EVERYWHERE
AGOSTO 2010
LIVING p.5
INSPIRATION p.33
Las matemáticas prueban que las jirafas
NOW p.59
creando un perfil en Twitter, Facebook y Tuenti.
Bere Casillas, the tailor that saved his business by embracing social networks.
GOOD p.77
Hazte coleccionista y cuelga en tu salón a Serge Gainsbourg metido en la bañera.
Become a collector and hang Serge Gainsbourg taking a bath in your living room.

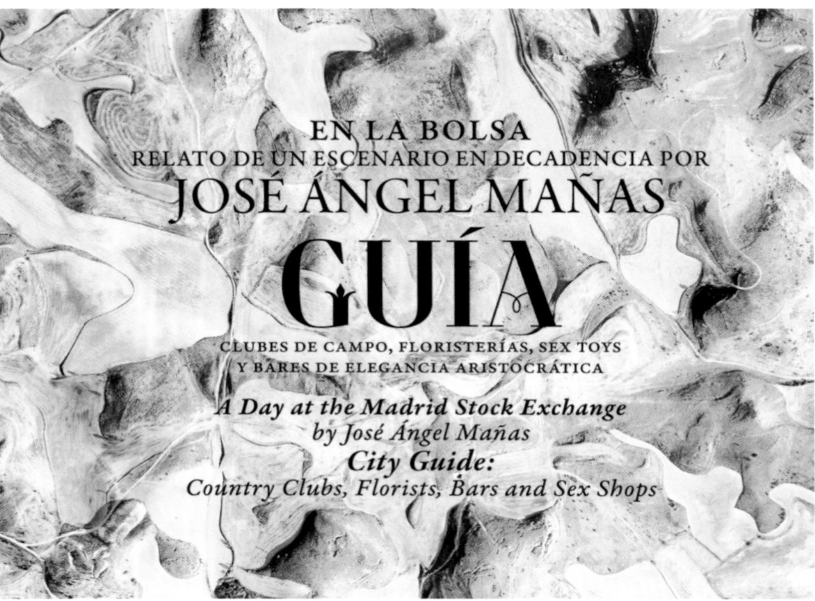

038

MADRIZ

CLIENT | Madriz

The cover for issue number 4 of *Madriz* (2009) is part of a series of photographs documenting the surroundings of Madrid seen from the sky. The goal was to capture the striking and unique beauty of a landscape that has been gradually transformed by the action of man. This series was conceived and performed by Fernando Maselli, a photographer who never before had ventured himself in aerial photography.

Long flying hours onboard a small two-seater helicopter were necessary to take these photographs during January and February, when it snowed with unusual frequency in Madrid. Unfortunately, Barajas airport's control tower did not authorize flying higher than an altitude of 5,000 feet, which meant that Fernando needed to invest another 200 hours assembling the landscapes with Photoshop in order to achieve these large vistas.

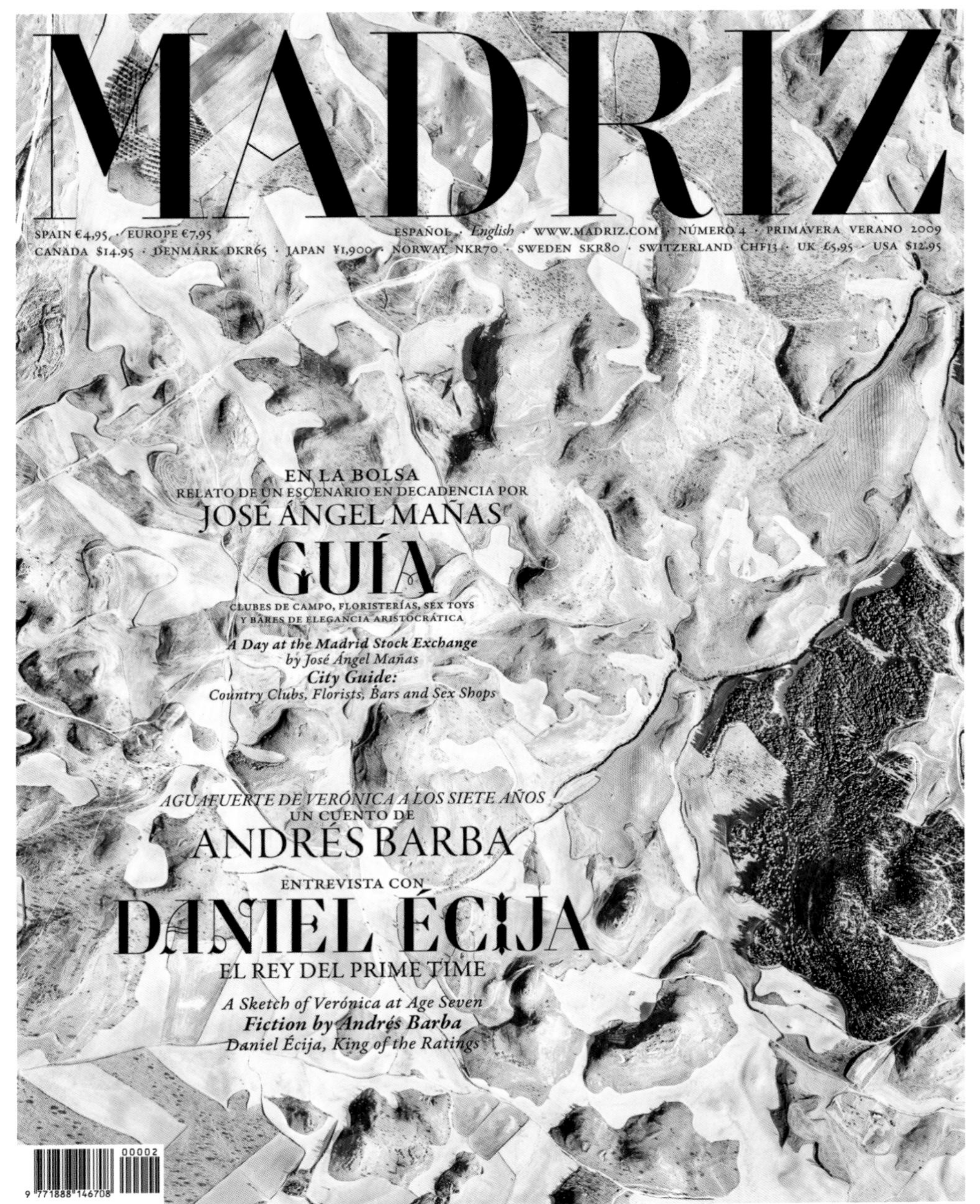
MADRIZ
SPAIN €4,95 · EUROPE €7,95
ESPAÑOL · English · WWW.MADRIZ.COM · NÚMERO 4 · PRIMAVERA VERANO 2009
CANADA $14.95 · DENMARK DKR65 · JAPAN ¥1,900 · NORWAY NKR70 · SWEDEN SKR80 · SWITZERLAND CHF13 · UK £5,95 · USA $12.95
EN LA BOLSA
RELATO DE UN ESCENARIO EN DECADENCIA POR
JOSÉ ÁNGEL MAÑAS
GUÍA
CLUBES DE CAMPO, FLORISTERÍAS, SEX TOYS
Y BARES DE ELEGANCIA ARISTOCRÁTICA
A Day at the Madrid Stock Exchange
by José Ángel Mañas
City Guide:
Country Clubs, Florists, Bars and Sex Shops
AGUAFUERTE DE VERÓNICA A LOS SIETE AÑOS
UN CUENTO DE
ANDRÉS BARBA
ENTREVISTA CON
DANIEL ÉCIJA
EL REY DEL PRIME TIME
A Sketch of Verónica at Age Seven
Fiction by Andrés Barba
Daniel Écija, King of the Ratings
000002
9 771888 146708

039

MAGMA BRAND DESIGN

CLIENT | Slanted, www.slanted.de

Slanted #15 – Experimental deals with experimental design strategies in typography and graphic design. This issue presents projects incorporating the accident into the design process, works based on mistakes and inaccuracy, fonts that derive from a concept or a system – in the end work that experiments or goes unconventional ways in design.

The playful handling of tools, forms and concept is a popular procedure to broaden the consciousness in typography.

It seems to be (regarding the huge amount of entries for this issue) a widespread phenomenon, very popular at design schools and universities. This is not a surprising fact – especially in interaction with a model, experimental results are the foundation of a theory.

We placed a special experimental type section with 48 pages in this issue to be able to present a large collection of typographical experiments.

This issue's cover is realized in an oldfashioned, experimental procedure, too: Its print sheet has been produced in rainbow printing using HKS colours.

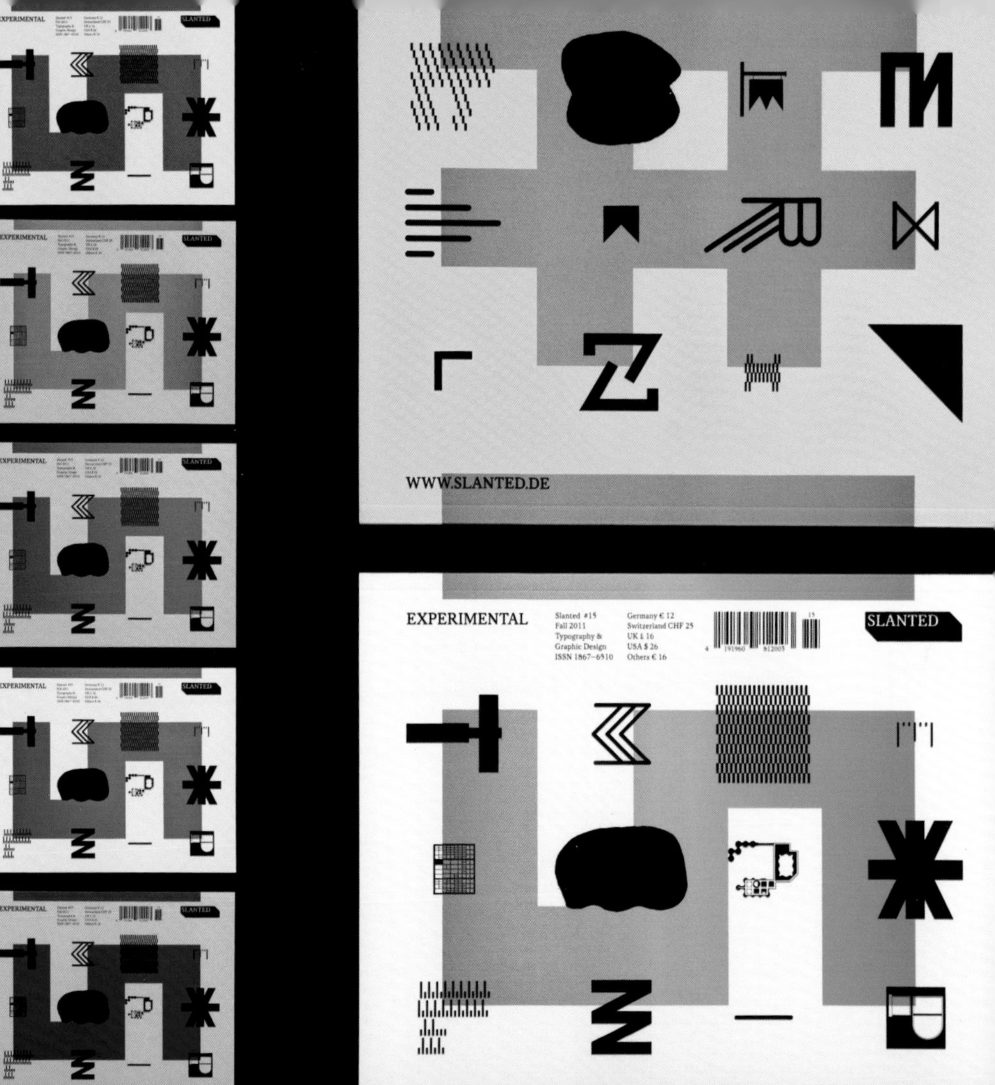
WWW.SLANTED.DE
EXPERIMENTAL
Slanted #15
Fall 2011
Typography &
Graphic Design
ISSN 1867–6510
Germany € 12
Switzerland CHF 25
UK £ 16
USA $ 26
Others € 16
SLANTED

INFORME

DESMENUZAMOS LAS MEJORES PANADERÍAS DE MADRID

040

RODRIGO SÁNCHEZ

CLIENT | Unidad Editorial Revistas SLU

What better way to represent something related to bread than the crumbs that are left when it's finished? It's the best way to show that it was delicious.

LA LUNA DE
INFORME
DESMENUZAMOS
LAS
MEJORES
PANADERÍAS
DE MADRID

LA LUNA

METROPOLI

LA REVISTA
DE OCIO
PARA EL FIN
DE SEMANA DE
EL MUNDO.
Nº 424.
DEL 15
AL 21 DE JUNIO
DE 2012

CON UN EXCEPCIONAL REPARTO, WES ANDERSON RECREA CÓMO ERAN LOS CAMPAMENTOS JUVENILES EN LOS AÑOS 60 EN LA COMEDIA MOONRISE KINGDOM...

...Y SELECCIONAMOS LOS MEJORES CAMPAMENTOS INFANTILES Y JUVENILES DEL VERANO DE 2012

041

RODRIGO SÁNCHEZ

CLIENT | Unidad Editorial Revistas SLU

The Wes Anderson film tells a story of adolescent love, almost juvenile, between a young Boy Scout and a student. Nature, love and youth are brought together in this cover.

DE SEMANA DE
EL MUNDO.
Nº 424.
DEL 15
AL 21 DE JUNIO
DE 2012
PO
CON UN
EXCEPCIONAL
REPARTO,
WES ANDERSO
RECREA CÓMO
ERAN LOS

FIN DE SEMANA DE **EL MUNDO**. Nº416.

LA LUNA DE

042

RODRIGO SÁNCHEZ

CLIENT | Unidad Editorial Revistas SLU

The cover, made from nuts, refers to the origins of the story and the consequences of the game.

LA REVISTA DE OCIO PARA EL FIN DE SEMANA DE **EL MUNDO**. Nº416. DEL 20 AL 26 DE ABRIL DE 2012

LA LUNA DE

LOS JUEGOS DEL HAMBRE

DESVELAMOS LAS 12 CLAVES DEL GRAN FENÓMENO LITERARIO Y CINEMATOGRÁFICO DE 2012

Ling

NUMERO 28, JUNIO 2009

A MAGAZINE ABOUT PEOPLE AND THEIR CITIES *exclusively for vueling passengers*

LAS COSAS QUE

043

FERICHE & BLACK

CLIENT | Vueling/La Fábrica

Magazine for the airline Vueling. It was created with the idea of distancing itself as much as possible from the typical onboard magazine. We envisioned an accessible, human and contemporary magazine. From this concept, we also came up with the manual title headline. In this case, the cover is a collage of everyday objects to illustrate the title "The Things We Love". Very personal things, it's clear.

SLANTED 17 — CARTOON / COMIC
SLANTED 17 — CARTOON / COMIC
SLANTED 17 — CARTOON / COMIC
SLANTED 17 — CARTOON / COMIC
SLANTED 17 — CARTOON / COMIC
17
CARTOON

SLANTED
TYPOGRAFIE & GRAFIK DESIGN
17
CARTOON
COMIC
17
CARTOON
COMIC
SLANTED

SLANTED
TYPOGRAFIE & GRAFIK DESIGN
17
CARTOON
COMIC
WWW.SLANTED.DE — TYPOGRAFIE & GRAFIK DESIGN

SLANTED
COMIC
CARTOON
17
TYPOGRAFIE & GRAFIK DESIGN

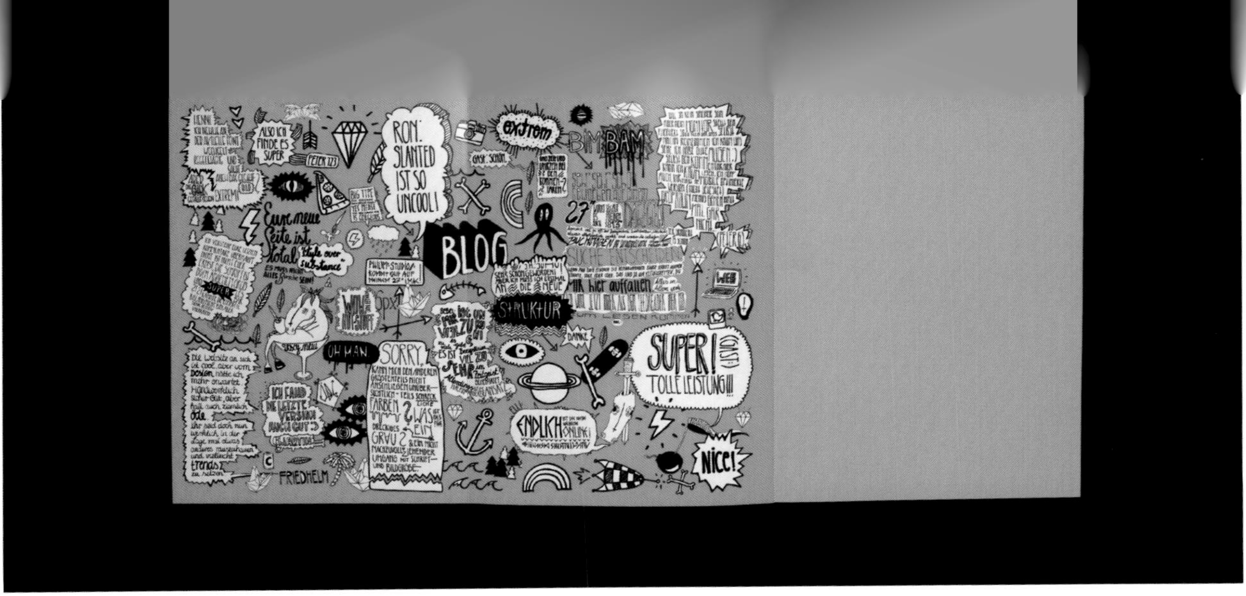

044

MAGMA BRAND DESIGN

CLIENT | Slanted, www.slanted.de

Comics consist of a sequence of images (strip) that tell a story. In cartoons, the narrative point is condensed into one image. The *Slanted issue # 17 – Cartoon / Comic* is packed cover to cover full of naratives and typographic explosion!

Along with the New Year, the first *Slanted* issue of 2012 has a new face. A new oversized format, 16 more pages, and a more tightening sequence in content and layout to create more space for projects and activities.

Also the appearance of the new magazine is marked throughout the comic book world. The eight-page fold-out cover glows in red and green on the outside, while the inside are comments of readers from our blog www.slanted.de, which were posted online last November.

WWW.NO
MAKING-
rechts ...
ne ...

045

PAPERLUX

CLIENT | Stiebner Publishing House

For the cover of the November 2011 issue we pulled out all the stops to produce something truly special after a long preparation period.

In 48,000 passes and with 104 extremely detailed die cuts per magazine, we created six differently coloured versions of the cover, without exposing the plates again each time. Our aim was to change the tangibility of the material only by "scribing" the paper. The result is a metamorphosis of paper, inspired by the one and only Richard Buckminster Fuller.

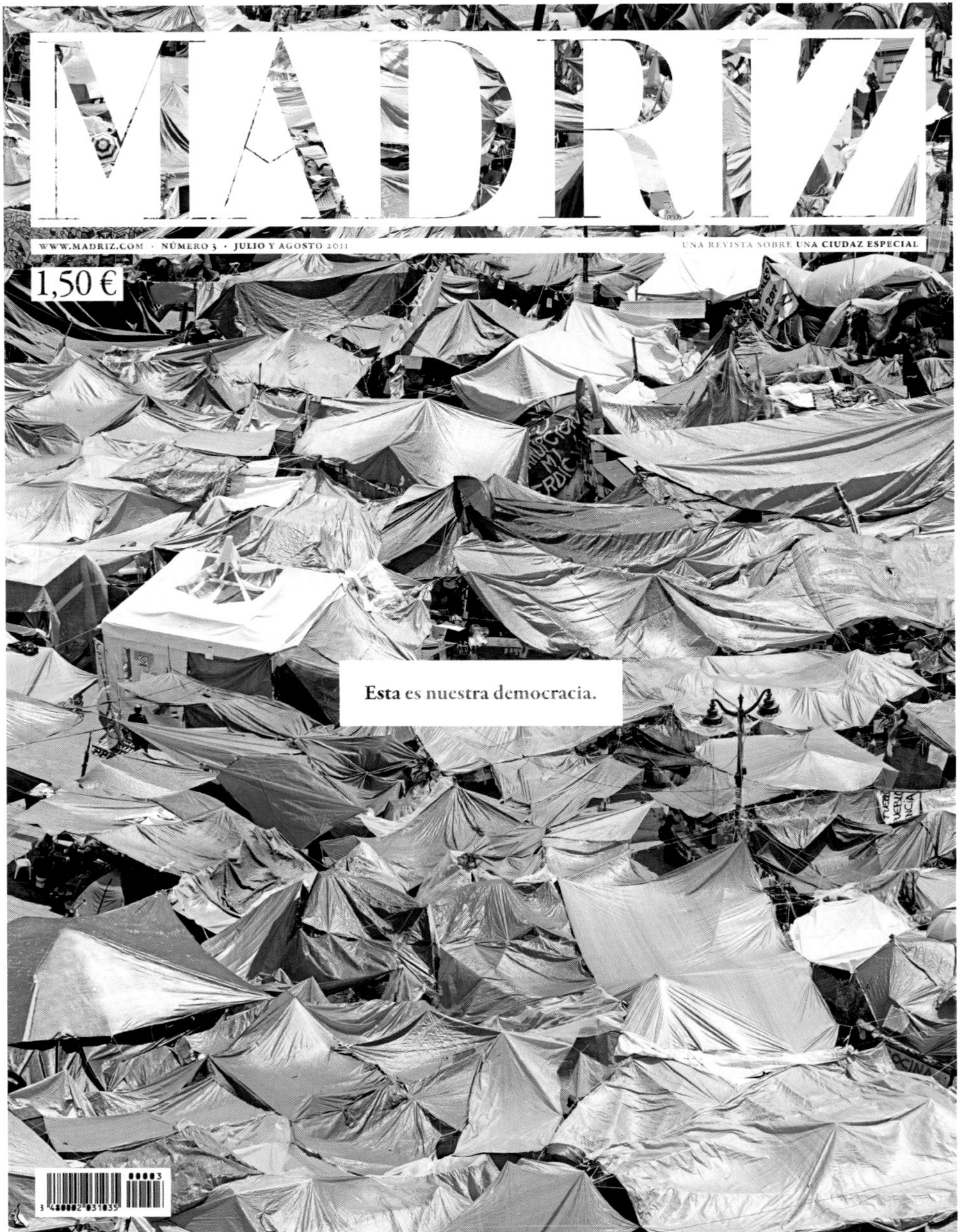
MADRIZ
WWW.MADRIZ.COM · NÚMERO 3 · JULIO Y AGOSTO 2011
UNA REVISTA SOBRE UNA CIUDAZ ESPECIAL
1,50 €
Esta es nuestra democracia.
3 480002 031035
00003

La única lucha que se pierde
es la que se abandona.

046

MADRIZ

CLIENT I Madriz

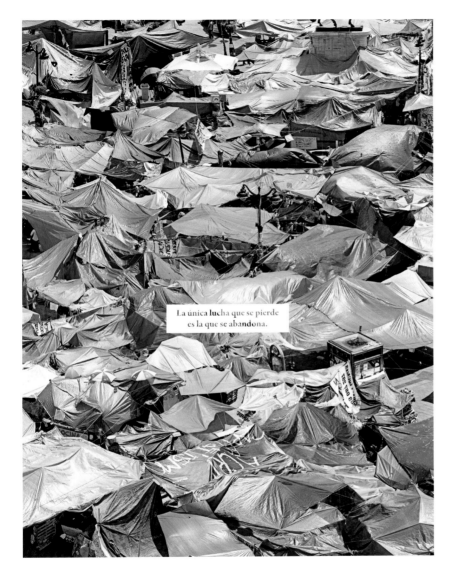

Issue number 3 of *Madriz* published in June 2011 was dedicated to the 15-M, a protest movement that took the streets of Spain and camped out for weeks in Puerta del Sol, Madrid's central square. Taken by Fernando Maselli, the photograph brings together through Photoshop a number of shots taken from different balconies surrounding Puerta del Sol. In order to create an aesthetic pattern, the tarpaulins were also digitally replicated. This visual exaggeration was aimed to highlight the public resonance and the political significance of this historical event.

The New York Times Style Magazine SUMMER 2009
Prism Break
ARTWORK BY PIERRE VANNI. PHOTOGRAPH BY MITCHELL FEINBERG.

he New York Times Style Magazine SUMMER 2009

047

PIERRE VANNI

CLIENT | New York Times Style Magazine

A fantastic example of creative direction for the Summer 2009 T Style well opener. Angular origami-like foreshadows the season's trend for colourful minimalism in this ocean cool and chiseled T sculpture.

048

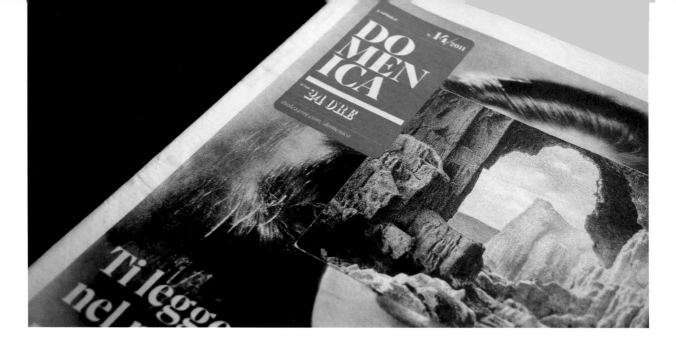

LUCA PITONI & ADRIANO ATTUS

CLIENT | Sole 24 Ore

Domenica, the most influential weekly cultural supplement of Italy.

A collage from English artist John Stezaker, "Mask XXXV".
The cover story is about neuroscience.
The title is "I read your thoughts"

Sold as an annex to *Sole 24 Ore* financial newspaper. Tabloid format, daily "pink" paper, 350.000 copies.
Year 2011, Editor-in-chief: Gianni Riotta.

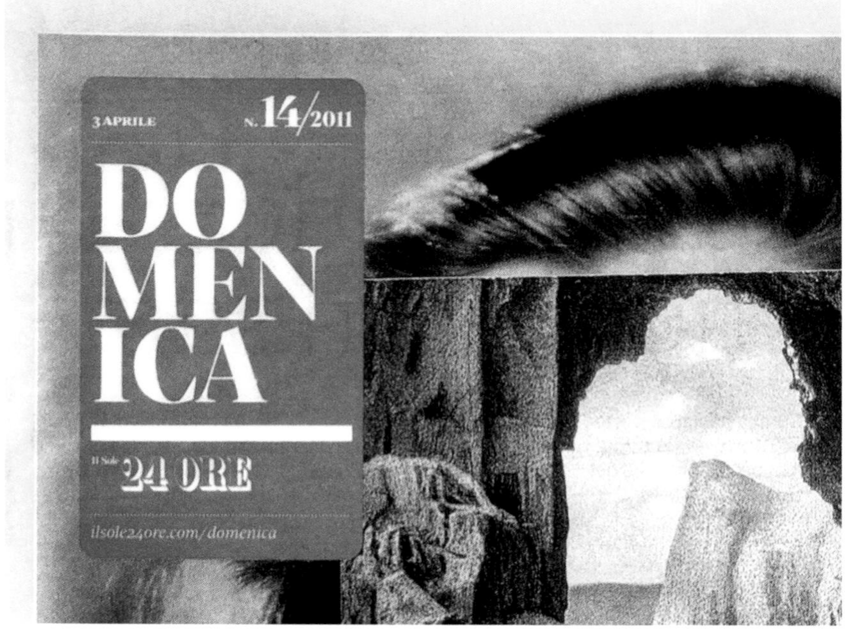

3 APRILE N. 14/2011

DOMENICA

Il Sole 24 ORE

ilsole24ore.com/domenica

Lydstep Cavern, nearTenby.

Ti leggo nel pensiero

Così le neuroscienze ci fanno scoprire i nostri supersensi E ne creano di nuovi

— pagg. 6-7

ORO DI NAPOLI

In mostra i gioielli di San Gennaro

— pp. 22-23

049

RODRIGO SÁNCHEZ

CLIENT | Unidad Editorial Revistas SLU

We wanted our cover to be a giant wave that destroyed everything in its path. Everything, including the cover title. Half of the page rushes over the other half.

LA OLA QUE HIZO LO IMPOSIBLE. JUAN ANTONIO BAYONA RECREA CON ESCALOFRIANTE REALISMO EL TSUNAMI DEL SUDESTE ASIÁTICO EN UNA PELÍCULA PROTAGONIZADA POR NAOMI WATTS Y EWAN McGREGOR

METROPOLI
LA REVISTA DE OCIO PARA EL ... DE EL MUNDO. Nº441. DEL 12 AL 18 DE OCTUBRE DE 2012
DEL 12 AL 18 DE OCTUBRE DE 2012
LA OLA QUE HIZO LO IMPOSIBLE. JUAN ANTONIO BAYONA RECREA CON ESCALOFRIANTE REALISMO EL TSUNAMI DEL SUDESTE ASIÁTICO EN UNA PELÍCULA PROTAGONIZADA POR NAOMI WATTS Y EWAN McGREGOR

050

LO SIENTO

CLIENT | +81

Graphic piece for the cover of the Japanese magazine *+81* magazine. The Fall 2011 edition was about "next creativity", which is why we proposed to create a typographic lettering through the use of bubble paper and injecting water with blue colouring. The bubble paper has a grid that allowed for putting concrete messages with only the use of a syringe as a drawing instrument.

Each typography was developed thinking about the brief, and was always inspired by its creation within the grid. Each existing grid can hide a typographic character and therefore, an alphabet. Experimental typography is a new layer or system within typographic design, as with today's tools you can achieve important results and create typographies without the exclusive use of a computer.

PLUS
EIGHTY
ONE
VOL.53 / AUTUMN 2011
Next Creativity Issue
ISBN978-4-309-90921-9
C0070 ¥1200E
9784309909219
定価 本体1200円 (税別)
発行:ディー・ディー・ウェーブ株式会社
発売:河出書房新社
1920070012002

051

FERICHE & BLACK

CLIENT | La Fábrica

A cultural travel magazine. What stands out most is the typographic treatment of the headline (which includes the number of the publication) and magazine title, which have the same weight and font. The photographic selection is always chosen very carefully. In these two cases we have an emblematic image taken by Masats during San Fermines, and a photograph of Oscar Tusquets (taken by Leopoldo Pomés), which reminds us of Italy with his harcut and exaggerated Roman profile. In this edition, Oscar was accompanied by Veneto, and we saw Scarpa and Canova.

OOM 6
DA BUENOS VIAJEROS
SQUETS
ADIO, CANOVA Y SCARPA
ROOM 2
REVISTA PARA BUENOS VIAJEROS
MASATS
DE VUELTA A LOS SANFERMINES / BACK TO SANFERMINES

052

GAIL BICHLER

CLIENT | The New York Times Magazine

The cover illustrates the contentious and eruptive nature of the geopolitical disputes between two Middle-Eastern powers, Iran and Israel. Ashed paper and smoke creates a cover that visually explains the rift these two sovereign nations are facing.

The New York Times Magazine
January 29, 2012
ISRAEL VS IRAN
WHEN WILL IT ERUPT? BY RONEN BERGMAN

y
o
r
o
k
o
b
u

053

DAVIDELFIN

CLIENT I Yorokobu

This is the cover that Davidelfin did for *Yorokobu*. It's open to different readings and interpretations, whereas, according to the artist, his proposal was more related to sculpture, secrets and mystery than to provocation. What happened was that the cover was filled with marks crossed out, which made us completely change the way we normally face this section: first they do the cover for us and then we write this text. Long live challenges and new scenes that make you think differently!

Davidelfin says that it's a metaphor for unconsciousness. "We're attracted to what we can't see, we want to read something that's crossed out even more than something that's perfectly legible...in our case, we love words and this is like a buried treasure."

And hidden in there, can you find the concept of "being happy" that is in implicit in the Japanese term Yorokobu? Well, yes. "It has to do with the work that we do, which makes us happy, and also with having the freedom to do what we want."

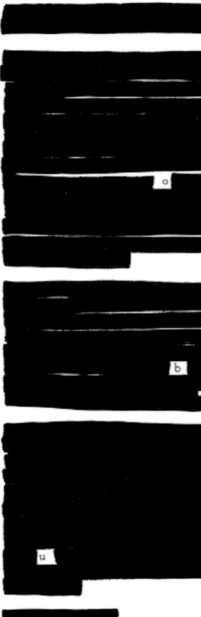

BREAKING THE MOLD

ARTWORK BY FABIEN BARON

054

FABIEN BARON

CLIENT | New York Times Style Magazine

The final T Style well opener in a series that spanned eight years of logo presentations. Created by Janet Froelich in 2004, this final T sculpture takes the fall as concrete shards seem to explode off the impact. Though broken, its form and essence remains intact. What more could a magazine concept page hope to impart as legacy?

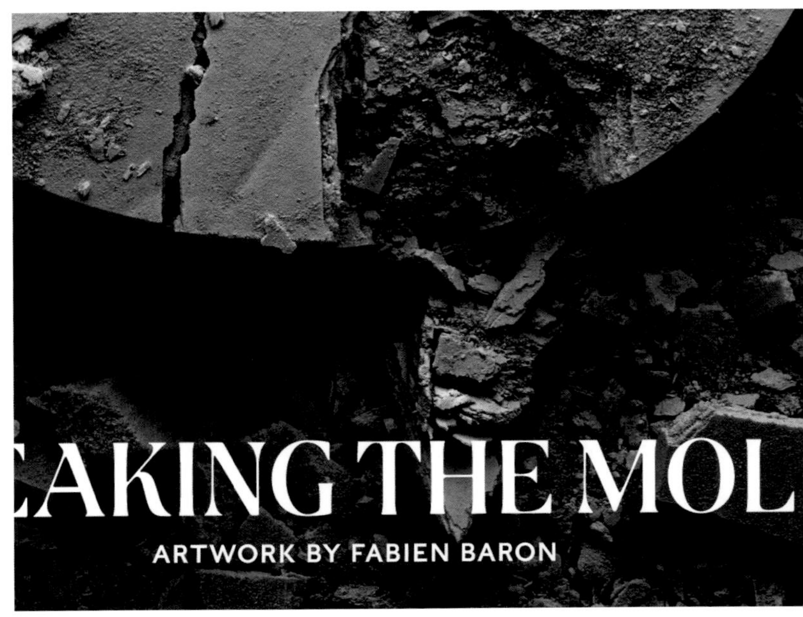

055

FRANCESCO FRANCHI

CLIENT | IL / Il Sole 24 ORE

Topic of the cover: the newspaper crisis.

SI CHIAMA CHIMURENGA IL NEW YORKER AFRICANO

Francesco Pacifico pag. 57

LA SVOLTA DI BEN SMITH BLOG, SIETE AL CAPOLINE

Jason Horowitz pag. 65

2

DIANO più letto al mon- apponese *Yomiuri Shim-* 14.532.694 copie, lo segue l'*Asahi Shimbun* con 12.601.375 copie diffuse.

IN ISLANDA IL 96 PER CENTO della popolazione legge tutti i giorni un quotidiano. Seguono giapponesi (92 per cento), norvegesi, svedesi, svizzeri e finlandesi.

NEL MONDO CI SONO 14.853 testate giornalistiche. Nel 2010 sono cresciute di 200 unità. In calo i giornali free press.

LA che pati mili sup do i of sh we stu c c

La notizia

ha causato in 5 anni cali menti pubblicitari del 23 , ma nell'ultimo anno il ato solo del 3 per cento.

IN GIAPPONE i quotidiani vendono in media 461 mila copie ciascuno. I giornali austriaci ne vendono 162 mila al giorno. In India invece si vendono più quotidiani rispetto agli Stati Uniti d'America e alla Germania.

L'INDUSTRIA INDIANA dei quotidiani cartacei è cresciuta di due terzi solo negli ultimi sei anni. Da oggi al 2014 si prevede che ci sarà un ulteriore boom del 18 per cento.

L' di pe ch ch sc N le de m ch in nu di ch de è pr

della mia

EA ASIA-PACIFICO la dif- delle copie è aumentata cento tra il 2009 e il 2010, er cento negli ultimi cin- . In America Latina più nto l'anno scorso e più ento negli ultimi 5 anni.

IL PRIMO ESEMPIO di "quotidiano", inteso come pubblicazione giornaliera del resoconto degli avvenimenti politici e di attualità, risale al 59 a.C. quando Giulio Cesare istituì gli *Acta Diurna populi Romani*.

NEL 2011 L'ECONOMIST ha superato il milione e mezzo di copie settimanali per la prima volta nella sua storia. «Ci abbiamo messo 160 anni per raggiungere il milione di copie diffuse, ma soltanto sette per arrivare a un milione e mezzo. E adesso ci aspettiamo di arrivare a due milioni di copie entro cinque anni». Nel 2006 una copertina dell'*Economist* aveva chiesto chi avesse ucciso i giornali. Quattro anni dopo, lo stesso settimanale della City ha raccontato «lo strano caso della sopravvivenza dell'inchiostro». I giornali sono sopravvissuti al cataclisma della crisi finanziaria diventando più snelli, più concentrati sulle proprie caratteristiche e soprattutto più calibrati sulle esigenze dei lettori.

morte

NTICO giornale? C'è una ancora aperta tra lo sve- *t-och Inrikes Tidningar* il tedesco *Einkommende* fondato a Lipsia nel 1650.

LA REGOLA DELLE 5 W del giornalismo anglosassone è legata al telegrafo: nell'800, il costo a parola dei telegrammi era elevato. I corrispondenti dettavano solo le cose fondamentali: who, what, where, when, why.

e fortemen

ACCESSORI proposti nel-

LE BICICLETTE Cigno del Gruppo

PER NON SEPARARSI mai dal pro-

PU

Marzo 2012

SI CHIAMA CHIMURENGA IL NEW YORKER AFRICANO
Francesco Pacifico pag. 57

LA SVOLTA DI BEN SMITH: BLOG, SIETE AL CAPOLINEA
Jason Horowitz pag. 65

COME FARE UN GIORNALE CINESE A MILANO
Carlo Piano pag. 73

La notizia della mia morte è fortemente esagerata

IL QUOTIDIANO più letto al mondo è il giapponese *Yomiuri Shimbun* con 14.532.694 copie, lo segue l'*Asahi Shimbun* con 12.601.375 copie diffuse.

IN ISLANDA IL 96 PER CENTO della popolazione legge tutti i giorni un quotidiano. Seguono giapponesi (92 per cento), norvegesi, svedesi, svizzeri e finlandesi.

NEL MONDO CI SONO 14.853 testate giornalistiche. Nel 2010 sono cresciute di 200 unità. In calo i giornali free press.

LA CARTA BATTE INTERNET anche nell'era web. I giornali stampati sono letti ogni giorno da 2,3 miliardi di persone. Un numero superiore del 20 per cento, secondo i dati della World Association of Newspapers and News Publishers, rispetto agli utenti globali web che sono 1,9 miliardi. Uno studio del *Financial Times* svela che i manager internazionali continuano a preferire la carta.

LA CRISI ha causato in 5 anni cali d'investimenti pubblicitari del 23 per cento, ma nell'ultimo anno il calo è stato solo del 3 per cento.

IN GIAPPONE i quotidiani vendono in media 461 mila copie ciascuno. I giornali austriaci ne vendono 162 mila al giorno. In India invece si vendono più quotidiani rispetto agli Stati Uniti d'America e alla Germania.

L'INDUSTRIA INDIANA dei quotidiani cartacei è cresciuta di due terzi solo negli ultimi sei anni. Da oggi al 2014 si prevede che ci sarà un ulteriore boom del 18 per cento.

L'autoironia di Mark Twain per smentire chi dice che i giornali sono finiti. Nessuno nega le difficoltà della stampa, ma le storie che raccontiamo in questo numero dimostrano che l'epitaffio della carta è quantomeno prematuro

NELL'AREA ASIA-PACIFICO la diffusione delle copie è aumentata del 7 per cento tra il 2009 e il 2010, e del 16 per cento negli ultimi cinque anni. In America Latina più 2 per cento l'anno scorso e più 4,5 per cento negli ultimi 5 anni.

IL PRIMO ESEMPIO di "quotidiano", inteso come pubblicazione giornaliera del resoconto degli avvenimenti politici e di attualità, risale al 59 a.C. quando Giulio Cesare istituì gli *Acta Diurna populi Romani*.

NEL 2011 L'ECONOMIST ha superato il milione e mezzo di copie settimanali per la prima volta nella sua storia. «Ci abbiamo messo 160 anni per raggiungere il milione di copie diffuse, ma soltanto sette per arrivare a un milione e mezzo. E adesso ci aspettiamo di arrivare a due milioni di copie entro cinque anni». Nel 2006 una copertina dell'*Economist* aveva chiesto chi avesse ucciso i giornali. Quattro anni dopo, lo stesso settimanale della City ha raccontato «lo strano caso della sopravvivenza dell'inchiostro». I giornali sono sopravvissuti al cataclisma della crisi finanziaria diventando più snelli, più concentrati sulle proprie caratteristiche e soprattutto più calibrati sulle esigenze dei lettori.

IL PIÙ ANTICO giornale? C'è una disputa ancora aperta tra lo svedese *Post-och Inrikes Tidningar* del 1645 e il tedesco *Einkommende Zeitung*, fondato a Lipsia nel 1650.

LA REGOLA DELLE 5 W del giornalismo anglosassone è legata al telegrafo: nell'800, il costo a parola dei telegrammi era elevato. I corrispondenti dettavano solo le cose fondamentali: who, what, where, when, why.

TRA GLI ACCESSORI proposti nelle ultime collezioni moda (tra cui tanti porta iPad) ne spicca uno in controtendenza: disegnato da Raf Simons per Jil Sander, è un contenitore avvolgi-giornale in pelle semirigida preziosa.

LE BICICLETTE Cigno del Gruppo Bernardi offrono un elegante accessorio recuperato tra i brevetti originali degli anni 50: si tratta del porta-giornale in acciaio da montare sul manubrio e disponibile nei colori oro o grigio cromato.

PER NON SEPARARSI mai dal proprio quotidiano preferito, Woolrich Woolen Mills e il suo designer Mark McNairy ripropongono per il prossimo inverno la giacca-camicia con maxi tasca verticale porta-giornale.

PUBBLICITÀ IN PRIMA PAGINA del *New York Times*: il 5 gennaio 2009, per la prima volta nella sua storia, il quotidiano americano ha venduto uno spazio nella *front page*. Si trattava di una striscia a colori di 6 cm della rete tv CBS.

IL – Il maschile del Sole 24 ORE n.39 del 16/03/2012 mensile PI Sped. in AP

D.L.353/2003 CONV. L.46/2004 Art.1, C.1, DCB MILANO Venerdì 16/03 in abbinamento obbligatorio con Il Sole 24 ORE a € 2,00 Da sabato 17/03 solo IL – Il maschile del Sole 24 ORE a € 0,50

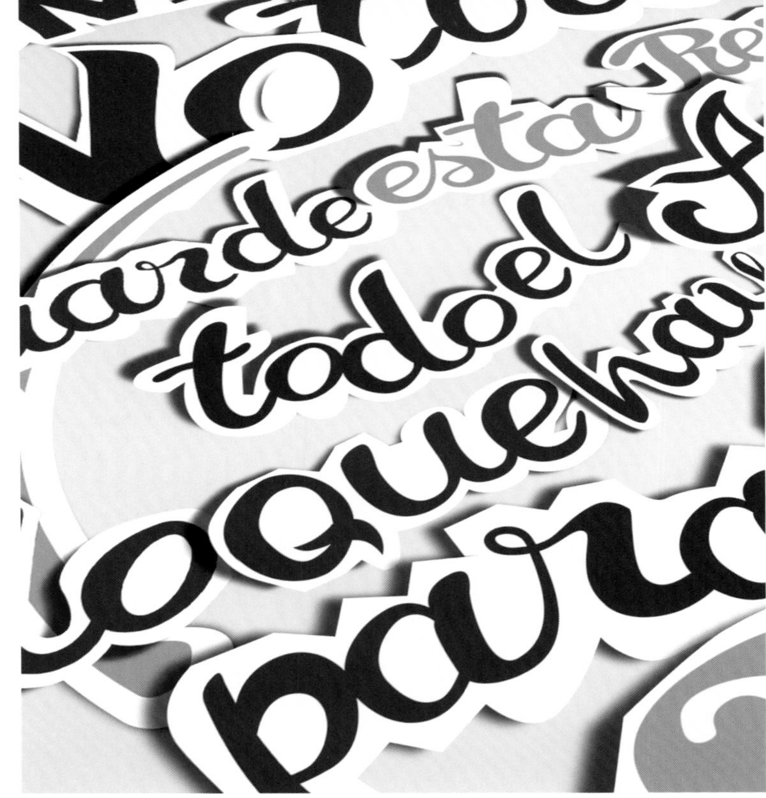

056

SERGIO JIMÉNEZ - SUBCOOLTURE

CLIENT | El Periódico de Catalunya

Covered created for the first issue of the year of the magazine *Dominical* (in the newspaper *El Periódico de Catalunya*). It's based on lettering constructed around cut-out words, alluding to an exercise of encouragement and survival confronting the difficult years that are coming with the economic crisis. Published in a bilingual double edition (Spanish and Catalan).

DOMINICAL
No
la llenceu
guardeu aquesta Revista
tot l'Any
el que s'ha de saber
per sobreviure
al 2011

EL FUTURO SIEMPRE VUELVE AL PASADO... Y VICEVERSA
LA LUNA DE
LA REVISTA DE OCIO PARA EL FIN DE SEMANA DE EL MUNDO
Nº442. DEL 19 AL 25 DE OCTUBRE DE 2012
METROPOLI
LOOPER
BRUCE WILLIS ES LA ESTRELLA DE "LOOPER", UNA PELÍCULA DE CIENCIA FICCIÓN SOBRE ASESINOS A SUELDO QUE VIAJAN EN EL TIEMPO

057

RODRIGO SÁNCHEZ

CLIENT | Unidad Editorial Revistas SLU

The past, the future and the paradoxes of time travel. A clock that goes forward and back. Metrópoli became personally involved in the themes that were brought to the cover, forwardwards and backwards.

058

RODRIGO SÁNCHEZ

CLIENT | Unidad Editorial Revistas SLU

Cover drawn with pen on the outer edge of various books all together.

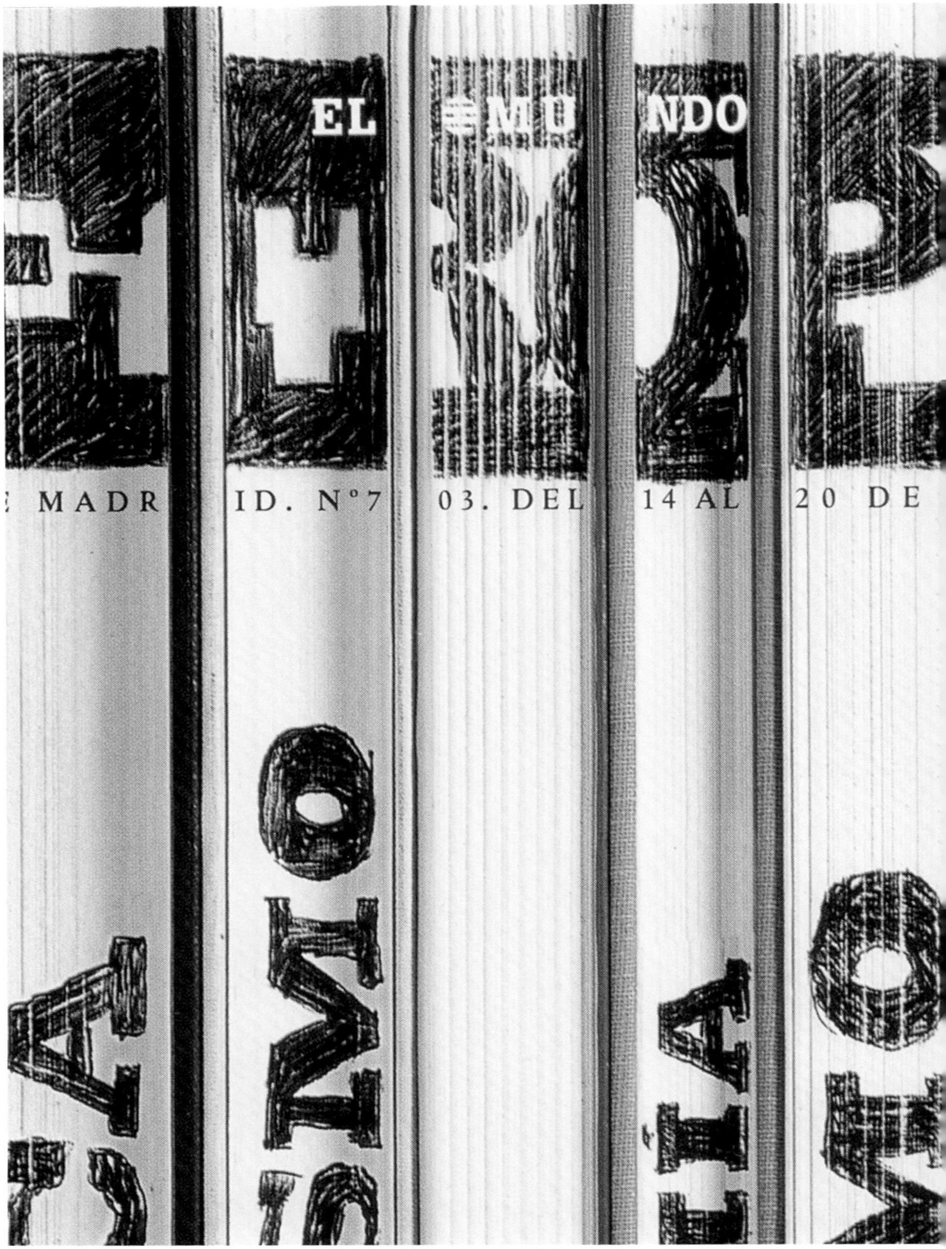

EL MUNDO
LA REVISTA DE MADRID. Nº703. DEL 14 AL 20 DE NOVIEMBRE DE 2003
VIAJES
CÓMIC
BOTÁNICA
ESOTERISMO
CINE
GASTRONOMÍA
EROTISMO
EDICIONES ÚNICAS
NATURISMO
RELIGIÓN
AQUÍ ENCONTRARÁ LOS LIBROS
MÁS RAROS

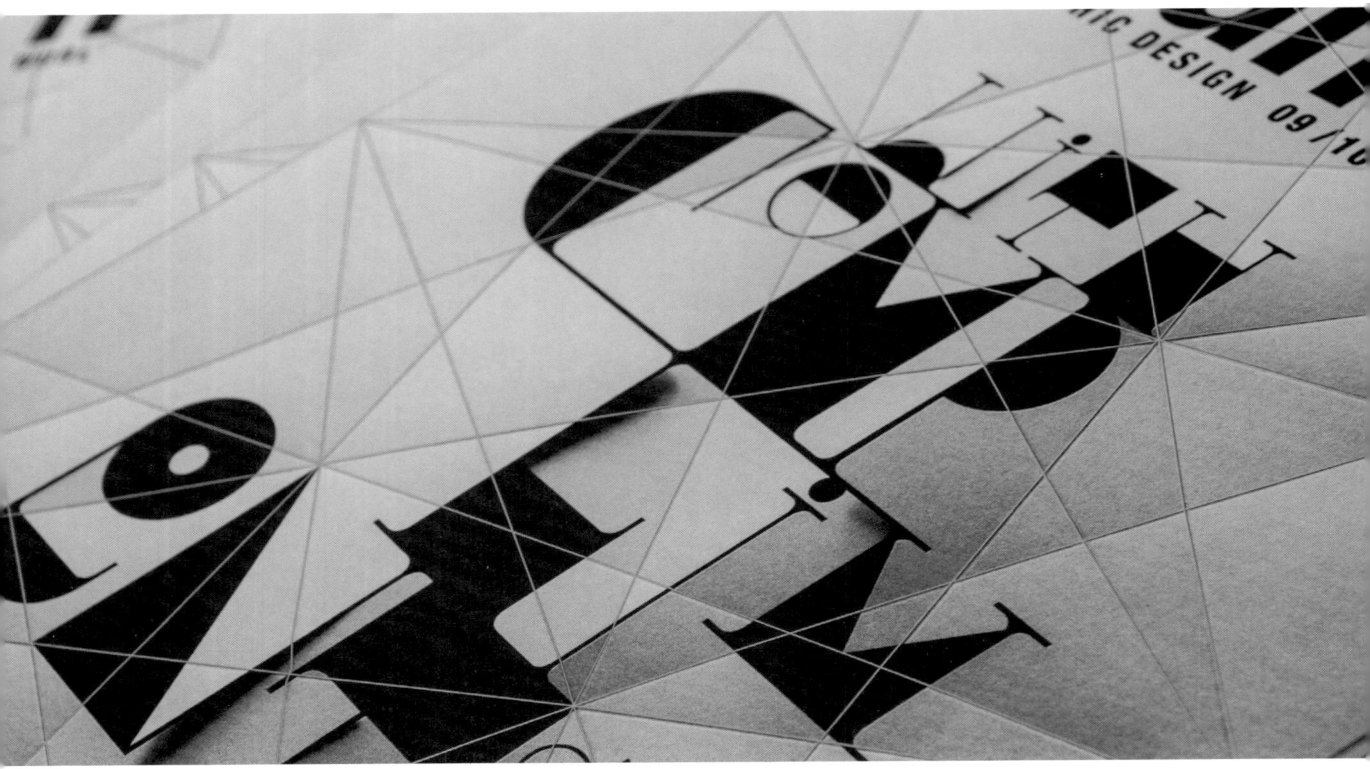

059

PAPERLUX

CLIENT | Stiebner Publishing House

Space or illusion? Typo cuts through a folded paper area, the shadows are caught on a photo - while the folds are tangible through a silkscreen relief printing. Three cover versions were available, each with the fine silkscreen lines, but in different colours.

Cultura, moda e geopolitica del mangiare tra *foodies*, *gastroindignados* e nuove rivoluzioni

L'APPETITO NEL MONDO

THE FOOD ISSUE

THE FICTION ISSUE

Racconti inediti di grandi scrittori italiani e stranieri in esclusiva per IL

RANE

DICEMBRE 2012

060

FRANCESCO FRANCHI

CLIENT | IL / Il Sole 24 ORE

Topic of the cover: special double issue, food and fiction.

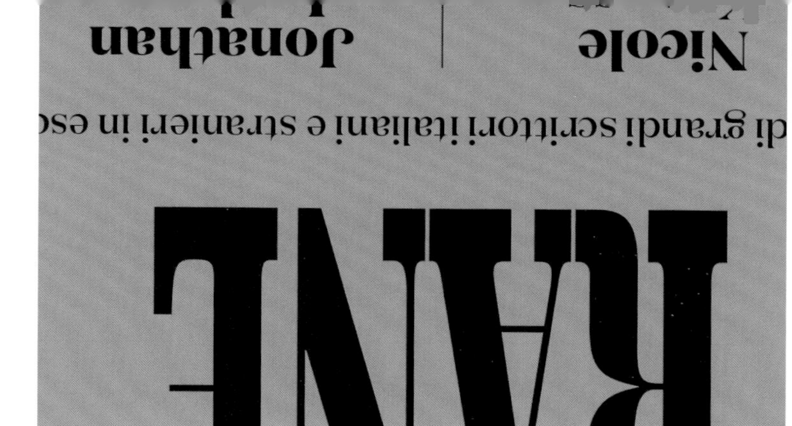

THE
ISSUE
FICTION
THE
ISSUE

Filippo Bologna
Gli attori sono cani – p.156
Rick Moody
Si dimenticava – p.163

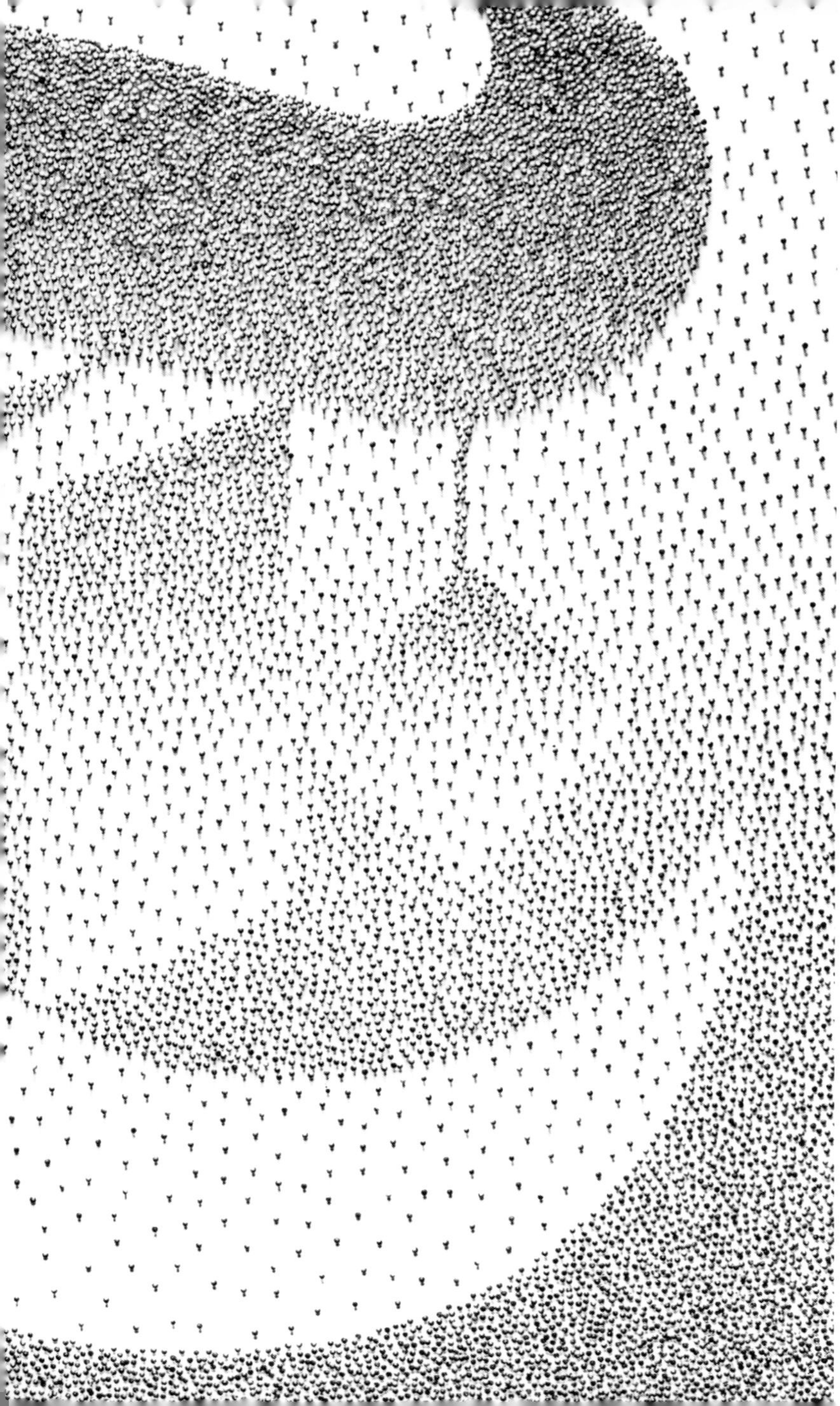

061

TARA DONOVAN

CLIENT | New York Times Style Magazine

Pointillism at its best. A magnificently executed collection of steel pins create a memorable Travel Spring 2011 well opener. Take note Google, dropping a pin, or many, can do more than mark territory.

The New York Times Style Magazine TRAVEL SPRING 2011
PHOTOGRAPH BY STEPHEN LEWIS
DROP A PIN
81

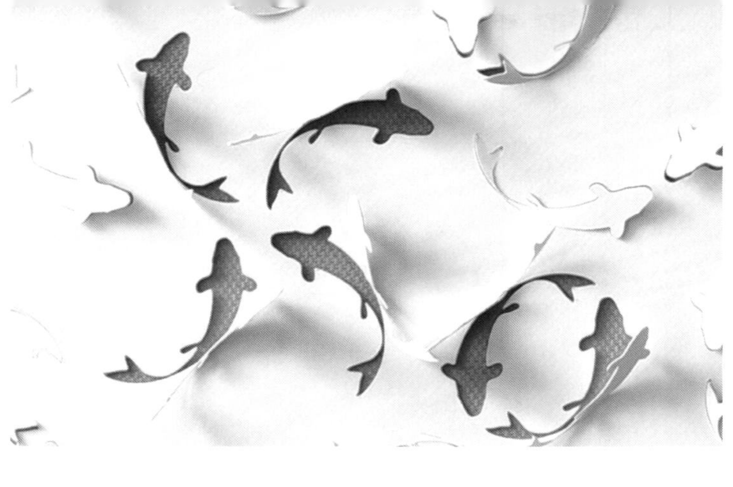

062

WANDA BARCELONA

CLIENT | Yorokobu

There's a lake on the cover, though it's white, not blue. Maybe it's the foam that makes the golden carp splash around. And between jumps, they draw shapes in the air. There are two that seem to be following each other and form a circle. Sometimes, a third joins this dance. On occasion, one of the fish can be seen jumping alone and sometimes several coincide in a jump, forming a star before re-entering their habitat, the fresh water.

It's a reading. But there's another, the one we ask of all of the artists who do the cover: to be able to read the word Yorokobu. That is to say, that they invent some lettering. And in this case, the letters are formed by some of the many carp that are on the cover, the ones who show their golden colour when jumping.

And why fish? Because this animal says a lot about the work of its artists, Inti, Daniel and Iris, the members of Wanda. "We're specialists in ephemeral architecture and our materials are paper and cardboard. Is there anything more ephemeral than a fish's memory? They say that every three seconds a fish forgets its previous life. It even forgets what it's eaten," comments Inti.

The carp is something else that's related to the origen of the word in question, Yorokobu. As happens to a good number of the people who pass by this space, Wanda looked for some kind Japanese icon. In a handmade way, like all of the work, they constructed a sea of paper and filled it with carp. And luck would have it that, in the moment of the photo, some of them jumped out of the water while the rest remained placidly swimming below.

A Blanc Slate JUST ADD COLOR.

ARTWORK BY KAMO. PHOTOGRAPH BY KAZUNARI TAJIMA.

A Blanc Sla

ARTWORK B

063

KAMO

CLIENT | New York Times Style Magazine

A beautifully detaild collection of paper roses and flowers, pieced together by artist Kamo, in a monastic yet intricate well opener for the Spring 2003 Style Issue. This sculpture, along with many others, form the T style logo the Times Syle magazine became well known for.

nox

TENDENCIAS DISEÑO

ARQUITECTURA MODA ARTE

PANAMERICANA: LA AVENTURA DE CRUZAR UN CONTINENTE

LOS MEJORES APARTAMENTOS CON FIRMA

COCHES CON ESPÍRITU F-1

TECNOLOGÍA PUNTA PARA VIAJEROS

JOAQUIN

064

FERICHE & BLACK

CLIENT | Focus ediciones

A trend magazine.
Black and white. A centered image. Openly smoking.
His name in an exaggerated font, half-hidden by the actor himself, that, apart from giving the title, also decorates and gives the image a certain volume. Without concessions.

065

NICOLA YEOMAN

CLIENT | New York Times Style Magazine

A ghostly fog surrounds translucent white chiffon, arranged and strung in a rural forest scene, inviting the reader to the then coming 2010 Fall fashion trends. The well opener, like the fabric used, almost floats off the page, creating a delicate balance between the constant and the ephemeral.

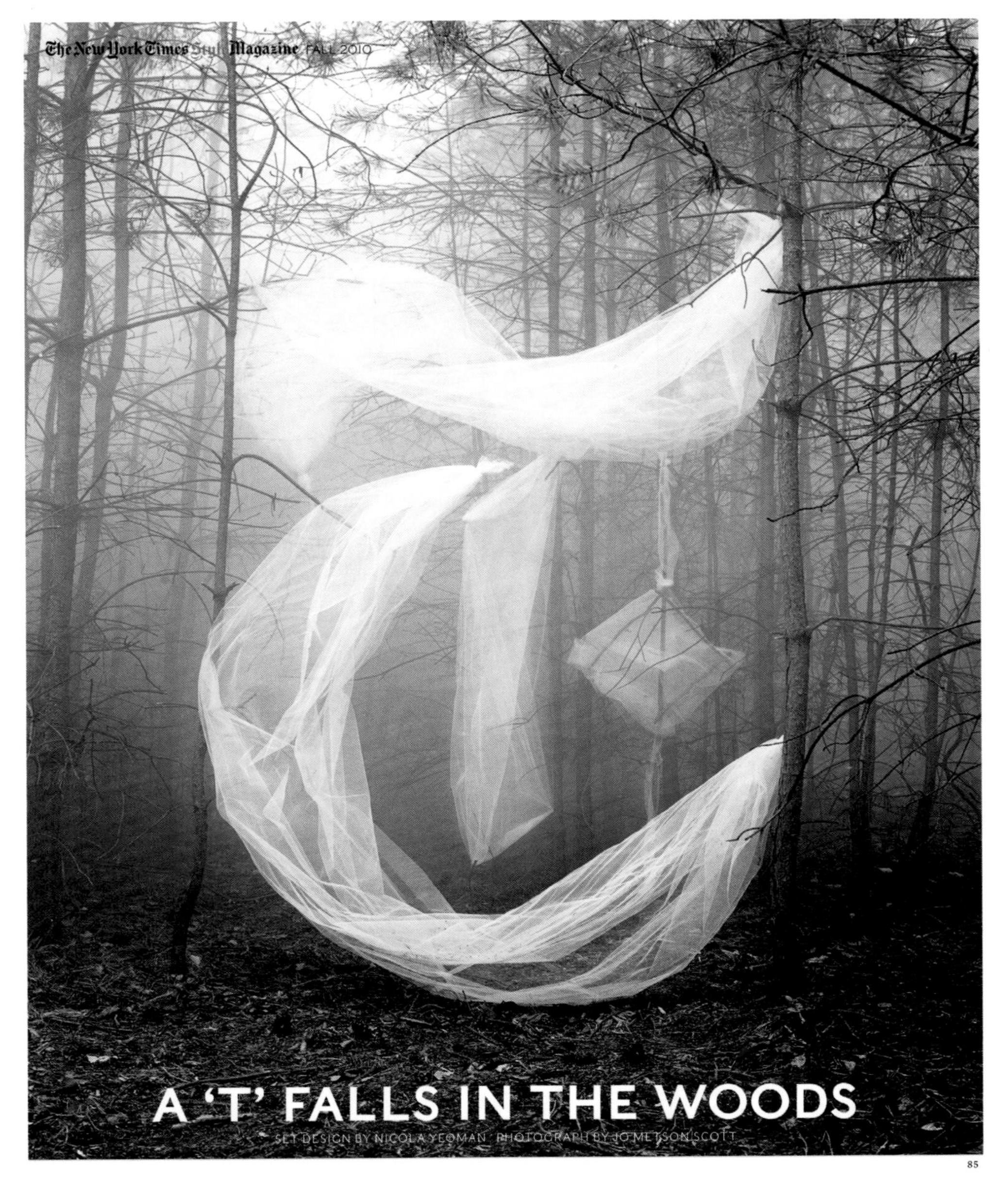
The New York Times Style Magazine FALL 2010
A 'T' FALLS IN THE WOODS
SET DESIGN BY NICOLA YEOMAN PHOTOGRAPH BY JO METSON SCOTT
85

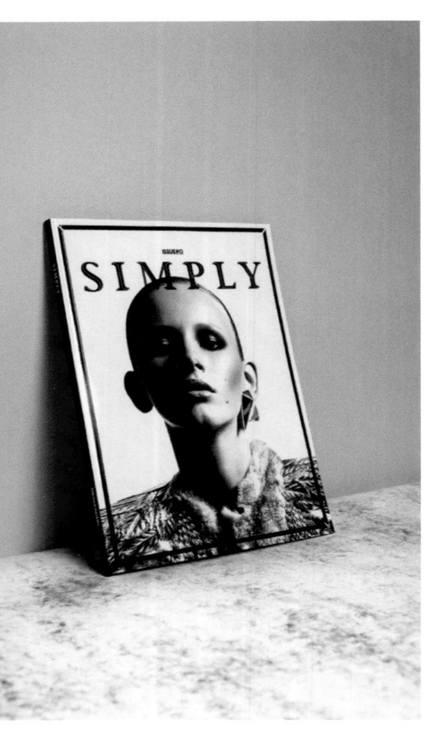

066

PABLO ABAD

CLIENT | Simplyprorsum

SIMPLY THE MAG comes from the desire to editorialise our vision of fashion. The result is a heterogeneous combination of the stories that it aims to tell, under the same creative direction, and the essence of each one of the collaborators. Twelve editorials divided in two acts, three pieces of art and a central interview, with homages to Newton and Hepburn, make up the offer of this issue #0.

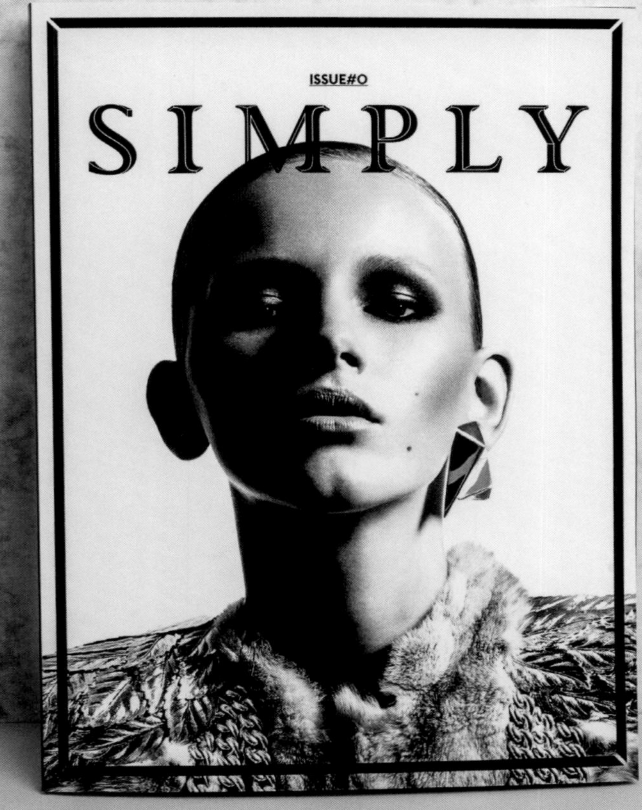

ISSUE#0
SIMPLY

YOROKOBU / TAKE A WALK ON THE SLOW SIDE / Nº 35 - 2012
5€

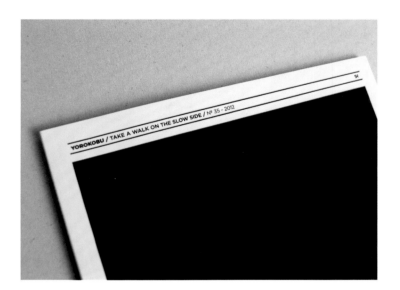

067

YOROKOBU

CLIENT | Yorokobu

This cover is a chalkboard that's waiting for you to draw the word Yorokobu. Do it however you want. You have five colours of chalk. This is our invitation for you the write Yorokobu however you like and as many times as you'd like.

This chalkboard is a birthday celebration. Our third birthday. We want to celebrate it with you and your drawings.

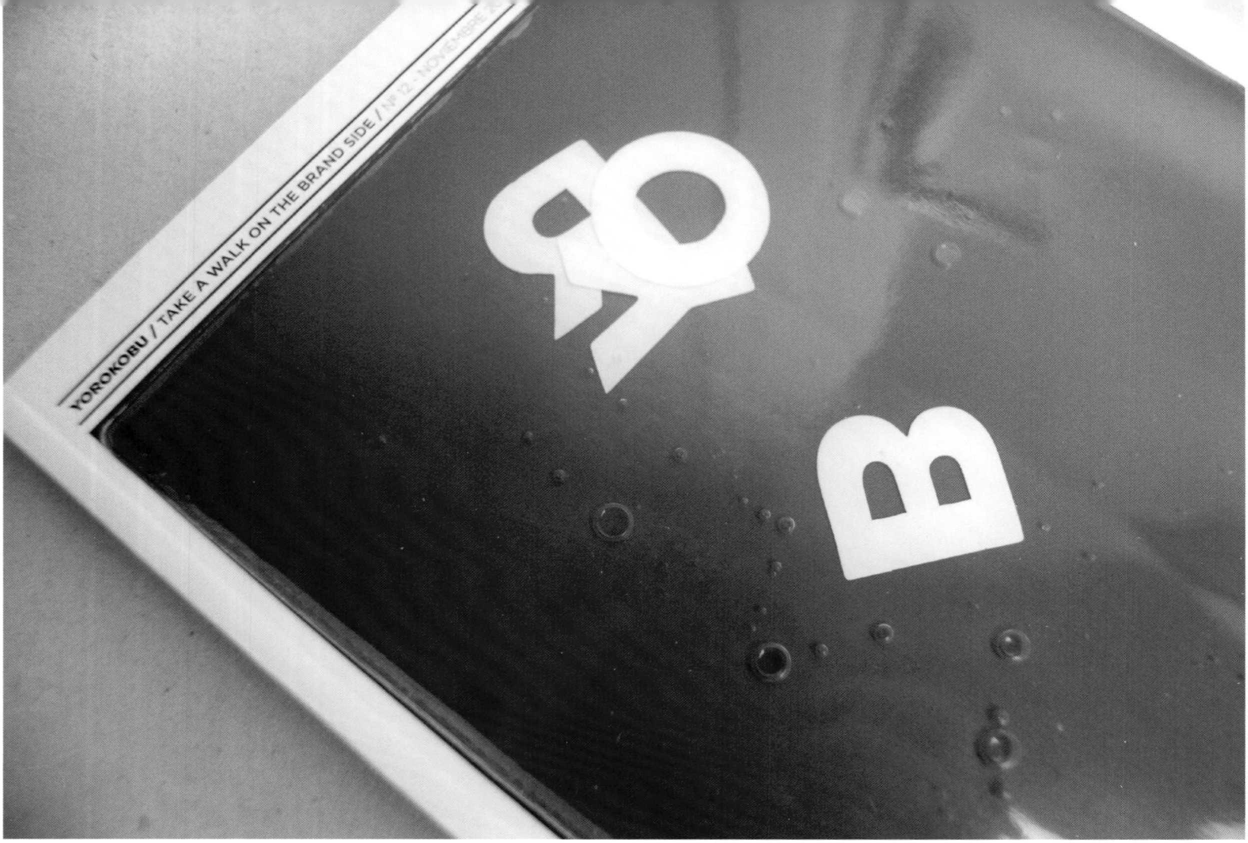

068

YOROKOBU

CLIENT | Yorokobu

This time it's your turn to make the cover. Why you? Because it's *Yorokobu's* first birthday and we're going to celebrate it by playing with letters with you. It's easy. Take the magazine with two hands. Put your face in front of the cover. Stare at the disorganized letters that move among the water and try to construct the word Yorokobu with them.

YOROKOBU / TAKE A WALK ON THE BRAND SIDE /

YOROKOBU / TAKE A WALK ON THE BRAND SIDE /

YOROKOBU / TAKE A WALK ON THE BRAND SIDE /

YOROKOBU / TAKE A WALK ON THE BRAND SIDE /

069

MAGMA BRAND DESIGN

CLIENT | Slanted, www.slanted.de

SLAB! Slanted Magazine #20 – Slab Serif is entirely dedicated to the early 19th century born »serifenbetonte Linear-Antiqua,« broadly known as Egyptienne, Slab Serif, Square Serif or Mécanes outside German classification. Developing during Industrial Revolution in Great Britain, these typefaces fastly spread on advertising posters and flyers. Back in these days it was the main purpose of the slab serifs to attract attention by their strong visual expression. In this issue we want to bring back some of this (at least in Central Europe) rather gone attention to the often striking slab serifs.

The cover shows Hank Aaron in full batting position after his famous 714 career home run. The other pages of the fold-out cover are featuring other athletes and disciplines in American Sports. A popular choice and common to see on their jerseys and shirts: Slab Serifs.

SLANTED

TYPOGRAFIE & GRAFIK DESIGN

20

SLAB SERIF

WINTER 2012/13 — ISSN 1867-6510
DE EUR 14 / CH CHF 25 / UK £ 16 / US $ 26 / OTHERS EUR 16

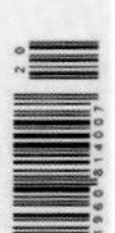

WWW.SLANTED.DE — TYPOGRAFIE & GRAFIK DESIGN

esse

arts + opinions

76

L'IDÉE DE LA
PEINTURE

THE IDEA
OF PAINTING

070

FEED

CLIENT | Esse - Contemporary art magazine

Cover for *Esse* (contemporary art magazine) on the theme “The Idea of Painting”.

A JOURNAL OF HIDDEN CREATIVITY

MAKE SHIFT

ISSUE 01 FALL 2011

ONE WORLD'S WASTE...
How most of the world's population finds opportunity in re-culture

HACKONOMICS
Everyday cost-saving product hacks in Kenya

TEXTILES REBORN
India's textile recyclers breathe new life into old fabric

SCIENCE OF SCARCITY
The struggle to bridge science with indigenous knowledge

Re-culture

Reuse, repair, and recycle at the grassroots

071

SANTOS HENAREJOS

CLIENT | Analogue Digital, Inc.

Makeshift is a magazine about creativity in unexpected places, like the favelas of Río or the alleys of Delhi. These are places where the resources might be scarce but where were genious is used daily, with the creation of companies and self-expression. *Makeshift* is about people, the things they make and the places where the make them. It's a quarterly publication based in New York and each edition has a central theme that all the articles are structured around. There are now four editions published: Re-culture, Mobility, Resistance and Communication.

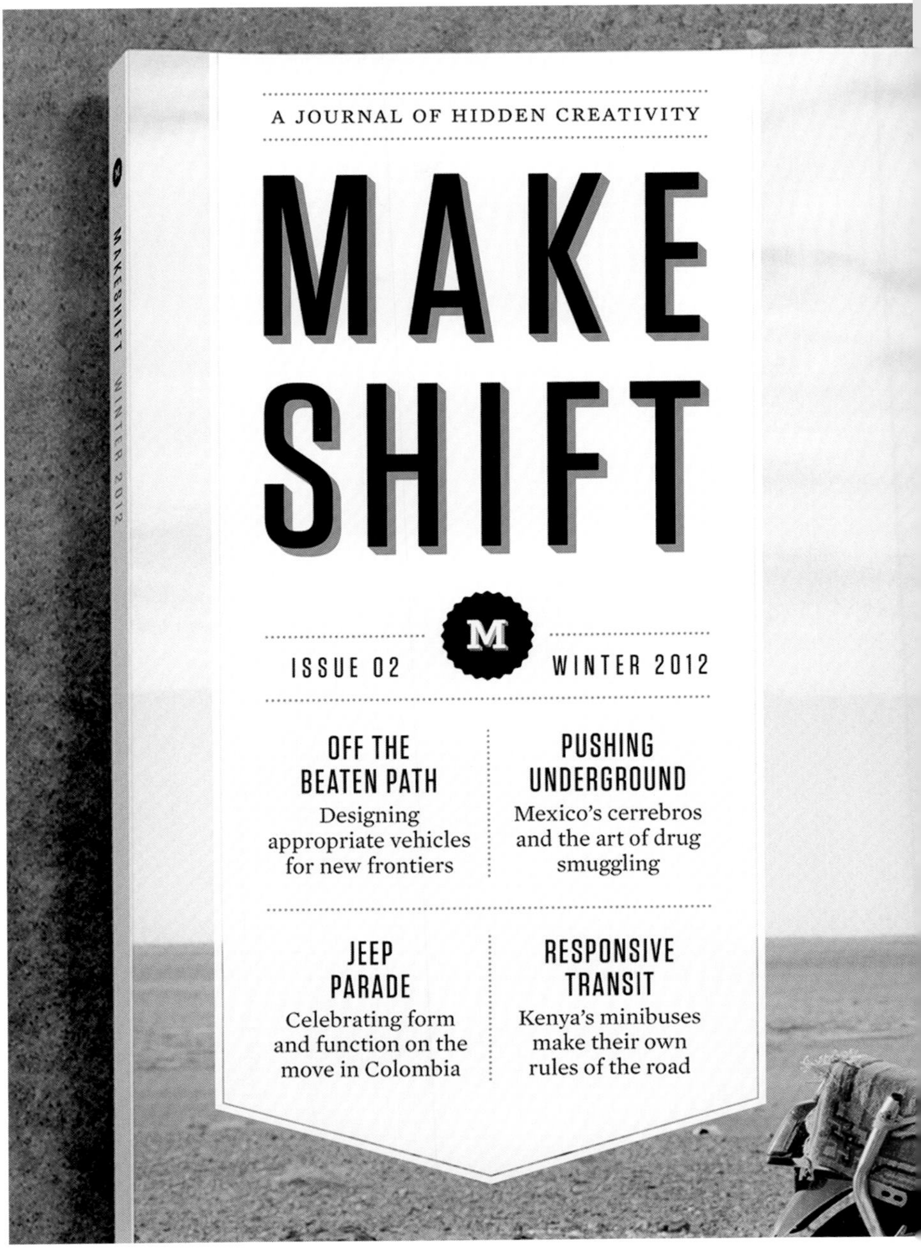

072

BELIEVE IN®

CLIENT | The Dartington Hall Trust

Scene is a bi-annual magazine published by The Dartington Hall Trust covering topics central to their three programmes of work: Arts, Social Justice and Sustainability.

The magazine cover features work by a different local artist for every issue and has been designed to allow the artwork to wrap the publication.

you know
you can

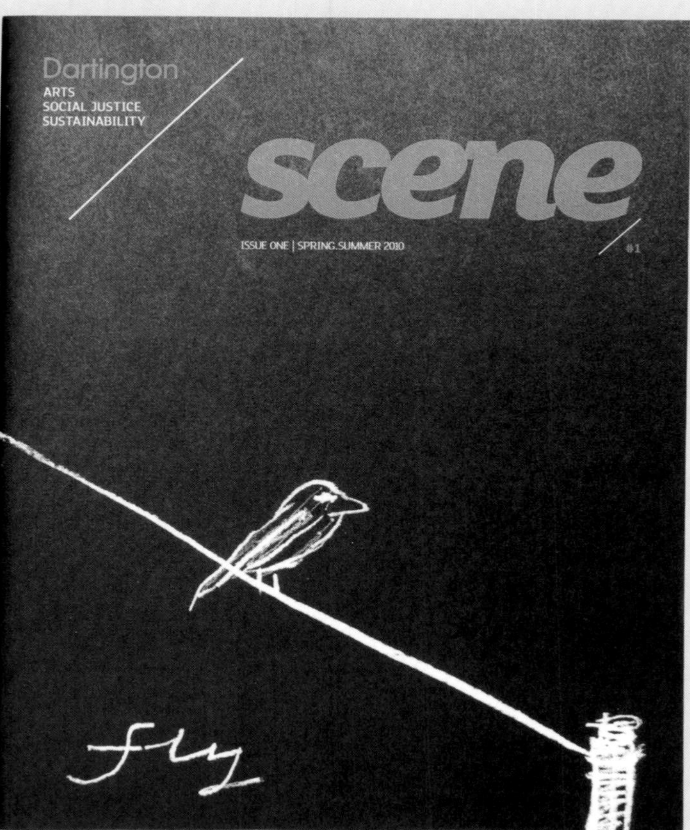
Dartington
ARTS
SOCIAL JUSTICE
SUSTAINABILITY
scene
ISSUE ONE | SPRING.SUMMER 2010
#1
fly

073

ZIM&ZOU

CLIENT | Le Monde

Representation of a collision of protons (based on a graph from the CERN). The rings range from infinitely large, to infinitely small.

· 1
Higgs boson is the last piece of a puzzle assembled by physicists 50 years ago to describe the matter of the Universe.

· 2
Higgs boson is the particle that gives other particles their mass.

· 3
The matter is a blend of multiple scales of elements. Quarks assemble into protons or neutrons. They are forming nuclei which, by combining with electrons, creates atoms.

· 4
By studying the relationship of the Higgs boson with other particles, physicists hope to better understand the universe.

M
Le magazine du Monde
22 DÉCEMBRE 2012
Rétrospective 2012
LE BOSON DE HIGGS
Héros de l'année

8 MAGGIO N. 19/2011

DOMENICA

Il Sole 24 ORE

ilsole24ore.com/domenica

PAROLE D'ITALIA

PAROLE D'ITALIA

Al Salone del Libro di Torino gli studenti scelgono i termini che descrivono il Paese: dubbi e speranze. Cambia il linguaggio politico

pagg. 2-4

VENEZIA & BORGES

Isola di San Giorgio con verde labirinto

Giovanni Bazoli

— p. 37

074

LUCA PITONI & ADRIANO ATTUS

CLIENT | Sole 24 Ore

Domenica, the most influential weekly cultural supplement of Italy.

Artwork by Tipoalcuni (alias Luca Pitoni). The title is "Parole d'Italia" (Italian Words).

Sold as an annex to *Sole 24 Ore* financial newspaper. Tabloid format, daily "pink" paper, 350.000 copies.
Year 2011, Editor-in-chief: Gianni Riotta.

RYAN MCGINLEY
JACK WALLS
DRIES VAN NOTEN
MAGNUS BERGER
MICHAEL STIPE
CAROLINE TRENTINI
PHILIP CRANGI
MIRABELLE MARDEN
HUMBERTO LEON
JASON KIBBLER
CASEY SPOONER
CHRIS BOLLEN
DAVID STRETTEL
BRIAN PHILLIPS
GARDAR EIDE
EINARSSON
AND MORE
ISSUE 6

075

HOMEWORK

CLIENT | HE magazine

HE magazine brings men's fashion into the new. Every issue of *HE* features an international look at the latest in men's style, as seen by an intensely talented collection of top photographers, designers and stylists.

HE magazine's contributors range from the newest stars in men's fashion (including Patrik Ervell, Adam Kimmel and many more) to today's most well-regarded menswear designers, including Hedi Slimane, Ann Demeulemeester and Junya Watanabe. *HE* features one-of-a-kind contributions from international artists such as Casey Spooner, Michael Stipe and Chloë Sevigny, and provides its readers with original content from the creative minds of Greg Foley, Gerhard Steidl, Humberto Leon and many more. With a unique, modern take on contemporary culture, *HE* is a must-read guide for men of style.

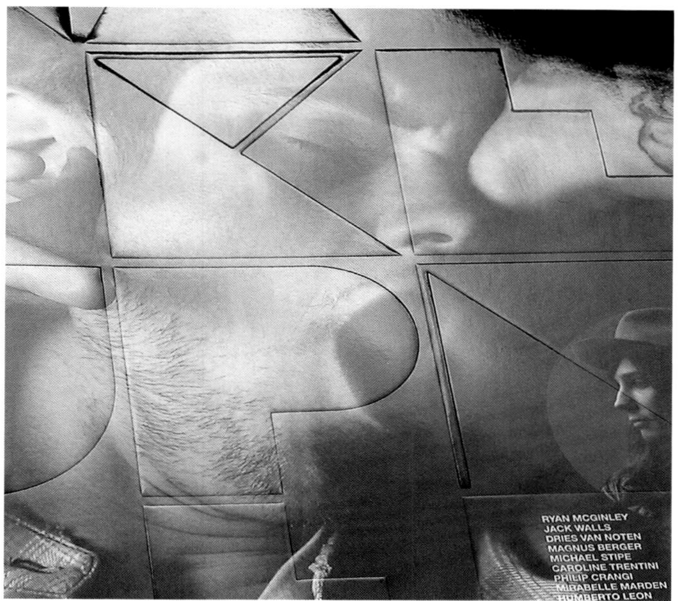

076

RICARDO CAVOLO

CLIENT | Yorokobu

The boy is Japanese. The father is from another continent. Which? The adult is a sailer and his skin is orange. Why? This cover's artist, Ricardo Cavalo, didn't draw any justification. He didn't illustrate the story behind these characters and this sea. He says that the story of this tattooed back, these waves, this ship and this impeccably dressed boy is the responsibility of whoever looks at it. It's the work of their fantasy.

"In all of my work I try to create an internal story, an intra-story," explains the illustrator. "In this case, I personified Yorokobu as a little Japanese boy with a sailer father from another continent (he has a reddish brown beard, so he can't be Japanese). And from there I leave it to the imagination of each person to reconstruct the story of the red-bearded sailer that ended up having a son in Japan. I tried to make it so that you can tell they have a relationship as positive as the expression that's reflected on the small Yorokobu in the boy's timid but happy face".

The technique used was ink and watercolour on paper. "I wanted to create a big mass of tattoos to reflect the huge quantity of information that a media form like Yorokobu deals with. This torso is like the universe of ideas, full of hundreds of sources of inspiration and diverse worlds to learn from," specifies the designer. Cavolo used his hands rather than the computer to draw this cover, as he does in all his work. "If there's something I try to maintain constant in my work it's that everything be done by hand. First, because it's the best way I know to explain things and second, because it seems to me that something handmade has more heat or more soul. I work with colour a lot because it's always powerful and grabs your attention. Regarding style, you could say it's simple or even naive, and I use that precisely to tell more complex stories. If the style is simple, it's more direct and reaches the spectatorcol more easily."

YOROKOBU / TAKE A WALK ON THE SLOW SIDE / Nº 26 - FEBRERO 2012
5€
yoroKobu
YRKB
L.P.M
LYNA
RICARDO·CAVOLO

077

NR2154

CLIENT | Rika

Rika Magazine is published twice-yearly by Amsterdam-based fashion brand Rika. Each issue features a new style of the custom-designed Rika typeface, a new hand-created element, and is printed with multiple covers.

LOVE
AFTER TASTE
CELEBRATING THE END OF ELEGANCE WITH
LINDA EVANGELISTA
LOVE ISSUE 7 ✦ AFTER TASTE ✦ S/S 2012

LOVE
LOVE ISSUE 7

078

NR2154

CLIENT | Love Magazine/Condé Nast

London-based *Love Magazine* is published twice-yearly by Condé Nast, under Editor-in-Chief Katie Grand.

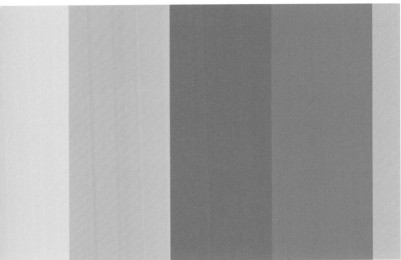

bcdefghijklm

079

RUIZ+COMPANY

CLIENT | Yorokobu

"Yorokobu means being happy". This is what is says on the cover. Maybe you didn't realize right away, but if you look carefully, you can see that there's a code in the colours. As the artist calls it, it's the "language of colours".

The key is to substitute the letters for colours until you uncover the phrase. "It's a playful cover", says David Ruiz. "We didn't want it to be merely pretty. The idea was to make people reflect when they read it, to make them think". And they've achieved it. The story of this cover has substance. To start, it involved the entire team at Ruiz + Company. "We wanted to do something really powerful and that, at the same time, would allow us to experiment. With such an open briefing, the best thing was to investigate a little. What would happen if we used some kind of code instead of typography?", said Ruiz. That was how they started to work with numbers. And this identification between numbers and letters to make numeric words evolved to the world of colours. A chromatic study confirmed that yellow and orange tones are most associated with happiness, which is why the majority of the letters that appear are found near colours that symbolise this state.

The final sentence, from the design, was the easiest: you only had to identify the colours with letters. "What could happen is that nobody would get it and they would say, 'What a beautiful colour-blocked cover', and that's it. But someone could also discover and see that there's something more in the pretty colour message. That's what makes this cover," explains David Ruiz.

YOROKOBU / TAKE A WALK ON THE BRAND SIDE / Nº 8 - JUNIO 2010
7€
abcdefghijklmnñopqrstuvwxyz

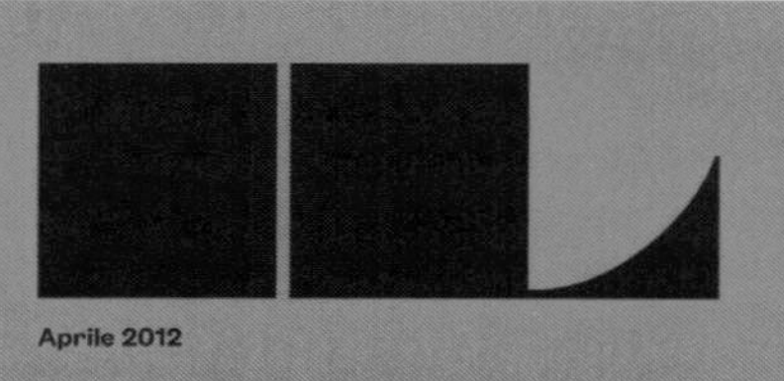

Aprile 2012

LA POLIZIA DEL PENSIERO

Orwell, l'Islam, la libertà di espressione e noi

Il nuovo saggio di Paul Berman

pagine 141-152

La nostra scuola di stile non esiste più ma per i creativi di tutto il mondo siamo diventati l'America

Design intelligente

IL – Il maschile del Sole 24 ORE n. 40 del 13/04/2012 mensile PI Sped. in AP D.L.353/2003 CONV. L.46/2004 Art.1, C.1, DCB MILANO
Venerdì 13/04 in abbinamento obbligatorio con Il Sole 24 ORE a € 2,00 Da sabato 14/04 solo IL – Il maschile del Sole 24 ORE a € 0,50

080

FRANCESCO FRANCHI

CLIENT | IL / Il Sole 24 ORE

Topic of the cover: design made in Italy.

number ||||||||||
STUDIO
Client
Country

Descriptive text.

034

SACHIKO AKINAGA

New York Times Style Magazine

Japan

Who doesn't like a party? Especially a rooftop pool party on a sunny day where the jazz quartet sounds out harmony to a perfect lego land jubilee. Travel in the winter? Yes, please. This beloved Akinaga well opener, entices the reader to saddle up to a luxurious hotel bar, catch the rays, and tell the bartenders, "I'll have what they're having".
Creative Director: David Sebbah / Photographer: Koichiro Doi.

035

JUDY KAMEON & ERIK OTSEA

New York Times Style Magazine

United States of America

We have all the seasons colours here. A whole year's worth of them in fact. Violets fall into sylvan mosses over a pebbled backdrop. The Fall Travel 2011 T logo articulately prompts the reader to expect change throughout the season. Plant textures juxtaposed by the chilly Autumn colour flux give the ensuing fall travel features an exotic, yet comforting opening remark.
Creative Director: David Sebbah.

036

NAKANO DESIGN OFFICE

Architectural Institute of Japan

Japan

The October edition of the magazine published by the Architectural Institute of Japan.
We visualised the Japanese intensity scale of the Great East Japan Earthquake that hit on March 11, 2011.
In this image, a vertical line indicates passage of time, and waveforms of intensity, scale of the area from Tohoku region to Kanto region, are spaced along the time-shift..
Art Director and Designer: Takeo Nakano / Edit: 2012-2013 Editorial Board of the Journal of Architecture and Building Science.

037

SANTOS HENAREJOS & ROC CANALS

Brands & Roses

Spain

Ling is the onboard magazine from Vueling. It's a monthly publication centered around the cities that the airline flies to. It's a bilingual magazine and is organised in four sections: living, inspiration, now and good.
Cover photos: Roc Canals.

038

MADRIZ

Madriz

Spain

The cover for issue number 4 of *Madriz* (2009) is part of a series of photographs documenting the surroundings of Madrid seen from the sky. The goal was to capture the striking and unique beauty of a landscape that has been gradually transformed by the action of man. This series was conceived and performed by Fernando Maselli, a photographer who never before had ventured himself in aerial photography.
Long flying hours onboard a small two-seater helicopter were necessary to take these photographs during January and February, when it snowed with unusual frequency in Madrid. Unfortunately, Barajas airport's control tower did not authorize flying higher than an altitude of 5,000 feet, which meant that Fernando needed to invest another 200 hours assembling the landscapes with Photoshop in order to achieve these large vistas..
Creative Director: Louis-Charles Tiar / Art Director: Sonia Bilbao / Photographer: Fernando Maselli.

039

MAGMA BRAND DESIGN

Slanted, www.slanted.de

Germany

Slanted #15 – Experimental deals with experimental design strategies in typography and graphic design. This issue presents projects incorporating the accident into the design process, works based on mistakes and inaccuracy, fonts that derive from a concept or a system – in the end work that experiments or goes unconventional ways in design.
The playful handling of tools, forms and concept is a popular procedure to broaden the consciousness in typography.
It seems to be (regarding the huge amount of entries for this issue) a widespread phenomenon, very popular at design schools and universities. This is not a surprising fact – especially in interaction with a model, experimental results are the foundation of a theory.
We placed a special experimental type section with 48 pages in this issue to be able to present a large collection of typographical experiments.
This issue's cover is realized in an oldfashioned, experimental procedure, too: Its print sheet has been produced in rainbow printing using HKS colours.

040

RODRIGO SÁNCHEZ

Unidad Editorial Revistas SLU

Spain

What better way to represent something related to bread than the crumbs that are left when it's finished? It's the best way to show that it was delicious.
Art Director and Designer: Rodrigo Sánchez / Photographer: Ángel Becerril.

041

RODRIGO SÁNCHEZ

Unidad Editorial Revistas SLU

Spain

The Wes Anderson film tells a story of adolescent love, almost juvenile, between a young Boy Scout and a student. Nature, love and youth are brought together in this cover.
Art Director and Designer: Rodrigo Sánchez / Lettering and Engraving: Lucía Martín / Photographer: Ángel Becerril.

042

RODRIGO SÁNCHEZ

Unidad Editorial Revistas SLU

Spain

The cover, made from nuts, refers to the origins of the story and the consequences of the game.
Art Director and Designer: Rodrigo Sánchez / Lettering and Illustration: Lucía Martín / Photographer: Ángel Becerril.

043

FERICHE & BLACK

Vueling/La Fábrica

Spain

Magazine for the airline Vueling. It was created with the idea of distancing itself as much as possible from the typical onboard magazine. We envisioned an accessible, human and contemporary magazine. From this concept, we also came up with the manual title headline. In this case, the cover is a collage of everyday objects to illustrate the title "The Things We Love". Very personal things, it's clear.

044

MAGMA BRAND DESIGN

Slanted, www.slanted.de

Germany

Comics consist of a sequence of images (strip) that tell a story. In cartoons, the narrative point is condensed into one image. The *Slanted issue # 17 – Cartoon / Comic* is packed cover to cover full of naratives and typographic explosion!
Along with the New Year, the first *Slanted* issue of 2012 has a new face. A new oversized format, 16 more pages, and a more tightening sequence in content and layout to create more space for projects and activities.
Also the appearance of the new magazine is marked throughout the comic book world. The eight-page fold-out cover glows in red and green on the outside, while the inside are comments of readers from our blog www.slanted.de, which were posted online last November.

045

PAPERLUX

Stiebner Publishing House

Germany

For the cover of the November 2011 issue we pulled out all the stops to produce something truly special after a long preparation period. In 48,000 passes and with 104 extremely detailed die cuts per magazine, we created six differently coloured versions of the cover, without exposing the plates again each time. Our aim was to change the tangibility of the material only by "scribing" the paper. The result is a metamorphosis of paper, inspired by the one and only Richard Buckminster Fuller.

046

MADRIZ

Madriz

Spain

Issue number 3 of *Madriz* published in June 2011 was dedicated to the 15-M, a protest movement that took the streets of Spain and camped out for weeks in Puerta del Sol, Madrid's central square. Taken by Fernando Maselli, the photograph brings together through Photoshop a number of shots taken from different balconies surrounding Puerta del Sol. In order to create an aesthetic pattern, the tarpaulins were also digitally replicated. This visual exaggeration was aimed to highlight the public resonance and the political significance of this historical event.
Creative Director: Louis-Charles Tiar / Art Director: Sonia Bilbao / Photographer: Fernando Maselli.

047

PIERRE VANNI

New York Times Style Magazine

France

A fantastic example of creative direction for the Summer 2009 T Style well opener. Angular origami-like foreshadows the season's trend for colourful minimalism in this ocean cool and chiseled T sculpture.
Creative director: David Sebbah / Photographer: Mitchell Feinberg.

048

LUCA PITONI & ADRIANO ATTUS

Sole 24 Ore

Italy

Domenica, the most influential weekly cultural supplement of Italy. A collage from English artist John Stezaker, "Mask XXXV". The cover story is about neuroscience. The title is "I read your thoughts". Sold as an annex to *Sole 24 Ore* financial newspaper. Tabloid format, daily "pink" paper, 350.000 copies.
Year 2011, Editor-in-chief: Gianni Riotta.
Creative Director: Luca Pitoni and Adriano Attus / Art Director: Luca Pitoni.

049

RODRIGO SÁNCHEZ

Unidad Editorial Revistas SLU

Spain

We wanted our cover to be a giant wave that destroyed everything in its path. Everything, including the cover title. Half of the page rushes over the other half.
Art Director and Designer: Rodrigo Sánchez / Photographer: Ángel Becerril.

050

LO SIENTO

+81

Spain

Graphic piece for the cover of the Japanese magazine *+81* magazine. The Fall 2011 edition was about "next creativity", which is why we proposed to create a typographic lettering through the use of bubble paper and injecting water with blue colouring. The bubble paper has a grid that allowed for putting concrete messages with only the use of a syringe as a drawing instrument.
Each typography was developed thinking about the brief, and was always inspired by its creation within the grid. Each existing grid can hide a typographic character and therefore, an alphabet. Experimental typography is a new layer or system within typographic design, as with today's tools you can achieve important results and create typographies without the exclusive use of a computer.

051

FERICHE & BLACK

La Fábrica

Spain

A cultural travel magazine. What stands out most is the typographic treatment of the headline (which includes the number of the publication) and magazine title, which have the same weight and font. The photographic selection is always chosen very carefully.
In these two cases we have an emblematic image taken by Masats during San Fermines, and a photograph of Oscar Tusquets (taken by Leopoldo Pomés), which reminds us of Italy with his harcut and exaggerated Roman profile. In this edition, Oscar was accompanied by Veneto, and we saw Scarpa and Canova.

052
GAIL BICHLER
New York Times Magazine
United States of America

The cover illustrates the contentious and eruptive nature of the geopolitical disputes between two Middle-Eastern powers, Iran and Israel. Ashed paper and smoke creates a cover that visually explains the rift these two sovereign nations are facing.
Art Director: Gail Bichler / Design Director: Arem Duplessis / Illustrator: Ash illustrator Sean Freeman / Smoke Photo Illustrator: Julian Wolkenstein / Story: Ronen Bergman.

053
DAVIDELFIN
Yorokobu
Spain

This is the cover that Davidelfin did for *Yorokobu*. It's open to different readings and interpretations, whereas, according to the artist, his proposal was more related to sculpture, secrets and mystery than to provocation. What happened was that the cover was filled with marks crossed out, which made us completely change the way we normally face this section: first they do the cover for us and then we write this text. Long live challenges and new scenes that make you think differently!
Davidelfin says that it's a metaphor for unconsciousness. "We're attracted to what we can't see, we want to read something that's crossed out even more than something that's perfectly legible...in our case, we love words and this is like a buried treasure."
And hidden in there, can you find the concept of "being happy" that is in implicit in the Japanese term Yorokobu? Well, yes. "It has to do with the work that we do, which makes us happy, and also with having the freedom to do what we want."

054
FABIEN BARON
New York Times Style Magazine
United States of America

The final T Style well opener in a series that spanned eight years of logo presentations. Created by Janet Froelich in 2004, this final T sculpture takes the fall as concrete shards seem to explode off the impact. Though broken, its form and essence remains intact. What more could a magazine concept page hope to impart as legacy?
Creative Director: David Sebbah.

055
FRANCESCO FRANCHI
IL / Il Sole 24 ORE
Italy

Topic of the cover: the newspaper crisis.
Typeface: Tiempos (by Klim Type Foundry).

056
SERGIO JIMÉNEZ - SUBCOOLTURE
El Periódico de Catalunya
Spain

Covered created for the first issue of the year of the magazine *Dominical* (in the newspaper *El Periódico de Catalunya*). It's based on lettering constructed around cut-out words, alluding to an exercise of encouragement and survival confronting the difficult years that are coming with the economic crisis. Published in a bilingual double edition (Spanish and Catalan).

057
RODRIGO SÁNCHEZ
Unidad Editorial Revistas SLU
Spain

The past, the future and the paradoxes of time travel. A clock that goes forward and back. Metrópoli became personally involved in the themes that were brought to the cover, forwardwards and backwards.
Art Director and Designer: Rodrigo Sánchez / Photographer: Ángel Becerril.

058
RODRIGO SÁNCHEZ
Unidad Editorial Revistas SLU
Spain

Cover drawn with pen on the outer edge of various books all together.
Art Director and Designer: Rodrigo Sánchez / Lettering: Ricardo Martínez and Rodrigo Sánchez / Photographer: Ángel Becerril.

059
PAPERLUX
Stiebner Publishing House
Germany

Space or illusion? Typo cuts through a folded paper area, the shadows are caught on a photo - while the folds are tangible through a silkscreen relief printing. Three cover versions were available, each with the fine silkscreen lines, but in different colours.

060

FRANCESCO FRANCHI

IL / Il Sole 24 ORE

Italy

Topic of the cover: special double issue, food and fiction.
Typeface: Domaine and Founders Grotesk (by Klim Type Foundry).

061

TARA DONOVAN

New York Times Magazine

United States of America

Pointillism at its best. A magnificently executed collection of steel pins create a memorable Travel Spring 2011 well opener. Take note Google, dropping a pin, or many, can do more than mark territory.
Creative Director: David Sebbah / Photographer: Stephen Lewis.

062

WANDA BARCELONA

Yorokobu

Spain

There's a lake on the cover, though it's white, not blue. Maybe it's the foam that makes the golden carp splash around. And between jumps, they draw shapes in the air. There are two that seem to be following each other and form a circle. Sometimes, a third joins this dance. On occasion, one of the fish can be seen jumping alone and sometimes several coincide in a jump, forming a star before re-entering their habitat, the fresh water.
It's a reading. But there's another, the one we ask of all of the artists who do the cover: to be able to read the word Yorokobu. That is to say, that they invent some lettering. And in this case, the letters are formed by some of the many carp that are on the cover, the ones who show their golden colour when jumping.
And why fish? Because this animal says a lot about the work of its artists, Inti, Daniel and Iris, the members of Wanda. "We're specialists in ephemeral architecture and our materials are paper and cardboard. Is there anything more ephemeral than a fish's memory? They say that every three seconds a fish forgets its previous life. It even forgets what it's eaten," comments Inti.
The carp is something else that's related to the origen of the word in question, Yorokobu. As happens to a good number of the people who pass by this space, Wanda looked for some kind Japanese icon. In a handmade way, like all of the work, they constructed a sea of paper and filled it with carp. And luck would have it that, in the moment of the photo, some of them jumped out of the water while the rest remained placidly swimming below.

063

KAMO

New York Times Style Magazine

Japan

A beautifully detaild collection of paper roses and flowers, pieced together by artist Kamo, in a monastic yet intricate well opener for the Spring 2003 Style Issue. This sculpture, along with many others, form the T style logo the Times Syle magazine became well known for.
Creative Director: Janet Froelich / Art Director: David Sebbah / Photographer: Kazunari Tajima.

064

FERICHE & BLACK

Focus ediciones

Spain

A trend magazine.
Black and white. A centered image. Openly smoking. His name in an exaggerated font, half-hidden by the actor himself, that, apart from giving the title, also decorates and gives the image a certain volume. Without concessions.

065

NICOLA YEOMAN

New York Times Style Magazine

United Kingdom

A ghostly fog surrounds translucent white chiffon, arranged and strung in a rural forest scene, inviting the reader to the then coming 2010 Fall fashion trends. The well opener, like the fabric used, almost floats off the page, creating a delicate balance between the constant and the ephemeral.
Set Design: Nicola Yeoman / Creative Director: David Sebbah / Photographer: Jo Metson Scott.

066

PABLO ABAD

Simplyprorsum

Spain

SIMPLY THE MAG comes from the desire to editorialise our vision of fashion. The result is a heterogeneous combination of the stories that it aims to tell, under the same creative direction, and the essence of each one of the collaborators. Twelve editorials divided in two acts, three pieces of art and a central interview, with homages to Newton and Hepburn, make up the offer of this issue #0. Photo Cover: Javier Garceche.

067

YOROKOBU

Yorokobu

Spain

This cover is a chalkboard that's waiting for you to draw the word Yorokobu. Do it however you want. You have five colours of chalk. This is our invitation for you the write Yorokobu however you like and as many times as you'd like. This chalkboard is a birthday celebration. Our third birthday. We want to celebrate it with you and your drawings.

068

YOROKOBU

Yorokobu

Spain

This time it's your turn to make the cover. Why you? Because it's *Yorokobu's* first birthday and we're going to celebrate it by playing with letters with you. It's easy. Taek the magazine with two hands. Put your face in front of the cover. Stare at the disorganized letters that move among the water and try to construct the word Yorokobu with them.

069

MAGMA BRAND DESIGN

Slanted, www.slanted.de

Germany

SLAB! Slanted Magazine #20 – Slab Serif is entirely dedicated to the early 19th century born »serifenbetonte Linear-Antiqua,« broadly known as Egyptienne, Slab Serif, Square Serif or Mécanes outside German classification. Developing during Industrial Revolution in Great Britain, these typefaces fastly spread on advertising posters and flyers. Back in these days it was the main purpose of the slab serifs to attract attention by their strong visual expression. In this issue we want to bring back some of this (at least in Central Europe) rather gone attention to the often striking slab serifs. The cover shows Hank Aaron in full batting position after his famous 714 career home run. The other pages of the fold-out cover are featuring other athletes and disciplines in American Sports. A popular choice and common to see on their jerseys and shirts: Slab Serifs.

070

FEED

Esse - Contemporary art magazine

Canada

Cover for *Esse* (contemporary art magazine) on the theme “The Idea of Painting”.

071

SANTOS HENAREJOS

Analogue Digital, Inc.

Spain

Makeshift is a magazine about creativity in unexpected places, like the favelas of Río or the alleys of Delhi. These are places where the resources might be scarce but where were genious is used daily, with the creation of companies and self-expression. *Makeshift* is about people, the things they make and the places where the make them. It's a quarterly publication based in New York and each edition has a central theme that all the articles are structured around. There are now four editions published: Re-culture, Mobility, Resistance and Communication.
Cover Photo issue 01: Tim Mitchell.
Cover Photo issue 02: Jeroen Toirkens.

072

BELIEVE IN®

The Dartington Hall Trust

United Kingdom

Scene is a bi-annual magazine published by The Dartington Hall Trust covering topics central to their three programmes of work: Arts, Social Justice and Sustainability.
The magazine cover features work by a different local artist for every issue and has been designed to allow the artwork to wrap the publication.

073 ZIM&ZOU

Le Monde

France

Representation of a collision of protons (based on a graph from the CERN).
The rings range from infinitely large, to infinitely small.

• 1
Higgs boson is the last piece of a puzzle assembled by physicists 50 years ago to describe the matter of the Universe.

• 2
Higgs boson is the particle that gives other particles their mass.

• 3
The matter is a blend of multiple scales of elements. Quarks assemble into protons or neutrons. They are forming nuclei which, by combining with electrons, creates atoms.

• 4
By studying the relationship of the Higgs boson with other particles, physicists hope to better understand the universe.

074 LUCA PITONI & ADRIANO ATTUS

Sole 24 Ore

Italy

Domenica, the most influential weekly cultural supplement of Italy. Artwork by Tipoalcuni (alias Luca Pitoni). The title is "Parole d'Italia" ("Italian Words). Sold as an annex to *Sole 24 Ore* financial newspaper. Tabloid format, daily "pink" paper, 350.000 copies.
Year 2011, Editor-in-chief: Gianni Riotta
Creative Director: Luca Pitoni and Adriano Attus / Art Director: Luca Pitoni.

075 HOMEWORK

HE Magazine

Denmark

HE magazine brings men's fashion into the new. Every issue of *HE* features an international look at the latest in men's style, as seen by an intensely talented collection of top photographers, designers and stylists.
HE magazine's contributors range from the newest stars in men's fashion (including Patrik Ervell, Adam Kimmel and many more) to today's most well-regarded menswear designers, including Hedi Slimane, Ann Demeulemeester and Junya Watanabe. *HE* features one-of-a-kind contributions from international artists such as Casey Spooner, Michael Stipe and Chloë Sevigny, and provides its readers with original content from the creative minds of Greg Foley, Gerhard Steidl, Humberto Leon and many more. With a unique, modern take on contemporary culture, *HE* is a must-read guide for men of style.

076 RICARDO CAVOLO

Yorokobu

Spain

The boy is Japanese. The father is from another continent. Which? The adult is a sailer and his skin is orange. Why? This cover's artist, Ricardo Cavalo, didn't draw any justification. He didn't illustrate the story behind these characters and this sea. He says that the story of this tattooed back, these waves, this ship and this impeccably dressed boy is the responsibility of whoever looks at it. It's the work of their fantasy.
"In all of my work I try to create an internal story, an intra-story," explains the illustrator. "In this case, I personified Yorokobu as a little Japanese boy with a sailer father from another continent (he has a reddish brown beard, so he can't be Japanese). And from there I leave it to the imagination of each person to reconstruct the story of the red-bearded sailer that ended up having a son in Japan. I tried to make it so that you can tell they have a relationship as positive as the expression that's reflected on the small Yorokobu in the boy's timid but happy face".
The technique used was ink and watercolour on paper. "I wanted to create a big mass of tattoos to reflect the huge quantity of information that a media form like Yorokobu deals with. This torso is like the universe of ideas, full of hundreds of sources of inspiration and diverse worlds to learn from," specifies the designer. Cavolo used his hands rather than the computer to draw this cover, as he does in all his work. "If there's something I try to maintain constant in my work it's that everything be done by hand. First, because it's the best way I know to explain things and second, because it seems to me that something handmade has more heat or more soul. I work with colour a lot because it's always powerful and grabs your attention. Regarding style, you could say it's simple or even naive, and I use that precisely to tell more complex stories. If the style is simple, it's more direct and reaches the spectatorcol more easily."

077 ||||||||||
NR2154

Rika

Denmark / United States of America

Rika Magazine is published twice-yearly by Amsterdam-based fashion brand Rika. Each issue features a new style of the custom-designed Rika typeface, a new hand-created element, and is printed with multiple covers.

078 ||||||||||
NR2154

Love Magazine/Condé Nast

Denmark / United States of America

London-based *Love Magazine* is published twice-yearly by Condé Nast, under Editor-in-Chief Katie Grande.

079 ||||||||||
RUIZ+COMPANY

Yorokobu

Spain

"Yorokobu means being happy". This is what is says on the cover. Maybe you didn't realize right away, but if you look carefully, you can see that there's a code in the colours. As the artist calls it, it's the "language of colours". The key is to substitute the letters for colours until you uncover the phrase. "It's a playful cover", says David Ruiz. "We didn't want it to be merely pretty. The idea was to make people reflect when they read it, to make them think". And they've achieved it. The story of this cover has substance. To start, it involved the entire team at Ruiz + Company. "We wanted to do something really powerful and that, at the same time, would allow us to experiment. With such an open briefing, the best thing was to investigate a little. What would happen if we used some kind of code instead of typography?", said Ruiz. That was how they started to work with numbers. And this identification between numbers and letters to make numeric words evolved to the world of colours. A chromatic study confirmed that yellow and orange tones are most associated with happiness, which is why the majority of the letters that appear are found near colours that symbolise this state.
The final sentence, from the design, was the easiest: you only had to identify the colours with letters. "What could happen is that nobody would get it and they would say, 'What a beautiful colour-blocked cover', and that's it. But someone could also discover and see that there's something more in the pretty colour message. That's what makes this cover," explains David Ruiz.

080 ||||||||||
FRANCESCO FRANCHI

IL / Il Sole 24 ORE

Italy

Topic of the cover: design made in Italy.
Art Director: Francesco Franchi /
Illustration: La Tigre.

188-247

ALBUMS

081

ENSERIO

CLIENT | Panxii Badii

A raw and simple graphic illustrates the naked and personal music of Panxii Badii. The six cards that are found in the interior, purposefully not ordered, form part of a puzzle and give the option of 24 distinct covers.

Panxii Badii Vuelta a ti
Panxii Badii Vuelta a ti
Panxii Badii Vuelta a ti
Panxii Badii Vuelta a ti

television pickup
Kinescope mountain

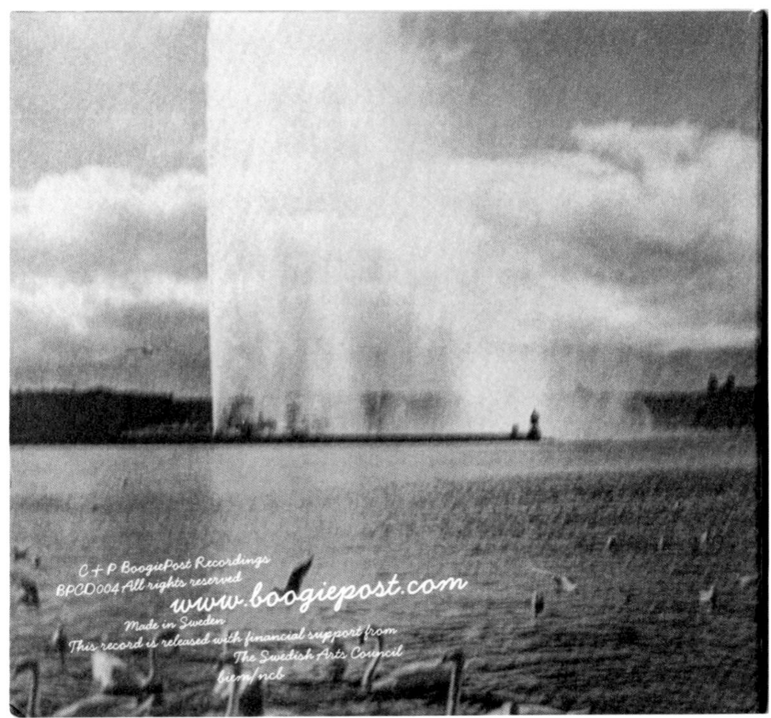

082

MAI-BRITT AMSLER

CLIENT | BoogiePost Recordings

CD in double carton sleeve with 12-page booklet.
Cover for Television Pickup, a half-electric, half-acoustic band. Television Pickup is an android cinema orchestra playing songs from films you wish you had seen: Haunting melodies covered in dirt, broken in pieces and served with a straw.

083

HVASS&HANNIBAL

CLIENT | number0 / Rallye Label

This is an album cover we designed for Japanese post-rock band number0. The artwork is made of spray painted glass layered with pieces of fabric that have been sewn together.

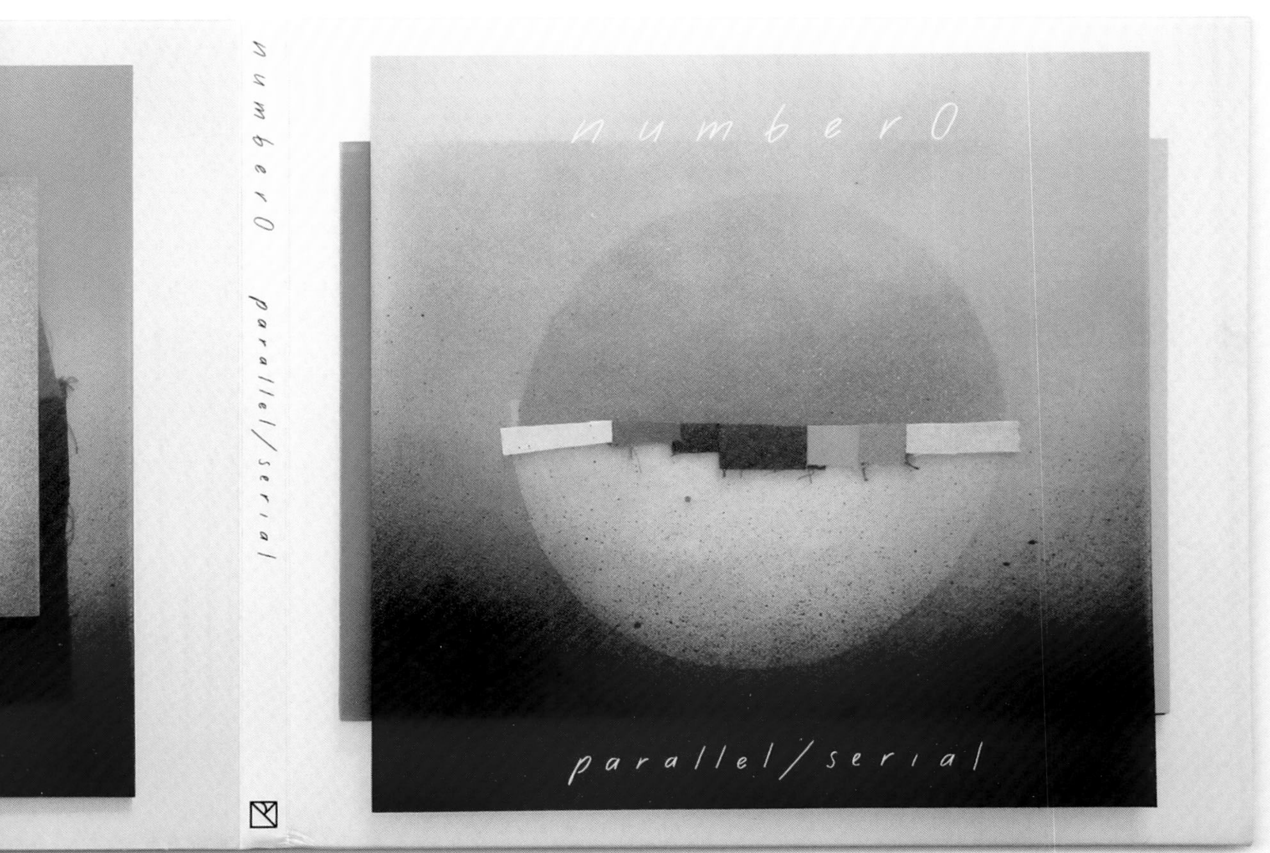
number0
parallel/serial
number0 parallel/serial

BARDOT

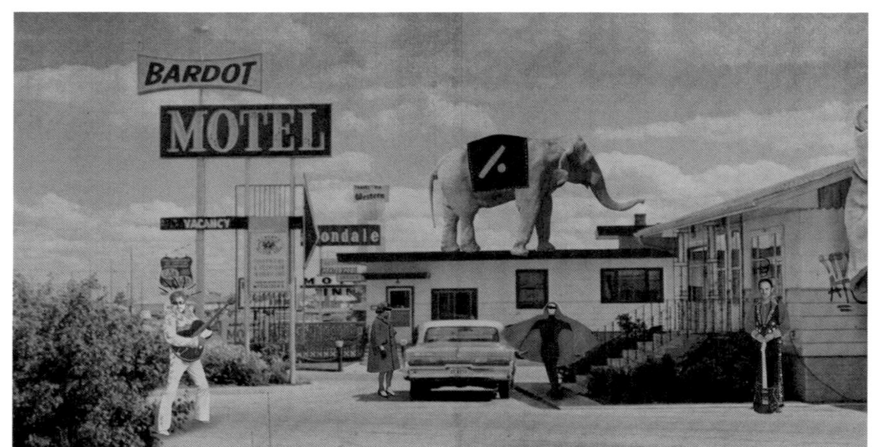

084

MAX-O-MATIC

CLIENT | Bardot

Design and illustration for *2*, the second album from Bardot, a pop group from Buenos Aires. The group's brief, guided by the lyrics and dark musical textures, asked for the incorporation of the following elements: elephants, love, landscapes, faded colours and a certain retro tone.

THE
HAUNTED
HOUSE
OF
HOUSE

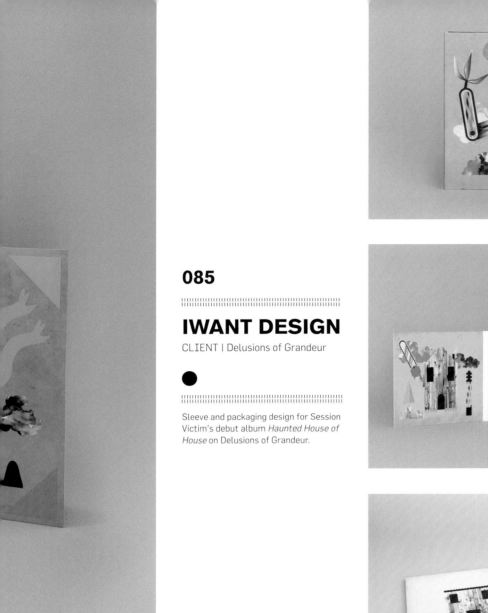

085

IWANT DESIGN

CLIENT | Delusions of Grandeur

Sleeve and packaging design for Session Victim's debut album *Haunted House of House* on Delusions of Grandeur.

086

HVASS&HANNIBAL

CLIENT | Canon Blue / Temporary Residence / Rumraket

We designed this album cover for American musician Daniel James, aka Canon Blue, who released his second album, *Rumspringa*, at Temporary Residence in the US and Rumraket in Scandinavia. The artwork is a tapestry made of fabric, and it is inspired by traditional Amish quiliting.

CANON BLUE
RUMSPRINGA

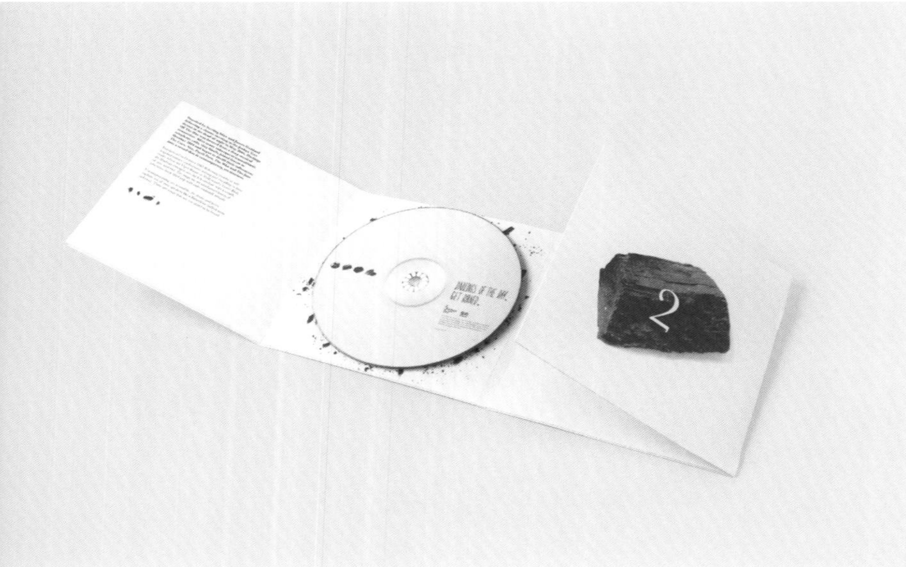

087

BELIEVE IN®

CLIENT | Darlings of the Day

8 page double gatefold CD cover for Hollywood-based band Darlings of the Day.

The cover portrays a photographic narrative inspired by the title *Get burned*. Four pieces of wood on the front cover represent each of the four tracks on the EP. Each piece is then revealed in a burnt state as the cover unfolds. The crow is taken from the band's identity marque. Hand-rendered typography has been created using charcoal for the cover title and back cover track listing.

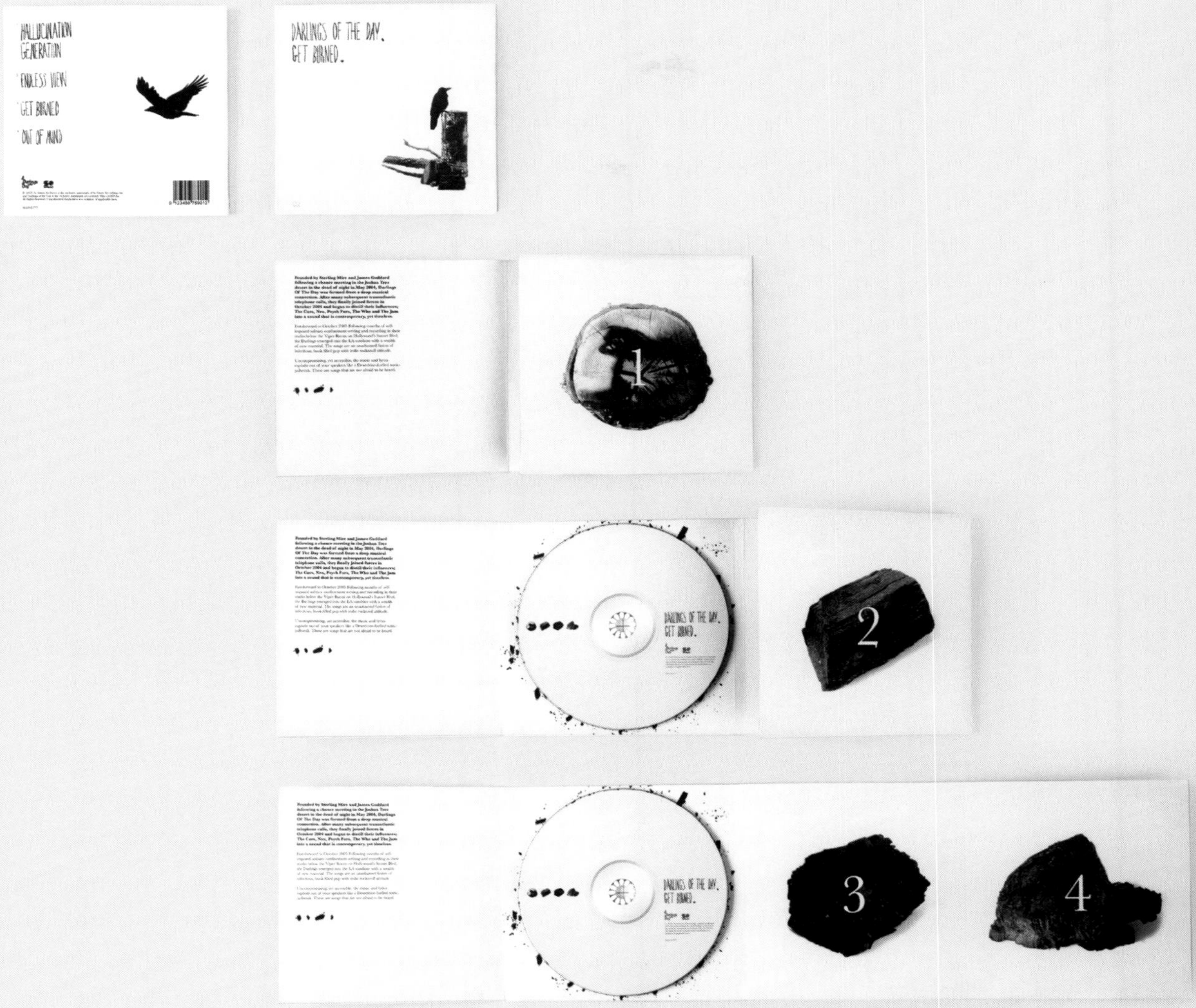

HALLUCINATION
GENERATION
ENDLESS VIEW
GET BURNED
OUT OF MIND

DARLINGS OF THE DAY.
GET BURNED.

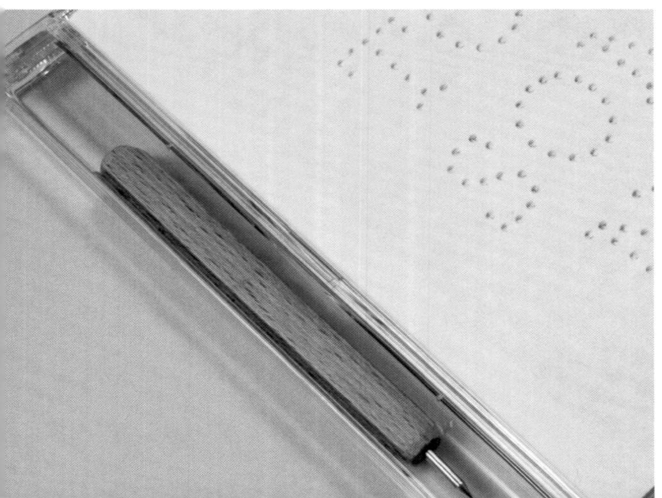

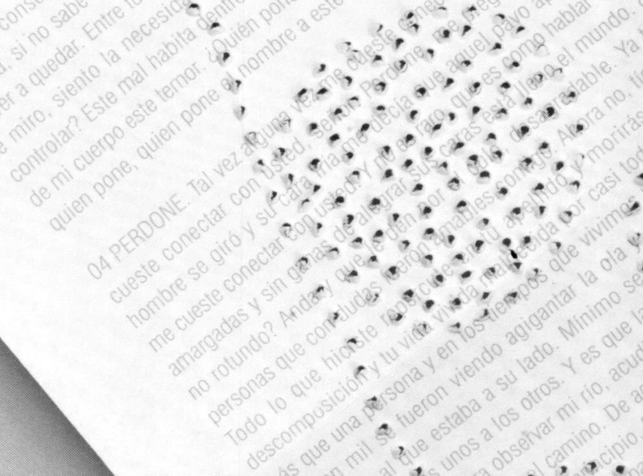

088

ENSERIO

CLIENT | Caiko

A handful of holes made by hand with a pick create an illustration on a completely blank poster that, once folded, serves as the cover of the first disc from the group Caiko. A limited series of 200 pieces with a convincing image created using an infantile technique.

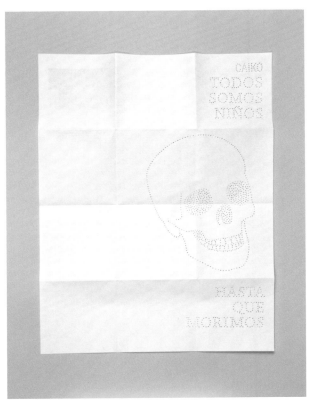

089

DRAWSWORDS & BARBARA HENNEQUIN

CLIENT | Face Tomorrow

Artwork for Dutch indie rock band Face Tomorrow's acoustic LP called *Move On*. This is their goodbye LP as a band, since they decided to call it quits after 10 years.

The decision was quickly made to make the mixed emotions about this ending of an era the base of the design - happy and sad at the same time. The 'punch holes' on the outer and inner sleeve reveal the vinyl's A (blue - happy) and B (red - sad) label on smiley-bright-yellow vinyl.

The glossy black stickers on the front and back cover were hand-stickered by the band themselves. Because of the possible combinations with the eyes (circle, cross or dash) and three different mouths (a happy smile, a sad smile and a curvy, undecided one) the artwork is different on every LP, which makes each one unique and an extra special goodbye gift.

Pressed in a limited edition of 300 (signed) copies.

1. Sign Up
2. My World Within
3. Paralusion
4. On My Own
5. Enlighten Me

6. All The Way
7. Saved
8. The Maze
9. Prop & Stay
10. The Stranger
11. Worth The Wait

090

MARTA VELUDO & RICARDO LEITE

CLIENT | Swinging Rabbits

Tricks are for Kids is the name of the album from the band Swinging Rabbits. With this delicious name we realised that exploring the visual world of our childhood was the right path to build a curious identity. We tried to achieve a perfect and playful combination with tactile process and typography, building up sets and hand-drawing types.

SWINGING RABBITS
Tricks Are For Kids
SWIN GING | RAB BITS
PRESENTS
TRICKS ARE FOR KIDS
EP
2011

091

DRAWSWORDS & BARBARA HENNEQUIN

CLIENT | Face Tomorrow

Artwork for Dutch indie rock band Face Tomorrow's 2010 full length self-titled LP and CD.

The 'blind spots' on the CD and LP were overprinted using a UV Spot varnish and the LP version was limited to 400 copies on black vinyl and only a 100 copies on marbled red/white vinyl all including the CD version as well.

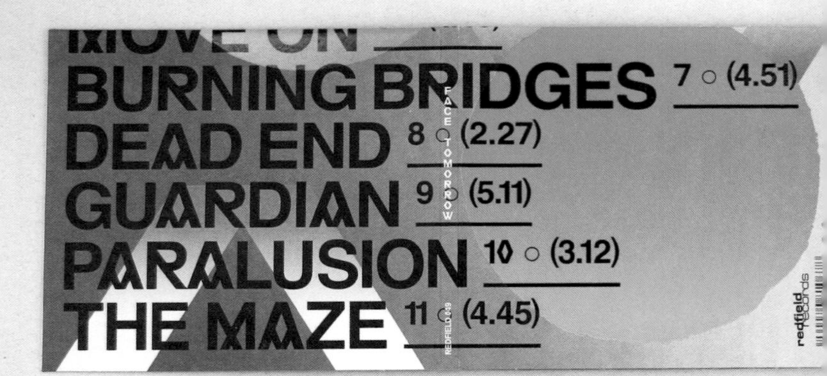

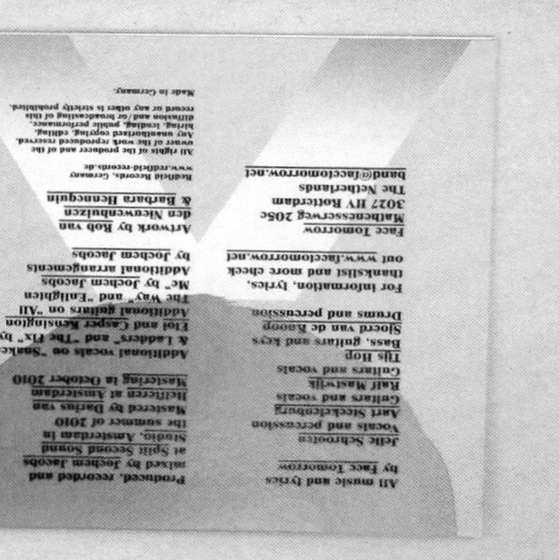

F T R
A O R
C M O
E O W

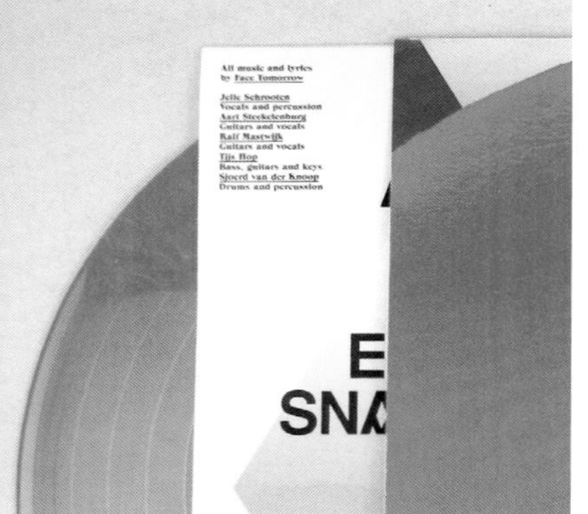
All music and lyrics
by Face Tomorrow
Jelle Schrooten
Vocals and percussion
Aart Steekelenburg
Guitars and vocals
Ralf Mastwijk
Guitars and vocals
Tijs Hop
Bass, guitars and keys
Sjoerd van der Knoop
Drums and percussion

092

THE CREATIVE CORPORATION

CLIENT | Third Rock Recordings

Cave Painting's elegant debut album reflects the band's belief in the artifact as a vital part of the listening experience.

The cover reveals a concertina of die cuts which, when closed, makes up the band's diamond logo. Inspired by Japanese paper engineering and binding techniques, the pack is made up of a spectrum of pastel shades fading into the next, with each panel containing an individual cut shape.

The design team felt it was clear that the packaging should reflect the band's understated but emotive music; aiming to produce a package that conveyed a feeling of depth and considerable beauty.

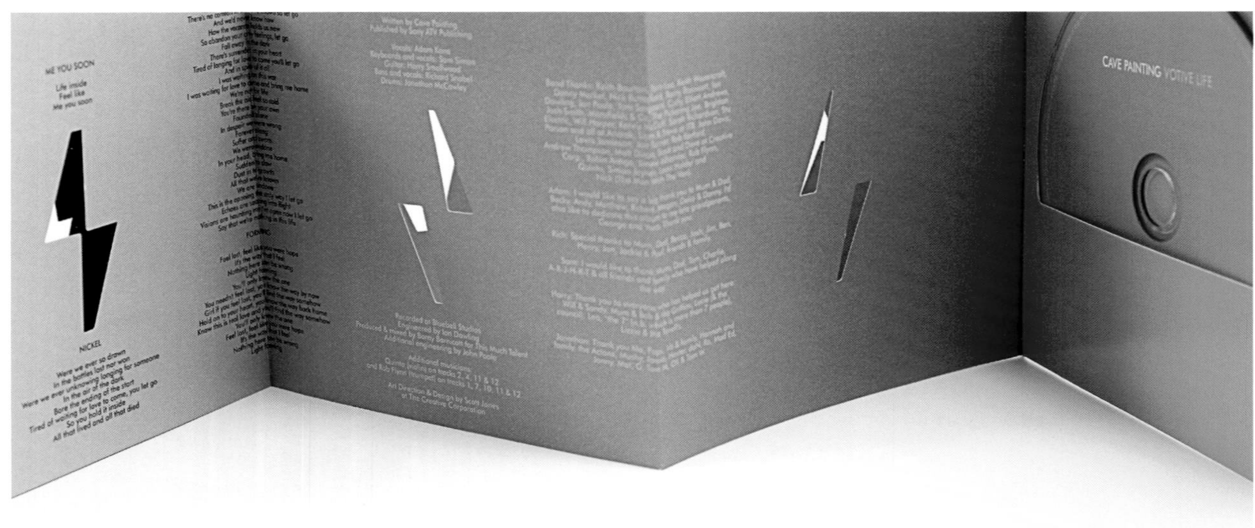

CAVE PAINTING
VOTIVE LIFE

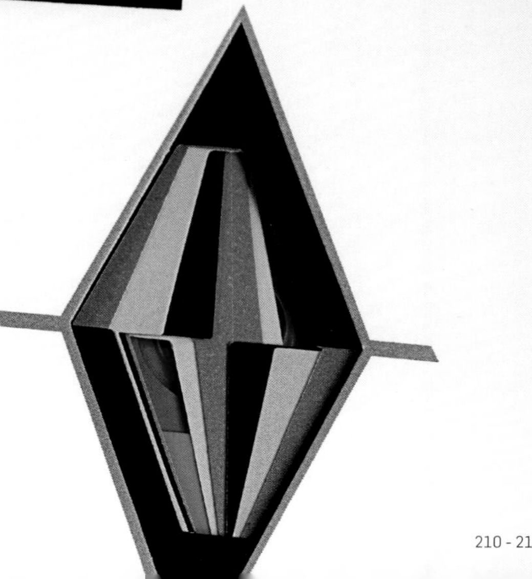

OUT
OF
THE
ASHES
OUT OF THE ASHES

A
Selection
of
Freerange
Rarities
&
Deletions
OUT OF THE ASHES

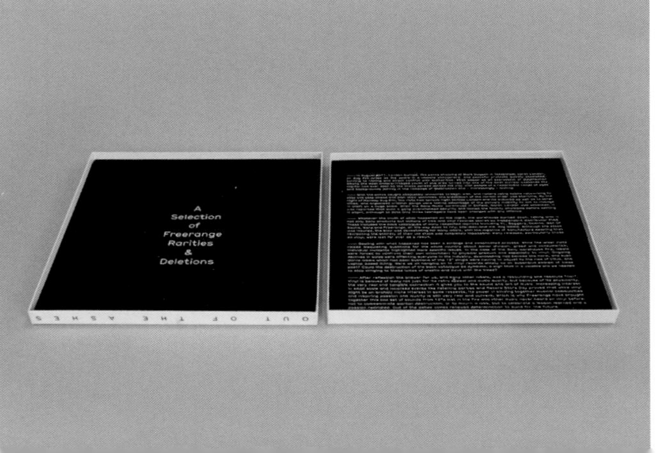
A
Selection
of
Freerange
Rarities
&
Deletions
OUT OF THE ASHES

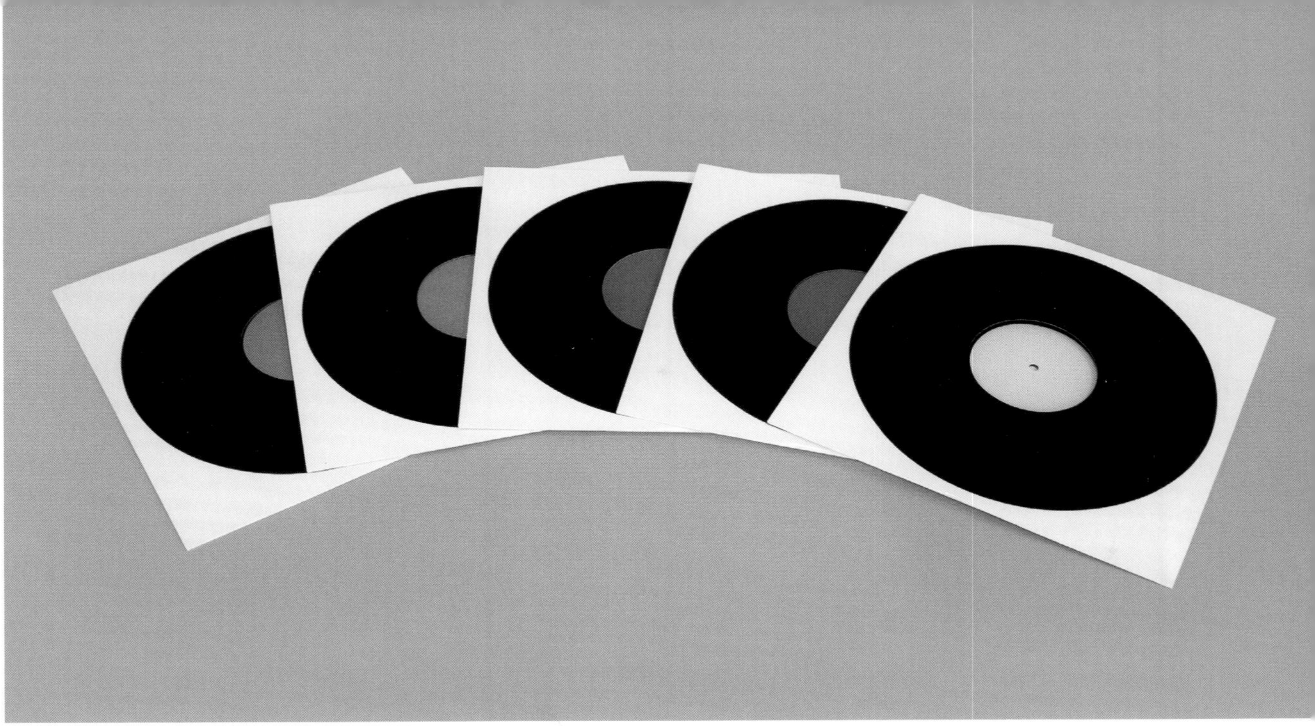

093

IWANT DESIGN

CLIENT | Freerange Records

On August 4th 2011, the Sony Music warehouse in Enfield, North London was attacked during riots and burnt to the ground. The blow was devastating for many labels and many releases have been lost forever as a result. One year on Freerange decided to release a box-set of classics and rarities and asked us to design the package. We wanted to do the project justice as it had affected many people we work with. We photographed ash in the form of a vinyl record, a kind of phoenix from the flames. The rest of the artwork was kept simple with clean back discs on the inner sleeves and single colour labels to identify each disc.

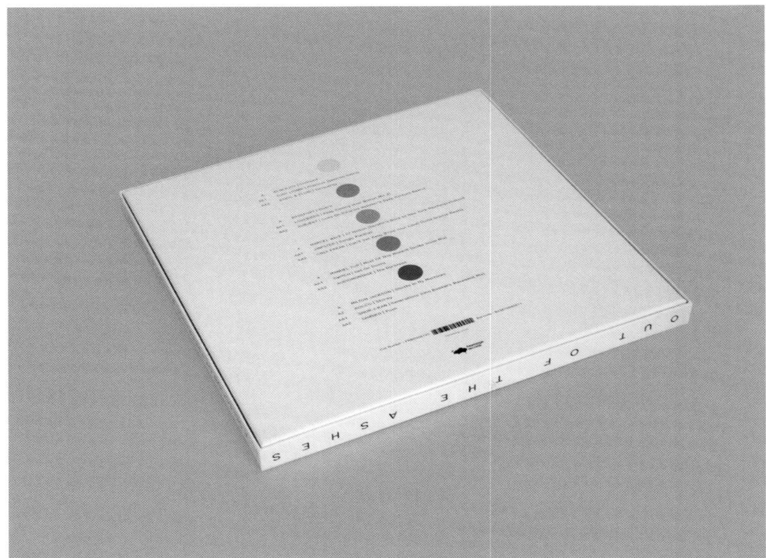

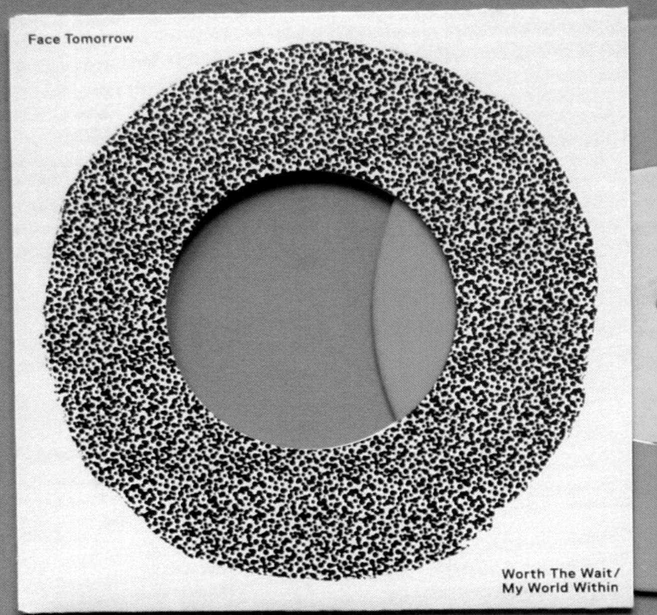
Face Tomorrow
Worth The Wait/
My World Within

Side A: Worth The Wait
Side B: My World Within

094

DRAWSWORDS & BARBARA HENNEQUIN

CLIENT | Face Tomorrow

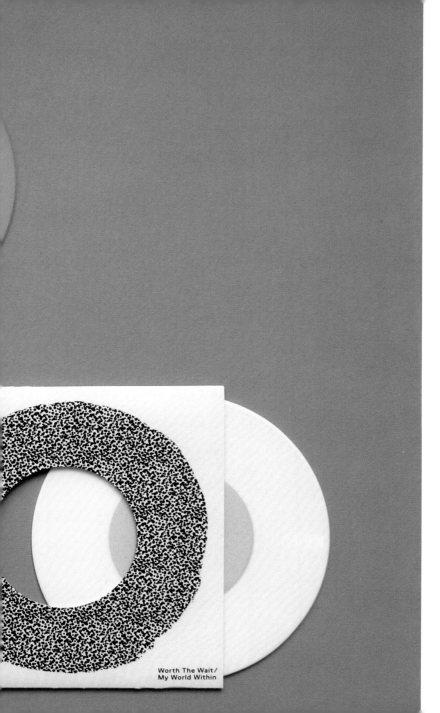

Artwork for Face Tomorrow's acoustic 7", featuring acoustic versions of "Worth the Wait" and "My World Within" as a preview for their upcoming acoustic album release. Available in three vinyl colours: white, purple (special edition for Record Store Day 2012) and orange (special edition for Groezrock 2012).

Pressed in a limited edition of 500 copies.

THE FREE FALL BAND
ELEPHANTS NEVER FORGET
BRO11LP LAV009LP

095

MAX-O-MATIC

CLIENT | LAV Records / BuenRitmo

Design and illustration for The Free Fall Band, a pop group from Barcelona. Influenced by bands from the '70s, like The Zombies, or more current bands like Belle & Sebastian, the cover of their first disc, *Elephants Never Forget*, had to be brilliant, luminous, happy and looking at the past through a fresh, modern lense. For the vinyl version of this album, we worked with a bi-tonal color scheme and emphasized the retro look with a halftone pattern texture for the collage.

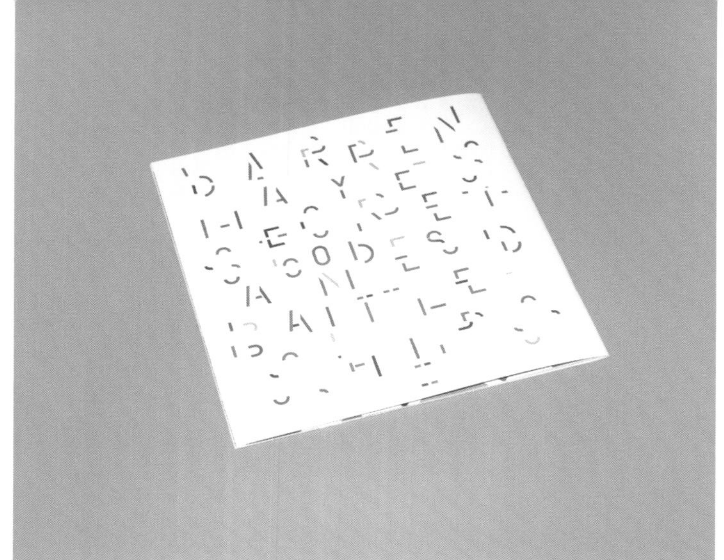

096

IWANT DESIGN

CLIENT | Darren Hayes

We worked closely with Darren Hayes for the better part of a year leading up to the release of his album *Secret Codes and Battleships*. We listened to Darren's ideas and thoughts on the record and began to slowly bring them to life. We initially created a pictorial code that was used to leak info about the release, then secrets were left in random places globally for people to discover more about the final reveal. The singles were all limited edition 7" 5 colour die-cut sleeves with heavy gloss covers and the main artwork printed inside the sleeve.

DARREN
HAYES
STUPID
MISTAKE

DARREN
HAYES
BLACK
OUT
THE
SUN

DARREN
HAYES
TALK
TALK
TALK

DARREN
HAYES
BLOOD
STAINED
HEART

097

MAX-O-MATIC

CLIENT | LAV Records / BuenRitmo

Design and illustration for The Free Fall Band, a pop group from Barcelona. Influenced by bands from the '70s, like The Zombies, or more current bands like Belle & Sebastian, the cover of their first disc, *Elephants Never Forget*, had to be brilliant, luminous, happy and looking at the past through a fresh, modern lense. With this in mind, the cover of the The Free Fall Band's first album was created as a mixture, with a base of colours, textures and hidden messages.

THE
FREE
FALL
BAND
ELEPHANTS
NEVER FORGET
BR011CD
LAV009

THE HOPE SLIDE

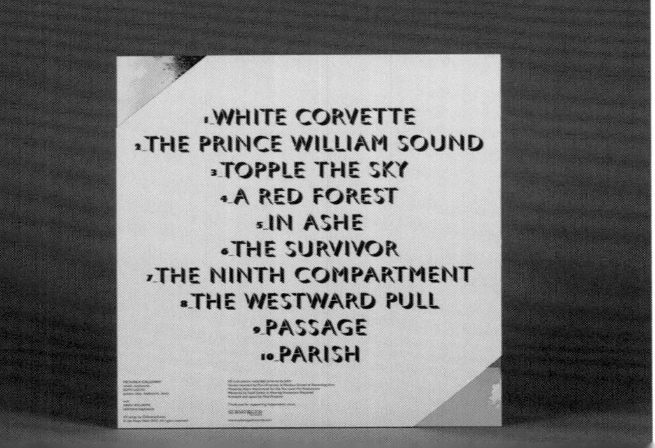

098

POST PROJECTS

CLIENT | The Hope Slide

Packaging and album art for Vancouver-based recording artists The Hope Slide. A limited edition vinyl release of their self-titled debut album – it features an intricate die-cut cover that forms the band's name out of a colour field on the record sleeve below.

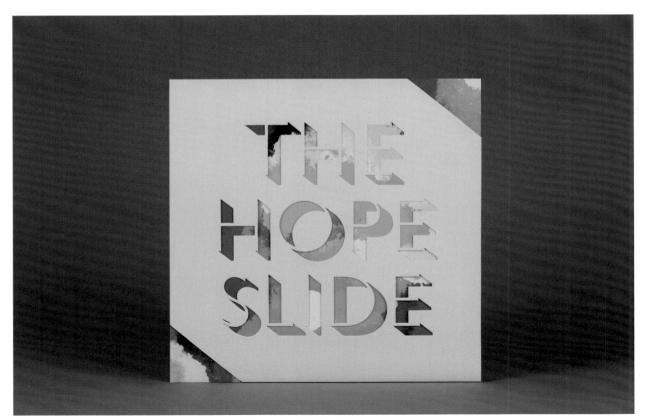

099

STUDIO IKNOKI

CLIENT | Aucan

For the artwork of Aucan's LP *Black Rainbow* a series of pictures of multi-coloured smoke were taken during a cold and rainy night; we wanted to "literally" recreate the black rainbow, trying to reproduce the feeling of a dark and explosive energy which emerges also from Aucan's music. Some basic and not so invasive typography has been added to the artwork in order to further stress the visual aspect.
The pictures of the coloured smoke, as well as the layout of the LP and CD were produced by Francesco D'abbraccio who is also one of Aucan's band members.

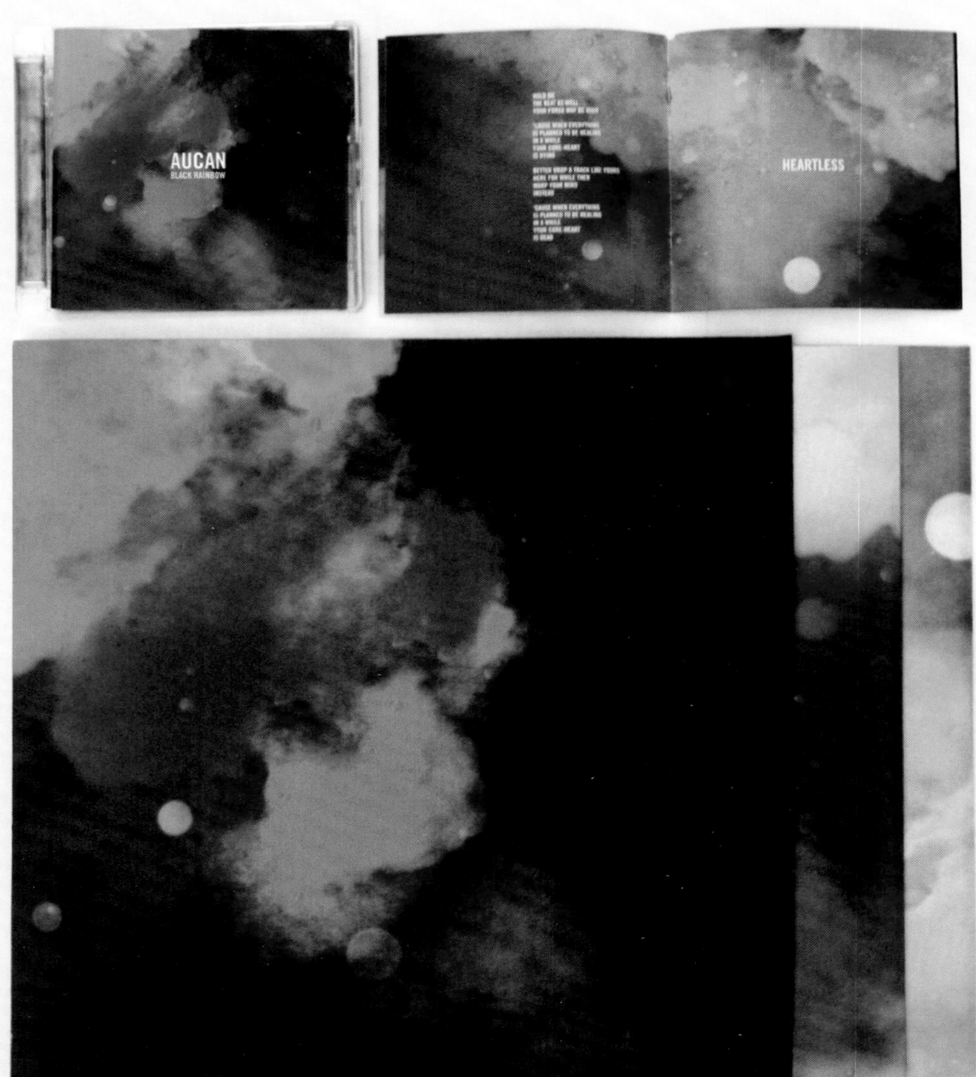
AUCAN
BLACK RAINBOW
HEARTLESS

ZINKPLAAT
MOOI
BESOEDELING

ZINKPLAAT
MOOI
BESOEDELING

ZINKPLAAT
MOOI
BESOEDELING

ZINKPLAAT
MOOI
BESOEDELING

100

FANAKALO

CLIENT | Zinkplaat

Zinkplaat is an Afrikaans pop-rock-blues-fusion band from South Africa. The name Zinkplaat is the Afrikaans word for corrugated metal.

This, their fourth album, comes shrink-wrapped with a scratch-off ink layer on the front and back, as well as a guitar pick to scratch the ink off with.

The album's name 'Mooi Besoedeling' translates to 'Beautiful Polution'. We believe this is a very good functional solution to the fact that a simplistic clean CD cover design stands out most from all the clutter on a store shelf, yet is very boring once bought. However if one wants to read the album as a concept, people seem to love the scratch-off part...

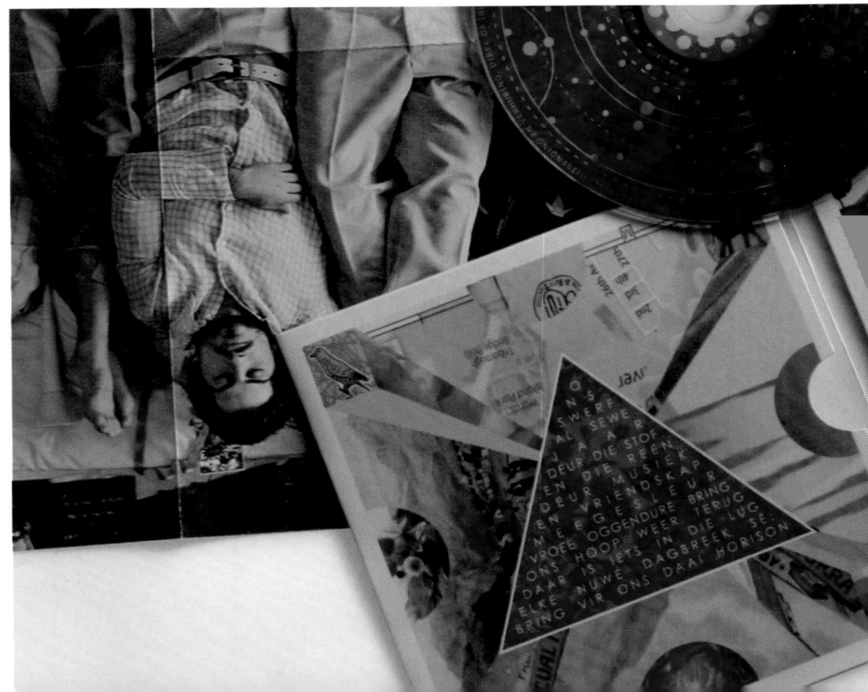

101

MAI-BRITT AMSLER

CLIENT | BoogiePost Recordings

6 page digipack. Cover for Østergaard Art Quartet, a collaboration between three countries and four unique musicians. With an unusual combination of instruments and a strong will to look beyond predefined musical roles, they are creating playful music in a improvised universe of sound.

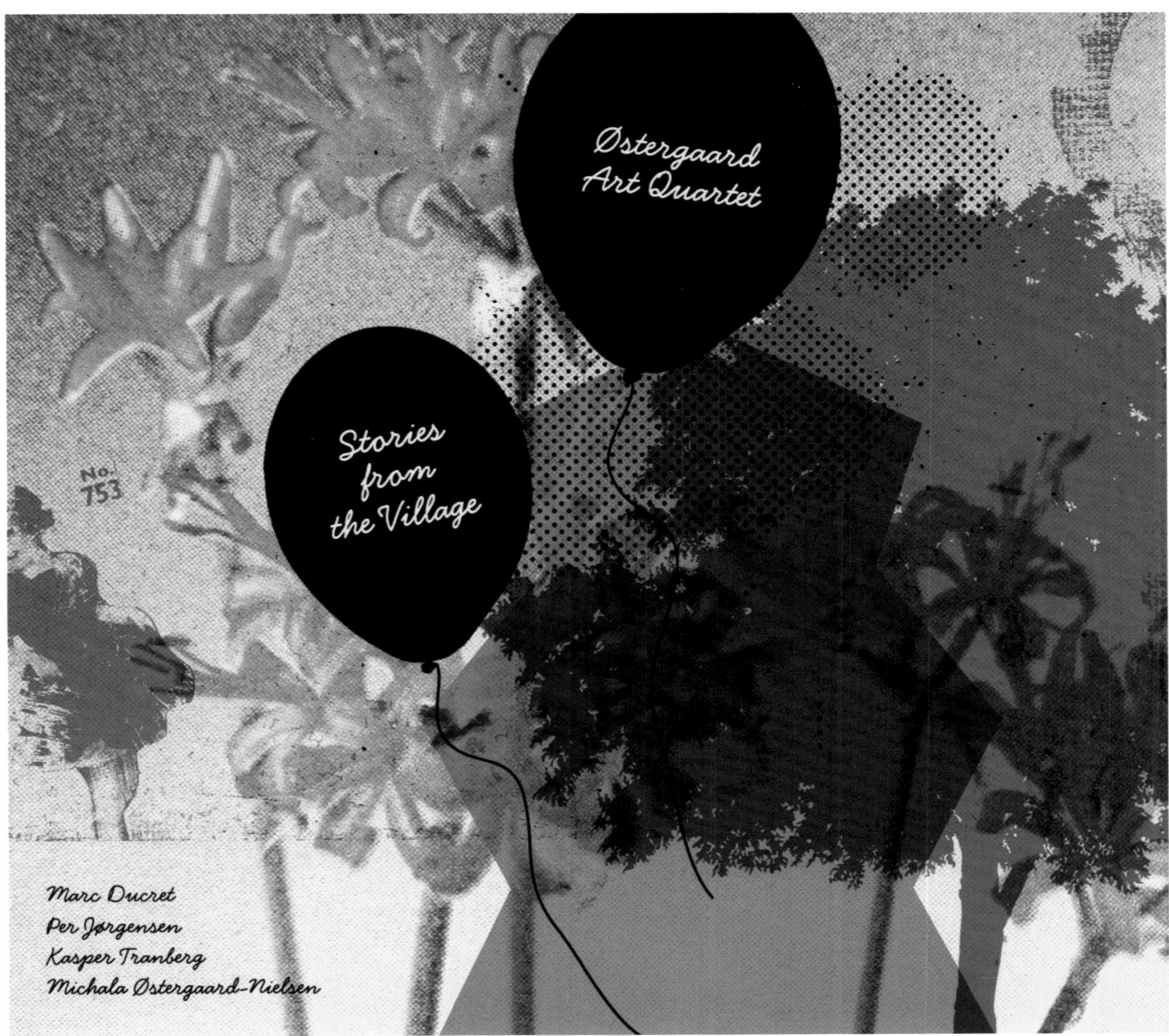
Østergaard
Art Quartet
Stories
from
the Village
No.
753
Marc Ducret
Per Jørgensen
Kasper Tranberg
Michala Østergaard-Nielsen

"comestible"

1-Marciano / 2-Al
7-Vuelve a los
COMESTIBL
Quedan reservados todos los derechos par
el ámbito doméstico. Queda prohibida cu
con la autorización de los titulares d

102

MAX-O-MATIC

CLIENT I Ombligo Records

Design and illustration for Comestible, an electro-pop group from Lima (Peru). In order to visualise the music of this group, who compose their music from samples, short fragments from other pre-existing songs cut and pasted together, the collage was a perfect tool, as it represents the fragmentation and the eclecticism of a very colourful and attractive style.

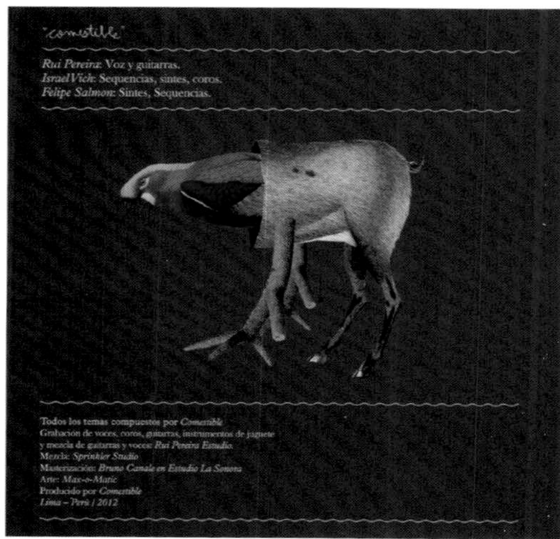

103

TWO TIMES ELLIOTT

CLIENT | Five Easy Pieces

Vinyl artwork for My Panda Shall Fly & Benjamin Jackson's debut EP on Five Easy Pieces. Printed 2 colour (black/805) on 300gsm reversed board sleeve. Pressed on 180g clear vinyl. Five Easy Pieces (FEP) curate experimental pop music and develop international artists, expanding networks and cultural communities.

MY PANDA SHALL FLY
& BENJAMIN JACKSON
MANTRA
* CLOUD BOAT REMIX
** CHAIRMAN KATO REMIX

104

IWANT DESIGN

CLIENT | Freerange Records

Identity and sleeve designs for Manual Tur's *Swans Reflecting Elephants*.

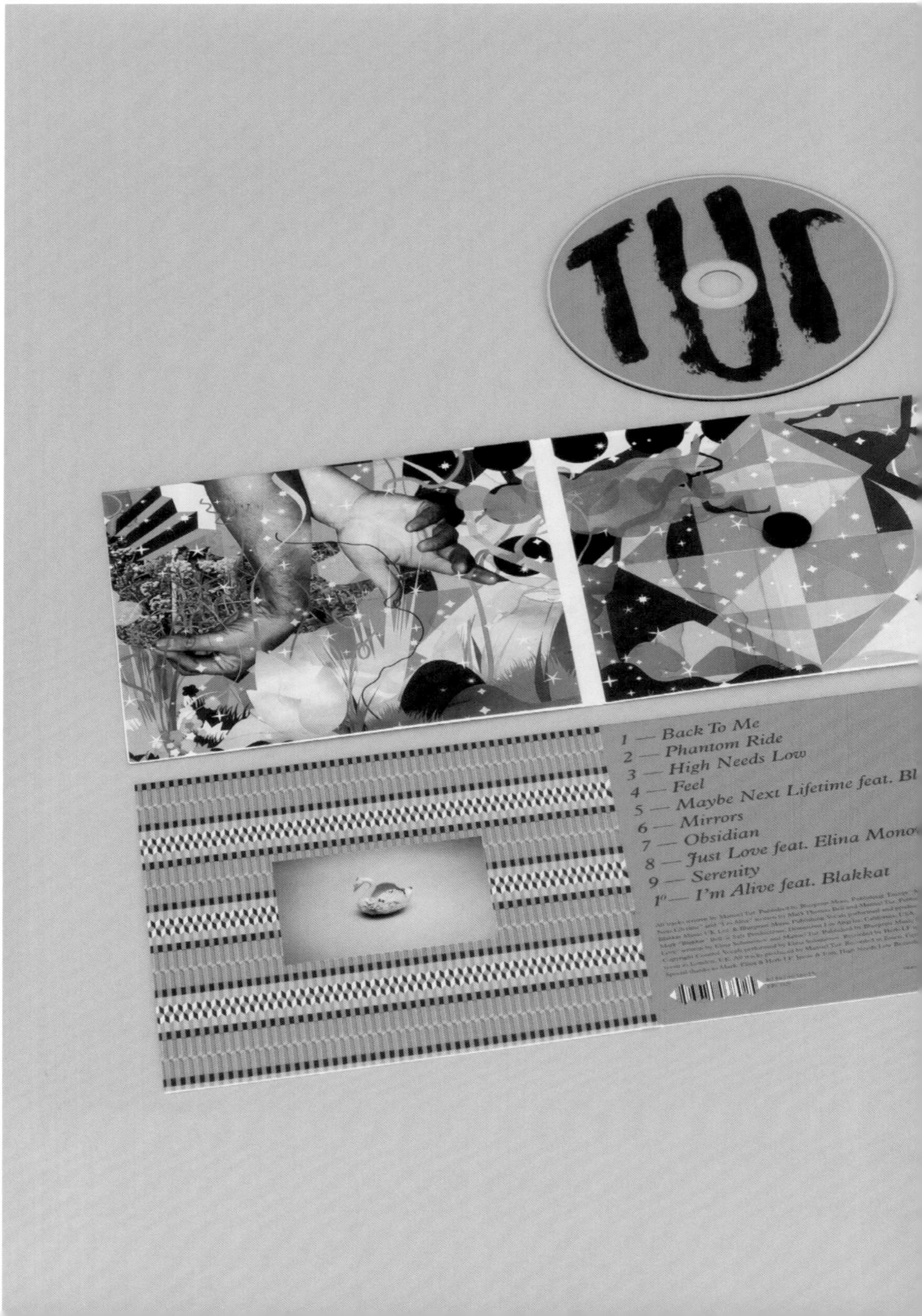

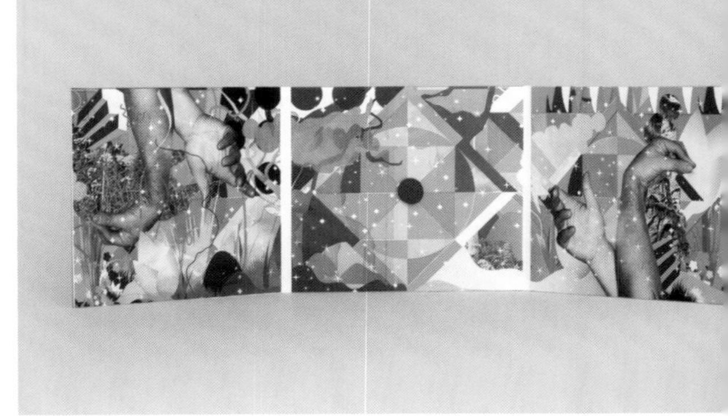

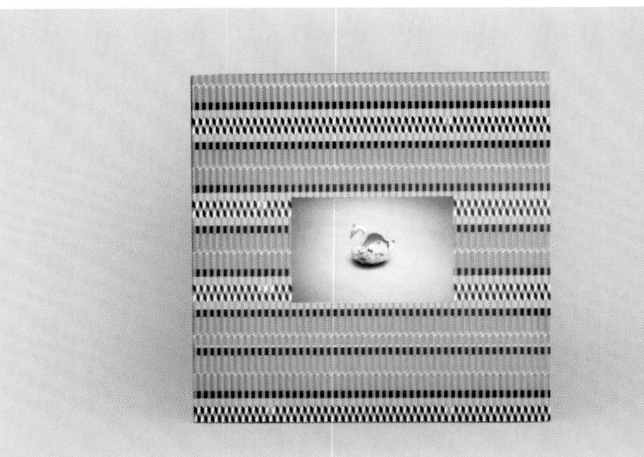

tur

105

FLOOR5

CLIENT | Xaver von Treyer
Supersoul Recordings

The Torino Scale is a method for categorising the impact hazard associated with near-Earth objects such as asteroids and comets. It is intended as a communication tool for astronomers and the public to assess the seriousness of collision predictions, by combining probability statistics and known kinetic damage potentials into a single threat value.

Xaver von Treyer adapted the name for his album, which also served as inspiration for the design process. We imagined the day after a possible collision. Smoking surface, darkness and hot lava underneath it all.

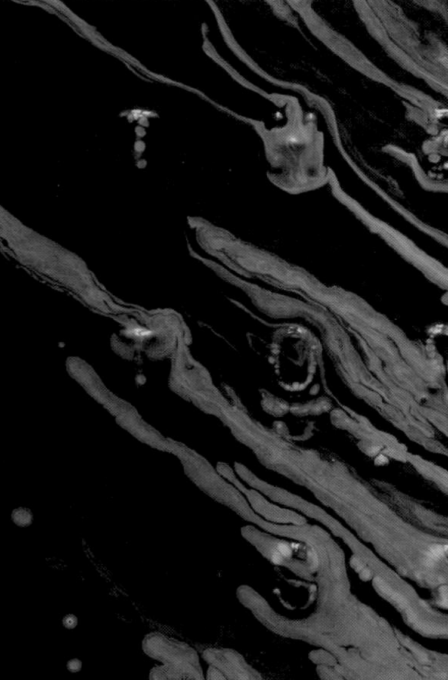

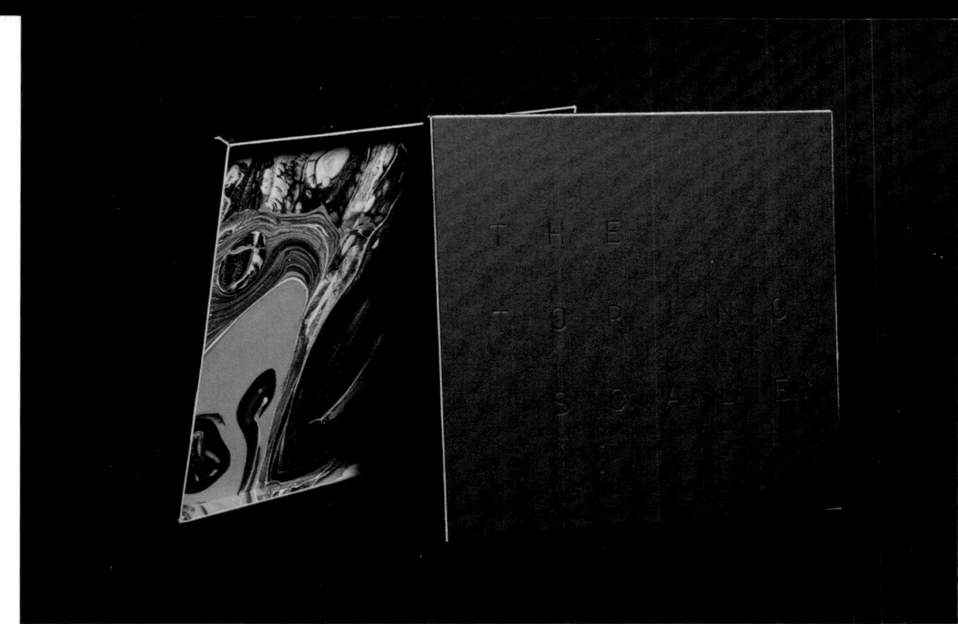
THE
TORINO
SCALE

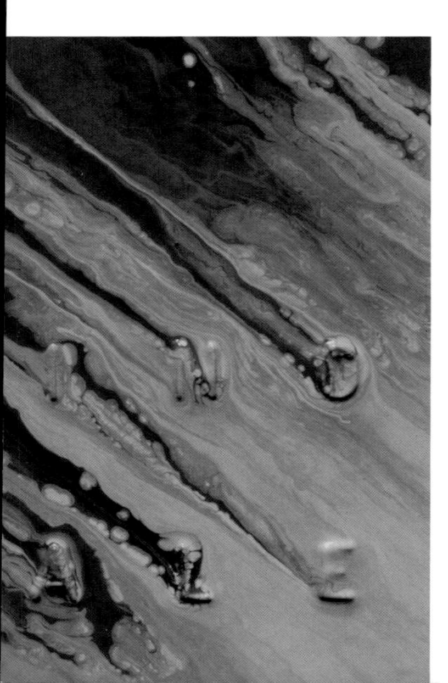

THE TORINO SCALE
33

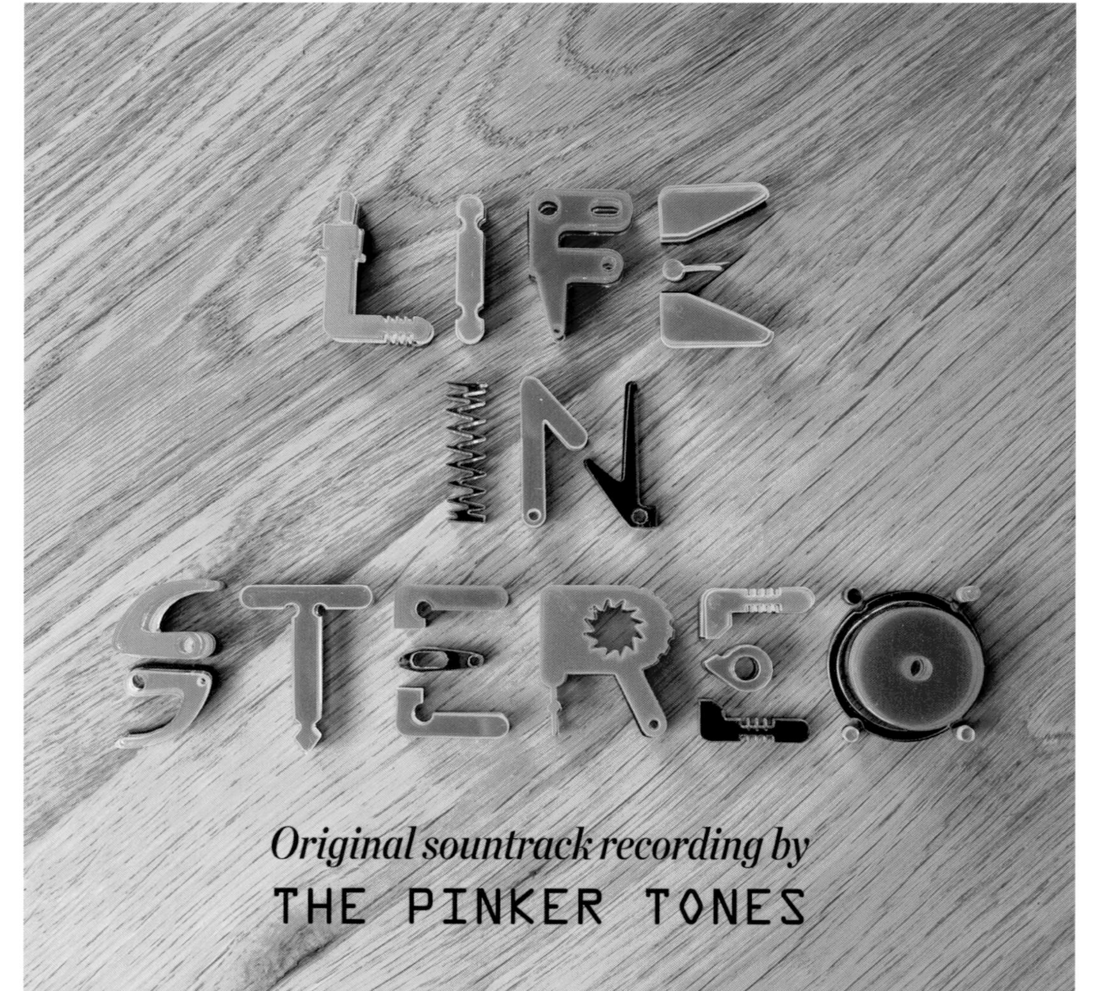
LIFE
IN
STEREO
Original soundtrack recording by
THE PINKER TONES

106

LO SIENTO

CLIENT | The Pinker Tones

"Life in Stereo", the new 2012 album from the electronic band. We designed a new alphabet converted into a layers of colours made of methacrylate pieces.

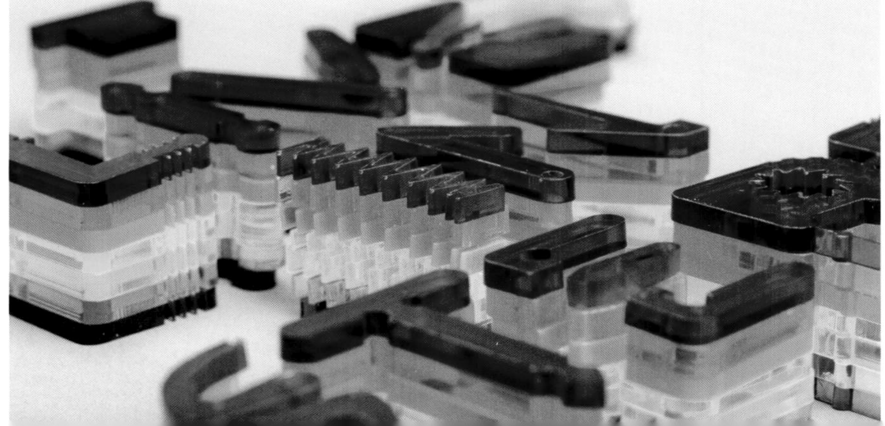

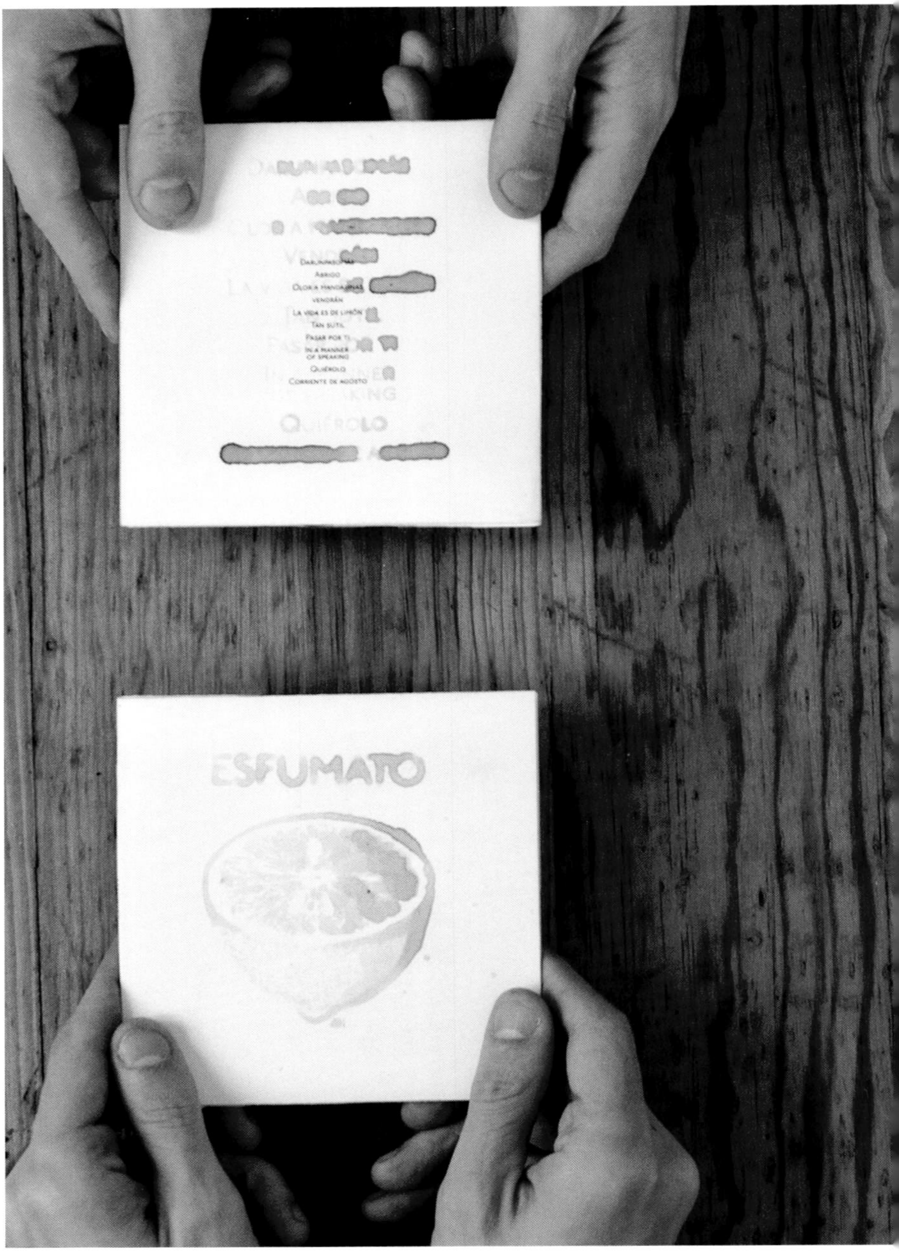

107

LA FRAGUA

CLIENT | Esfumato

Each copy of this album is a unique piece, stamped by hand with lemon juice and baked so that the ink appeared, like a kind of secret message. The result is extremely pictorial. The album *Limón*, from Esfumato, searches for the same magic and poetry that is transmitted their music.
The experimentation in the design process was fundamental to achieve this result, which makes it special, with numbered copies that are only distributed at their concerts.

ESFUMATO

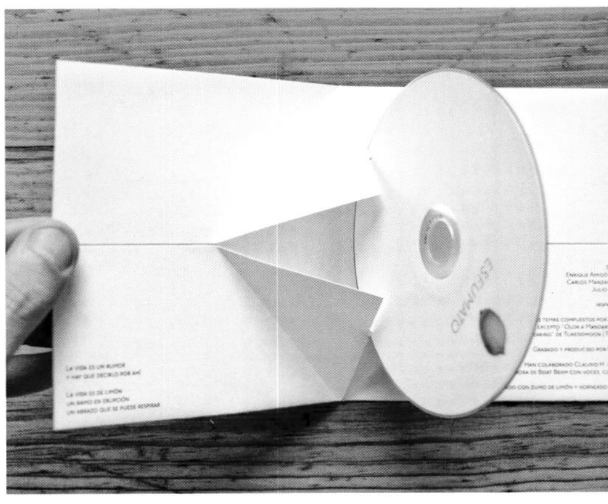
ESFUMATO

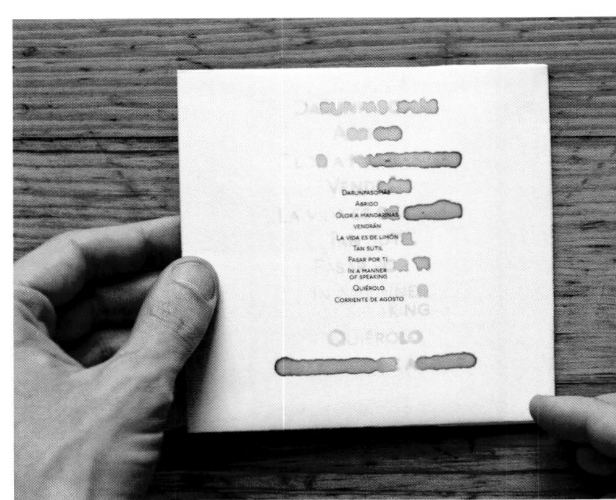
Darunpasomás
Abrigo
Olor a mandarinas
vendrán
La vida es de limón
Tan sutil
Pasar por ti
In a manner of speaking
Quiérolo
Corriente de agosto

number ||||||||||

STUDIO

Client

Country

Descriptive text.

081
ENSERIO
Panxii Badii
Spain

A raw and simple graphic illustrates the naked and personal music of Panxii Badii. The six cards that are found in the interior, purposefully not ordered, form part of a puzzle and give the option of 24 distinct covers.

082
MAI-BRITT AMSLER
BoogiePost Recordings
Denmark

CD in double carton sleeve with 12-page booklet. Cover for Television Pickup, a half-electric, half-acoustic band. Television Pickup is an android cinema orchestra playing songs from films you wish you had seen: Haunting melodies covered in dirt, broken in pieces and served with a straw.

083
HVASS&HANNIBAL
number0 / Rallye Label
Denmark

This is an album cover we designed for Japanese post-rock band number0. The artwork is made of spray painted glass layered with pieces of fabric that have been sewn together.

084
MAX-O-MATIC
Bardot
Spain

Design and illustration for 2, the second album from Bardot, a pop group from Buenos Aires. The group's brief, guided by the lyrics and dark musical textures, asked for the incorporation of the following elements: elephants, love, landscapes, faded colours and a certain retro tone.

085
IWANT DESIGN
Delusions of Grandeur
United Kingdom

Sleeve and packaging design for Session Victim's debut album *Haunted House of House* on Delusions of Grandeur.

086
HVASS&HANNIBAL
Canon Blue / Rumraket / Temporary Residence
Denmark

We designed this album cover for American musician Daniel James, aka Canon Blue, who released his second album, Rumspringa, at Temporary Residence in the US and Rumraket in Scandinavia.
The artwork is a tapestry made of fabric, and it is inspired by traditional Amish quiliting.

087
BELIEVE IN®
Darlings of the Day
United States of America / United Kingdom

8 page double gatefold CD cover for Hollywood-based band Darlings of the Day. The cover portrays a photographic narrative inspired by the title *Get burned*. Four pieces of wood on the front cover represent each of the four tracks on the EP. Each piece is then revealed in a burnt state as the cover unfolds. The crow is taken from the band's identity marque. Hand-rendered typography has been created using charcoal for the cover title and back cover track listing.

088
ENSERIO
Caiko
Spain

A handful of holes made by hand with a pick create an illustration on a completely blank poster that, once folded, serves as the cover of the first disc from the group Caiko. A limited series of 200 pieces with a convincing image created using an infantile technique.

089
DRAWSWORDS & BARBARA HENNEQUIN
Face Tomorrow
The Netherlands

Artwork for Dutch indie rock band Face Tomorrow's acoustic LP called *Move On*. This is their goodbye LP as a band, since they decided to call it quits after 10 years.
The decision was quickly made to make the mixed emotions about this ending of an era the base of the design - happy and sad at the same time. The 'punch holes' on the outer and inner sleeve reveal the vinyl's A (blue - happy) and B (red - sad) label on smiley-bright-yellow vinyl. The glossy black stickers on the front and back cover were hand-stickered by the band themselves. Because of the possible combinations with the eyes (circle, cross or dash) and three different mouths (a happy smile, a sad smile and a curvy, undecided one) the artwork is different on every LP, which makes each one unique and an extra special goodbye gift. Pressed in a limited edition of 300 (signed) copies.
Designers: Rob van den Nieuwenhuizen (DRAWSWORDS), Barbara Hennequin.

090

MARTA VELUDO & RICARDO LEITE

Swinging Rabbits
Portugal

Tricks are for Kids is the name of the album from the band Swinging Rabbits. With this delicious name we realised that exploring the visual world of our childhood was the right path to build a curious identity. We tried to achieve a perfect and playful combination with tactile process and typography, building up sets and hand-drawing types.

091

DRAWSWORDS & BARBARA HENNEQUIN

Face Tomorrow
The Netherlands

Artwork for Dutch indie rock band Face Tomorrow's 2010 full length self-titled LP and CD. The 'blind spots' on the CD and LP were overprinted using a UV Spot varnish and the LP version was limited to 400 copies on black vinyl and only a 100 copies on marbled red/white vinyl all including the CD version as well.
Designers: Rob van den Nieuwenhuizen (DRAWSWORDS), Barbara Hennequin.

092

THE CREATIVE CORPORATION

Third Rock Recordings
United Kingdom

Cave Painting's elegant debut album reflects the band's belief in the artifact as a vital part of the listening experience.
The cover reveals a concertina of die cuts which, when closed, makes up the band's diamond logo. Inspired by Japanese paper engineering and binding techniques, the pack is made up of a spectrum of pastel shades fading into the next, with each panel containing an individual cut shape.
The design team felt it was clear that the packaging should reflect the band's understated but emotive music; aiming to produce a package that conveyed a feeling of depth and considerable beauty.
Art-Director: Scott Jones.

093

IWANT DESIGN

Freerange Records
United Kingdom

On August 4th 2011, the Sony Music warehouse in Enfield, North London was attacked during riots and burnt to the ground. The blow was devastating for many labels and many releases have been lost forever as a result. One year on Freerange decided to release a box-set of classics and rarities and asked us to design the package. We wanted to do the project justice as it had affected many people we work with. We photographed ash in the form of a vinyl record, a kind of phoenix from the flames. The rest of the artwork was kept simple with clean back discs on the inner sleeves and single colour labels to identify each disc.

094

DRAWSWORDS & BARBARA HENNEQUIN

Face Tomorrow
The Netherlands

Artwork for Face Tomorrow's acoustic 7", featuring acoustic versions of "Worth the Wait" and "My World Within" as a preview for their upcoming acoustic album release. Available in three vinyl colours: white, purple (special edition for Record Store Day 2012) and orange (special edition for Groezrock 2012).
Pressed in a limited edition of 500 copies.
Designers: Rob van den Nieuwenhuizen (DRAWSWORDS), Barbara Hennequin.

095

MAX-O-MATIC

LAV Records / BuenRitmo
Spain

Design and illustration for The Free Fall Band, a pop group from Barcelona. Influenced by bands from the '70s, like The Zombies, or more current bands like Belle & Sebastian, the cover of their first disc, *Elephants Never Forget*, had to be brilliant, luminous, happy and looking at the past through a fresh, modern lense.
For the vinyl version of this album, we worked with a bi-tonal color scheme and emphasized the retro look with a halftone pattern texture for the collage.

096

IWANT DESIGN

Darren Hayes

United Kingdom

We worked closely with Darren Hayes for the better part of a year leading up to the release of his album *Secret Codes and Battleships*. We listened to Darren's ideas and thoughts on the record and began to slowly bring them to life. We initially created a pictorial code that was used to leak info about the release, then secrets were left in random places globally for people to discover more about the final reveal. The singles were all limited edition 7" 5 colour die-cut sleeves with heavy gloss covers and the main artwork printed inside the sleeve.

097

MAX-O-MATIC

LAV Records / BuenRitmo

Spain

Design and illustration for The Free Fall Band, a pop group from Barcelona. Influenced by bands from the '70s, like The Zombies, or more current bands like Belle & Sebastian, the cover of their first disc, Elephants Never Forget, had to be brilliant, luminous, happy and looking at the past through a fresh, modern lense. With this in mind, the cover of the The Free Fall Band's first album was created as a mixture, with a base of colours, textures and hidden messages.

098

POST PROJECTS

The Hope Slide

Canada

Packaging and album art for Vancouver-based recording artists The Hope Slide. A limited edition vinyl release of their self-titled debut album – it features an intricate die-cut cover that forms the band's name out of a colour field on the record sleeve below.

099

STUDIO IKNOKI

Aucan

Italy

For the artwork of Aucan's LP Black Rainbow a series of pictures of multi-coloured smoke were taken during a cold and rainy night; we wanted to "literally" recreate the black rainbow, trying to reproduce the feeling of a dark and explosive energy which emerges also from Aucan's music.
Some basic and not so invasive typography has been added to the artwork in order to further stress the visual aspect.
The pictures of the colored smoke, as well as the layout of the LP and CD were produced by Francesco D'abbraccio who is also one of Aucan's band members.

100

FANAKALO

Zinkplaat

South Africa

Zinkplaat is an Afrikaans pop-rock-blues-fusion band from South Africa. The name Zinkplaat is the Afrikaans word for corrugated metal.
This, their fourth album, comes shrink-wrapped with a scratch-off ink layer on the front and back, as well as a guitar pick to scratch the ink off with.
The album's name 'Mooi Besoedeling' translates to 'Beautiful Polution'. We believe this is a very good functional solution to the fact that a simplistic clean CD cover design stands out most from all the clutter on a store shelf, yet is very boring once bought. However if one wants to read the album as a concept, people seem to love the scratch-off part...

101

MAI-BRITT AMSLER

BoogiePost Recordings

Denmark

6 page digipack. Cover for Østergaard Art Quartet, a collaboration between three countries and four unique musicians. With an unusual combination of instruments and a strong will to look beyond predefined musical roles, they are creating playful music in a improvised universe of sound.

102

MAX-O-MATIC

Ombligo Records

Spain

Design and illustration for Comestible, an electro-pop group from Lima (Peru). In order to visualize the music of this group, who compose their music from samples, short fragments from other pre-existing songs cut and pasted together, the collage was a perfect tool, as it represents the fragmentation and the eclecticism of a very colourful and attractive style.

103

TWO TIMES ELLIOTT

Five Easy Pieces

United Kingdom

Vinyl artwork for My Panda Shall Fly & Benjamin Jackson's debut EP on Five Easy Pieces. Printed 2 colour (black/805) on 300gsm reversed board sleeve. Pressed on 180g clear vinyl. Five Easy Pieces (FEP) curate experimental pop music and develop international artists, expanding networks and cultural communities.
Designer: Ross Gunter.

104

IWANT DESIGN

Freerange Records
United Kingdom

Identity and sleeve designs for Manual Tur's *Swans Reflecting Elephants*.

105

FLOOR5

Xaver von Treyer / Supersoul Recordings
Germany

The Torino Scale is a method for categorising the impact hazard associated with near-Earth objects such as asteroids and comets. It is intended as a communication tool for astronomers and the public to assess the seriousness of collision predictions, by combining probability statistics and known kinetic damage potentials into a single threat value.
Xaver von Treyer adapted the name for his album, which also served as inspiration for the design process. We imagined the day after a possible collision. Smoking surface, darkness and hot lava underneath it all.
Designers: Marek Polewski, Neven Cvijanovic / Photographers: Marcus Gaab, Daniel Reiter.

106

LO SIENTO

The Pinker Tones
Spain

"Life in Stereo", the new 2012 album from the electronic band. We designed a new alphabet converted into a layers of colours made of methacrylate pieces.

107

LA FRAGUA

Esfumato
Spain

Each copy of this album is a unique piece, stamped by hand with lemon juice and baked so that the ink appeared, like a kind of secret message.The result is extremely pictorial. The album *Limón*, from Esfumato, searches for the same magic and poetry that is transmitted their music.
The experimentation in the design process was fundamental to achieve this result, which makes it special, with numbered copies that are only distributed at their concerts.

250-303

CATALOGUES

TALENT

108

BILDI GRAFIKS

CLIENT | EADC - Generalitat de Catalunya

The catalogue of an exhibition of photography from 15 artists from different parts of the world. The typographic concept, given that the artists are from different places but found in the same space, starts with the informative panels found at airports; the challenge consisted in animating typography on support paper, and this was achieved by working with lenticular technology. The project won awards from Grand Laus, Red Dot Best of the Best, and was nominated by Deutschland Designpreis.

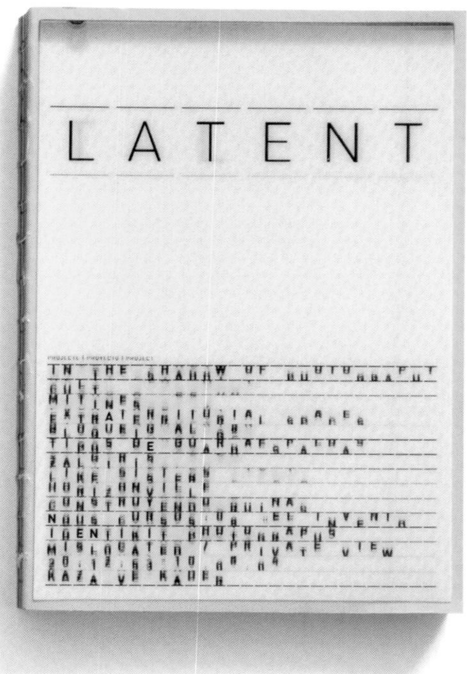

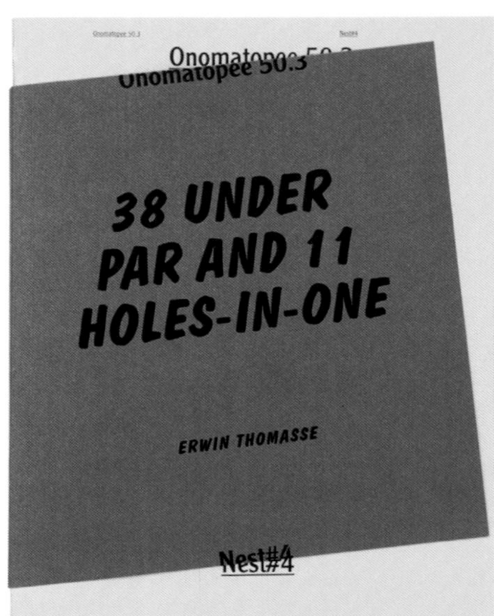
Onomatopee 50.3
38 UNDER PAR AND 11 HOLES-IN-ONE
ERWIN THOMASSE
Nest#4

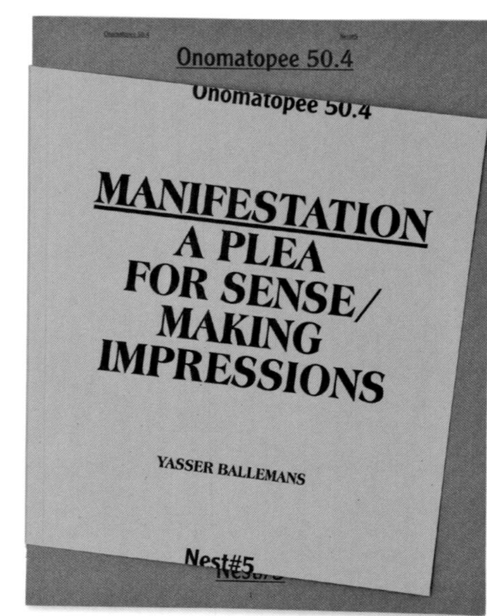
Onomatopee 50.4
MANIFESTATION
A PLEA FOR SENSE/ MAKING IMPRESSIONS
YASSER BALLEMANS
Nest#5

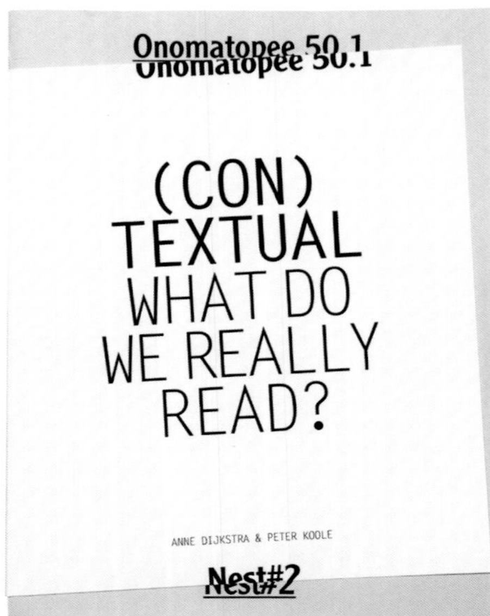
Onomatopee 50.1
(CON) TEXTUAL WHAT DO WE REALLY READ?
ANNE DIJKSTRA & PETER KOOLE
Nest#2

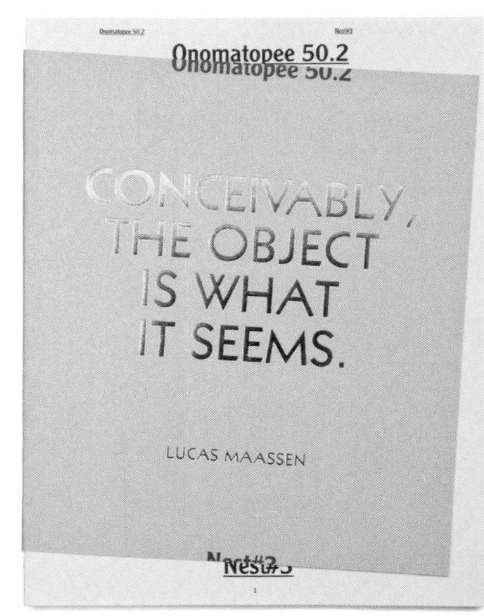
Onomatopee 50.2
CONCEIVABLY, THE OBJECT IS WHAT IT SEEMS.
LUCAS MAASSEN
Nest#3

109

RAW COLOR

CLIENT I Onomatopee

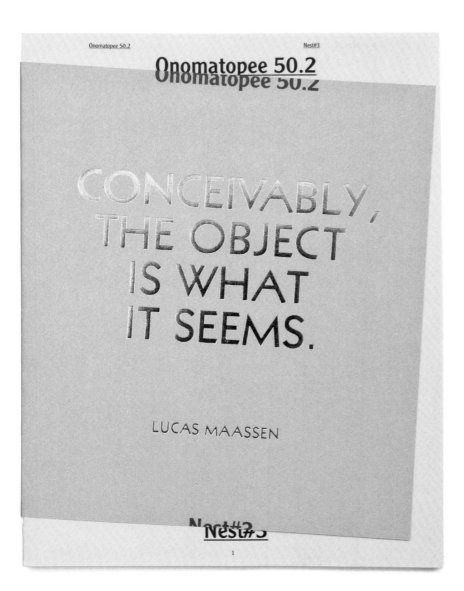

Onomatopee is a platform and publisher focusing on art projects reflecting on communication. They asked us to design a series of small books for the ongoing series "Nest", that spotlights emerging talent in art and design. Every publication represents one artist, who is also featured in an exhibition at the Onomatopee project space.

With this approach in mind we tried to translate this into a design, that creates a complete image as a series, but is at the same time able to highlight each artist's quality. Each booklet's cover is a folded oblique on the book block. It can be seen as a mismatching cover, in a way referring to the unadapted way of working of the featured artists. It exposes bits of the inside content of the book. This factor changes in colour and position during the series. The inside attempts a nice mixture of full colour and PMS printed pages. The work of the specific artist is enhanced by the text from different authors and a specific chosen lettertype.

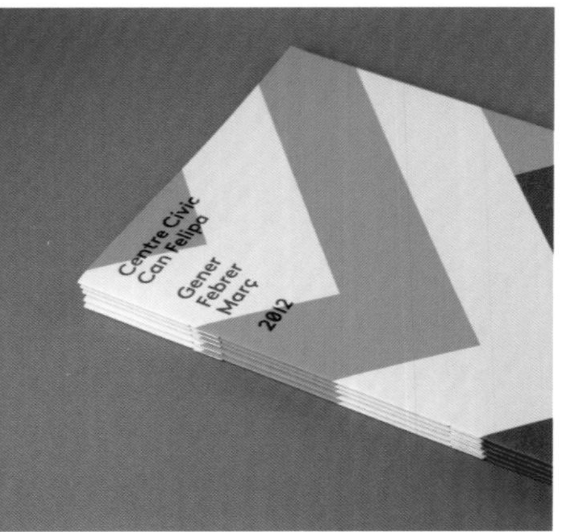

110

FORMA & CO

CLIENT | Centre Cívic Can Felipa

Cultural agenda for the civic center Can Felipa.

Centre Civic
Can Felipa
Abril
Maig
Juny
2012
Centre Civic
Can Felipa
Gener
Febrer
Març
2012
Ajuntament de Barcelona

Nest#7

Onomatopee 50.6

COMFORT
ZONE
AND
DISILLUSION
#2
SPATIAL
RUPTURE

BY WILLEM CLAASSEN

111

RAW COLOR

CLIENT | Onomatopee

The “Nest” series of 2011 is a follow up of the earlier series from 2010. Trying to keep a strong visual link with the earlier booklets we wanted to evolve their qualities into a new series. The booklets are based on a 8 page cover that is folded to the outside instead of to the inside.

The outer flap is slanted cut, resulting in two colour surfaces and scattered typography. This factor changes in colour and position during the series.

The inside attempts a nice mixture of full colour and duotonal pages. The work of the specific artist is enhanced by the text from different authors and a specific chosen font type.

The ongoing series “Nest”, spotlights emerging talent in art and design. Every publication represents one artist, who is also featured in an exhibition at the Onomatopee project space.

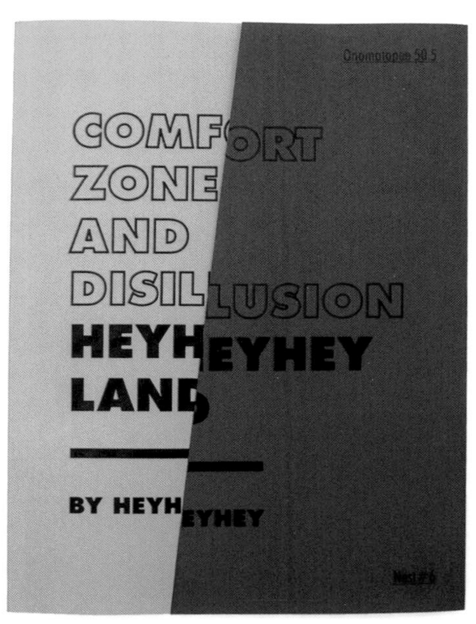
Onomatopee 50.5
COMFORT
ZONE
AND
DISILLUSION
HEYHEYHEY
LAND
BY HEYHEYHEY
Nest#6

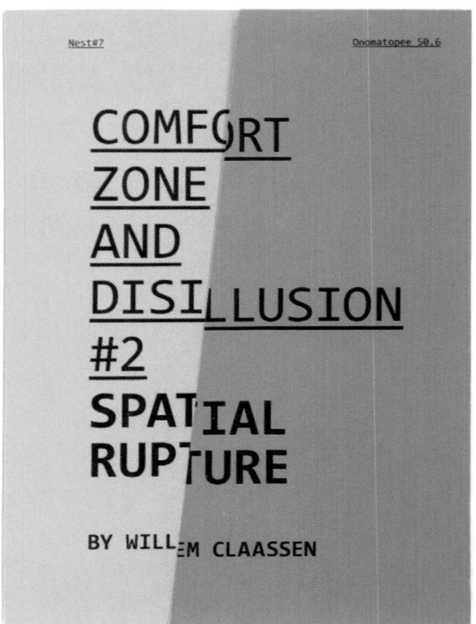
Nest#7
Onomatopee 50.6
COMFORT
ZONE
AND
DISILLUSION
#2
SPATIAL
RUPTURE
BY WILLEM CLAASSEN

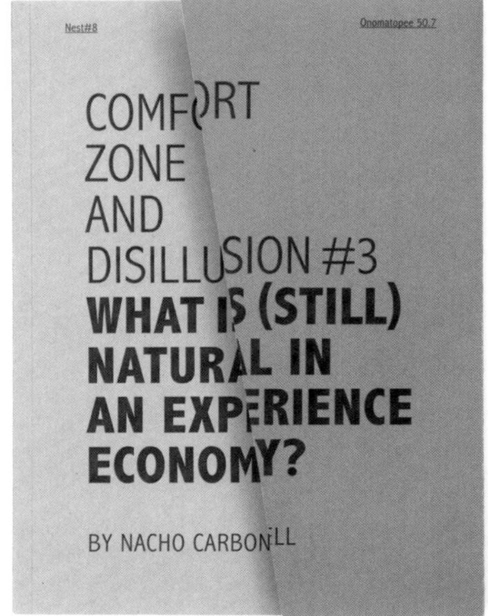
Nest#8
Onomatopee 50.7
COMFORT
ZONE
AND
DISILLUSION #3
WHAT IS (STILL)
NATURAL IN
AN EXPERIENCE
ECONOMY?
BY NACHO CARBONELL

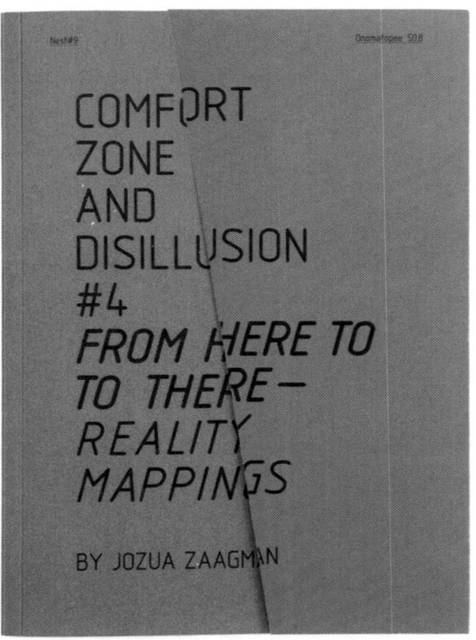
COMFORT
ZONE
AND
DISILLUSION
#4
FROM HERE TO
TO THERE—
REALITY
MAPPINGS
BY JOZUA ZAAGMAN

TYPEFORCE /
THE ANNUAL
CHICAGO SHOW
OF EMERGING
TYPOGRAPHIC
ALLSTARS
February | March 2010
The Annual Chicago Show of Emerging Typographic Allstars

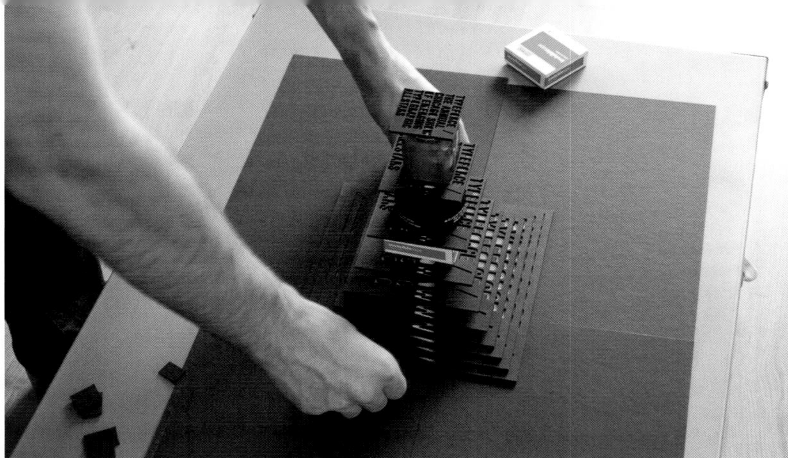

112

FIREBELLY DESIGN

CLIENT I TYPEFORCE 1 / The Annual Chicago Show of Emerging Typographic Allstars

This small format book was created to honor and document the inaugural TYPEFORCE exhibition, which occurred in 2010. It features the 23 largely Chicago-based designers/artists who participated in the event, separated within the book by neon orange spreads containing everything from flaming pastry type to sign language. The cover is the result of an overhead photograph taken of a pyramid made of matching and increasingly larger layers of laser cut mat board messages.

113

FIREBELLY DESIGN

CLIENT | TYPEFORCE 2 / The Annual Chicago Show of Emerging Typographic Allstars

The second TYPEFORCE catalogue showcases the 25 artists involved in the TYPEFORCE 2 exhibition, which opened on February 11, 2011. This book requires a physical commitment from the reader, as a fresh copy can only be accessed by ripping a hand-affixed, perforated tear seal on the cover. Strips on the front cover serve as a table of contents, labeling the work of the artists inside, where colour guides the viewer: motivation in blue, experience in red, with substance denoted by full-color printing.

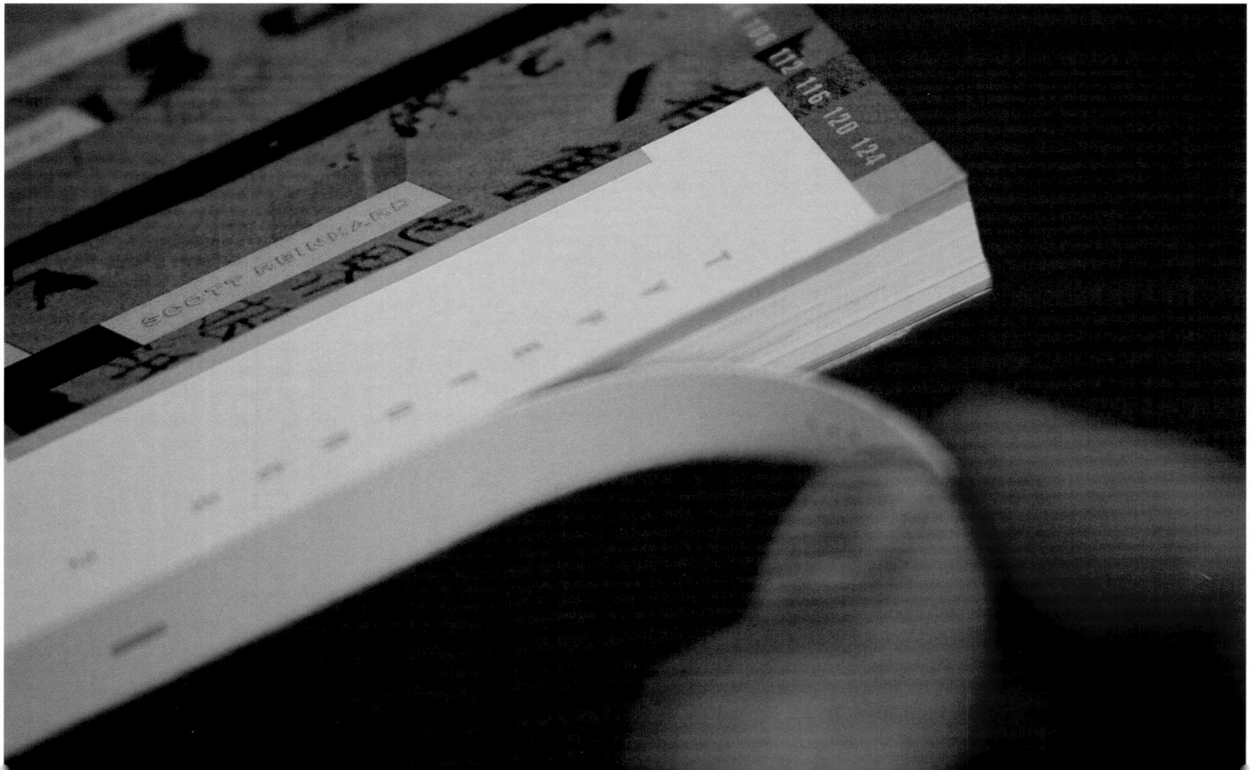

TYPEFORCE 3 / The Annual Show of Emerging Typographic Allstars

114

TALLER DE COMUNICACIÓN GRÁFICA

CLIENT | Fundación Amparo and Credit Suisse

Catalogue of the retrospective exhibition of the Mexican artist Betsabeé Romero at the Museo Amparo in the city of Puebla, Mexico. The show was also in Monterrey, Guadalajara, Mexico City and New York.

Interiors printed with 4 x 0 colours on 75g paper, with Japanese binding. Lining in 3mm cardboard bounded in boards with black flocking. The front and back of the lining are completely different and the flocking makes reference to a tire track intervened by the artist. Handsewn with dyed cotton thread.

115

NATIONAL FOREST DESIGN

CLIENT | Sixpack France

The 160-page *Peyote Poem* catalogue National Forest created for Sixpack France featured location photography of the capsule collection we designed as well as flats of the entire line. Printed entirely on aged recycled paper, the shamanist book of sorts was meant to feel like an artifact lost and later found on a dusty shelf somewhere in the high desert.

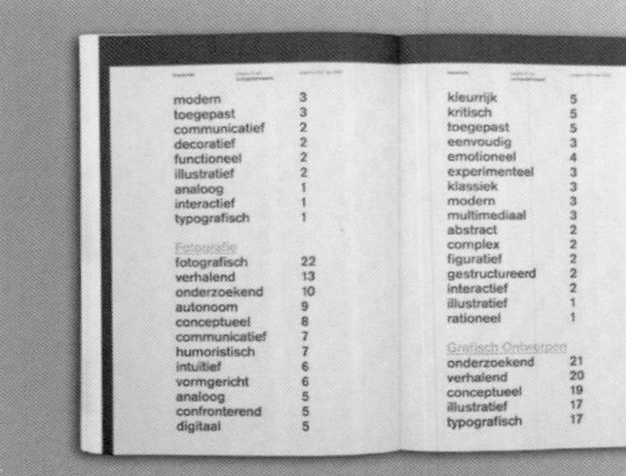

116

DRAWSWORDS

CLIENT I KABK (Royal Academy of Art, The Hague)

465-page catalogue containing all graduation projects of the students of the Royal Academy of Art in 2008-2009.

Instead of focusing on just the work the students produced during their graduation, we asked students about their future plans. These plans became the main design element - next to the images of their work - in the book.

We also asked the students to tag their work with predefined and self-defined keywords, which were then presented next to their work and also as clear, informative lists explaining how many times students from a certain course selected a specific tag or how many times a tag was selected in total amongst the 200 graduates. This information gave more insight in how students of specific courses think of their own work.

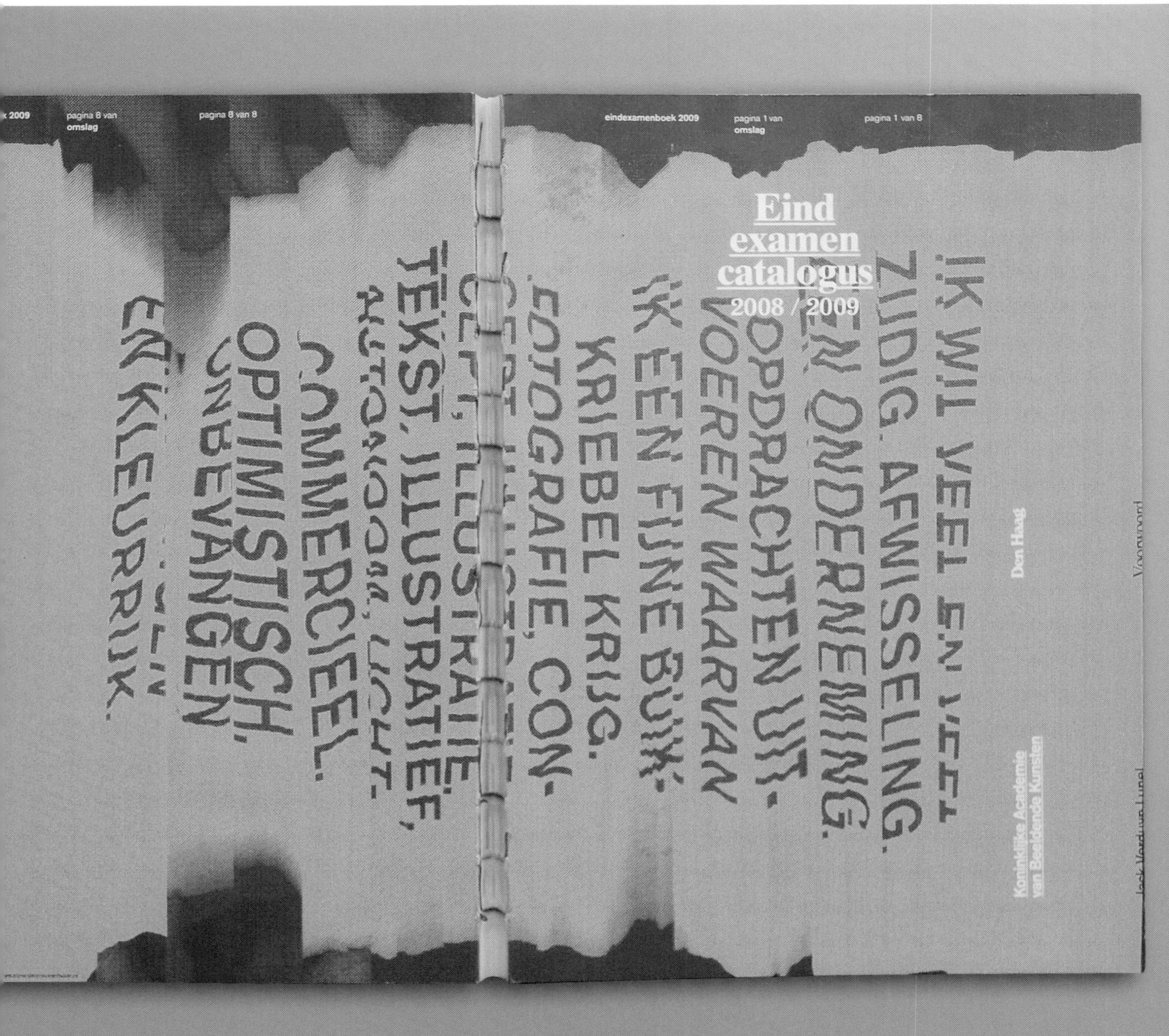
pagina 8 van
omslag
pagina 8 van 8
eindexamenboek 2009
pagina 1 van
omslag
pagina 1 van 8
Eind
examen
catalogus
2008 / 2009
Den Haag
Koninklijke Academie
van Beeldende Kunsten

117

NAKANO DESIGN OFFICE

CLIENT | Meguro Museum of Art, Tokyo

The retrospective exhibition of Kiyoo Kawamura, an artist from the Meiji period.

For the cover, we used a combination of vermillion red and gold leaf referring to the bookbinding which Kawamura did by himself.

For the body, we laid it out carefully so people can sense his delineations which are so sensitive but energetic at the same time.

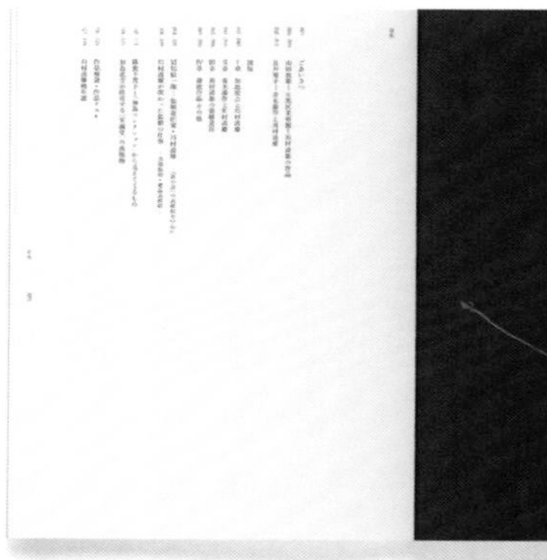

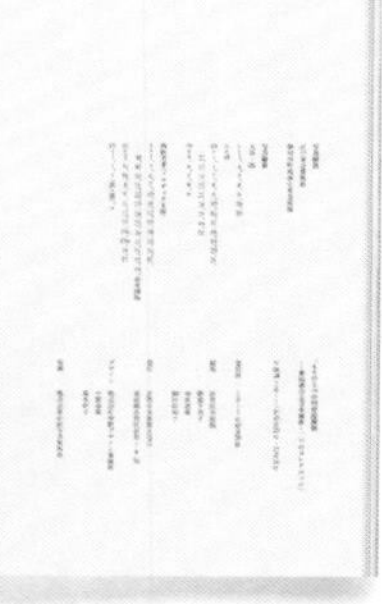

もうひとつの
川村清雄
展
加島虎吉と青木藤作・二つのコレクション
もうひとつの 川村清雄 展
加島虎吉と青木藤作・二つのコレクション
目黒区美術館
2012

118

TALLER DE COMUNICACIÓN GRÁFICA

CLIENT | Museo Nacional de Arte,
Instituto Nacional de Bellas Artes,
Fundación/colección Jumex

Catalogue for the exhibition *The Practice of Everyday Life* at the National Art Museum (Munal) in Mexico City. The exhibition is a dialogue between Munal's collection and the contemporary art collection from the Jumex Foundation.

Interiors printed on 4 x 4 colours on coated 150g paper with the lining padded with 3mm cardboard with 2mm foam, printed with 5 x 0 colours and laminated with shine. Square folding. The front and back images refer to a piece from each one of the collections.

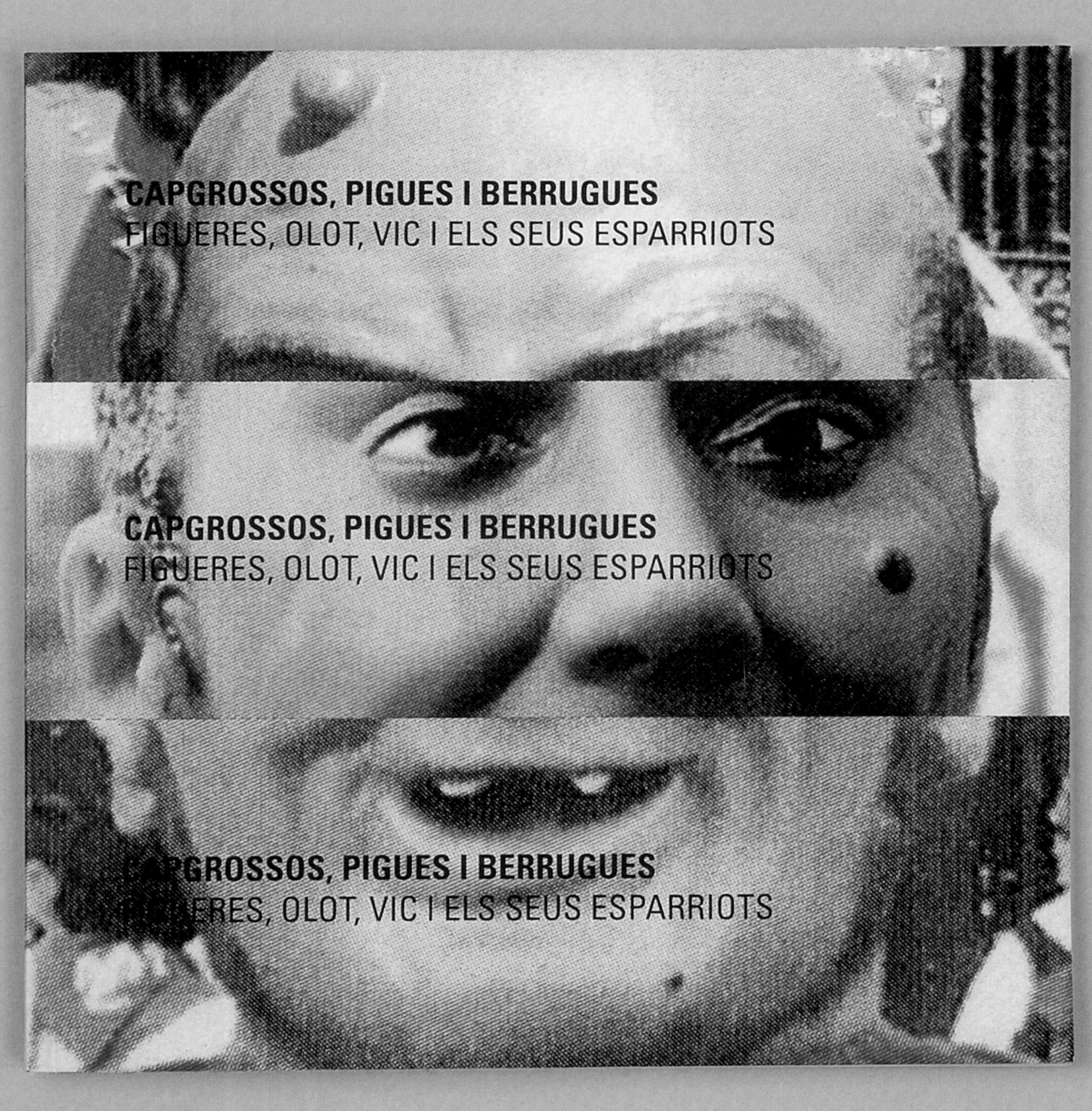
CAPGROSSOS, PIGUES I BERRUGUES
FIGUERES, OLOT, VIC I ELS SEUS ESPARRIOTS
CAPGROSSOS, PIGUES I BERRUGUES
FIGUERES, OLOT, VIC I ELS SEUS ESPARRIOTS
CAPGROSSOS, PIGUES I BERRUGUES
FIGUERES, OLOT, VIC I ELS SEUS ESPARRIOTS

119

ENSERIO

CLIENT | Museu dels Sants d'Olot

Catalogue edited for the itinerant exhibition *Capgrossos, pigues i berrugues. Figueres, Olot, Vic i els seus esparriots*, which brings together three traditional giant heads from three different cities with one characteristic in common: they come from the same mould. The catalogue is perforated and can be divided into three parts, an action which reinforces the concept of the exhibition.

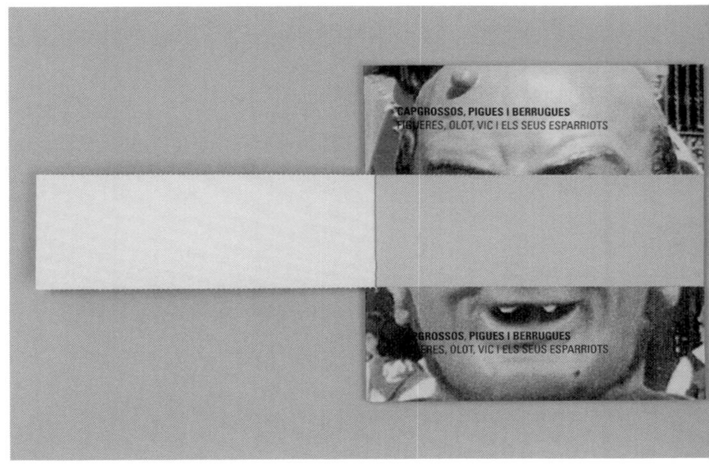

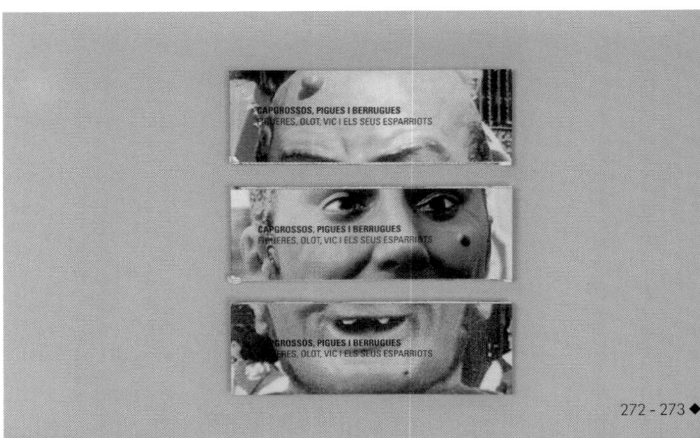

CLASE BCN

CLIENT | Arts Santa Mònica

The catalogue for the exhibition *Claret Serrahima de Cap a Peus* is a book object composed of four chapters, each one created in a graphically independent way that corresponds to the four main concepts of the show: head, stomach, hands and feet. The four books that form the catalogue are held together by a cover/poster que recreates the environment that surrounds Claret Serrahima and his studio, clase bcn, with images of his work spaces and graphic references. A selection of more than 100 works created from 1980 to now.

Title
Claret Serrahima
from head to feet
Subtitle
Graphic Design
Made in Barcelona
Description
Over 100 works by graphic designer
and cultural activist Claret Serrahima
and his clase bcn studio. The selection
is divided into four books that range
from the most conceptual and strategic
design to the freest and most irreverent
creations of a hyperactive talent.
Claret Serrahima from head to feet
CLARET SERRAHIMA FROM HEAD TO FEET
ACTAR
BON DIA
BRAVO
A TOUR WITH CARLES ABELL

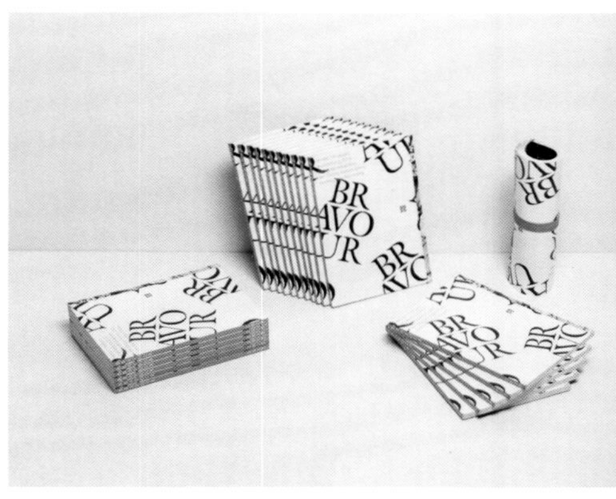

121

TEAM 505

CLIENT | GSO-University of Applied Sciences, Nuremberg (Germany)

We made the exhibition catalogue and poster for the graduates of the design faculty of the GSO-University in Nuremberg, Germany. Edition of 500 catalogues.

Bliss

Bliss

Freedom
"To imagine some incredible scenery and sensations which endure."
A feeling of freedom and lightness.

122

TOUS

CLIENT | Tous

The Bliss lookbook shows the principal pieces of the SS 2013 collection from the brand Tous, with the Bliss inspiration: galactic floral.

Bliss is a state of complete happiness and well-being to which we wanted give a modern component (galactic) and a floral touch, which is represented in the majority of the pieces from the collection.

The lookbook perfectly represents this inspirational concept in all of its pages, with the cover being the culmination: a perfect combination of tradition (natural thread) and modernity (plastic and flourescent) with a strong artisanal component (embroidery).

123

MIND DESIGN

CLIENT | Resonance FM

Catalogue, flyers, poster and press adverts for an exhibition on sound art in collaboration with Resonance FM. The exhibition took place in six different locations symbolised by the six speaker icons in the logo. The catalogue consists of a book and a CD held together by two rubber bands with punched slots on the side. In connection with the project a custom made font was designed which is inspired by volume scales on old stereo systems and expands when stretching the rubber bands.

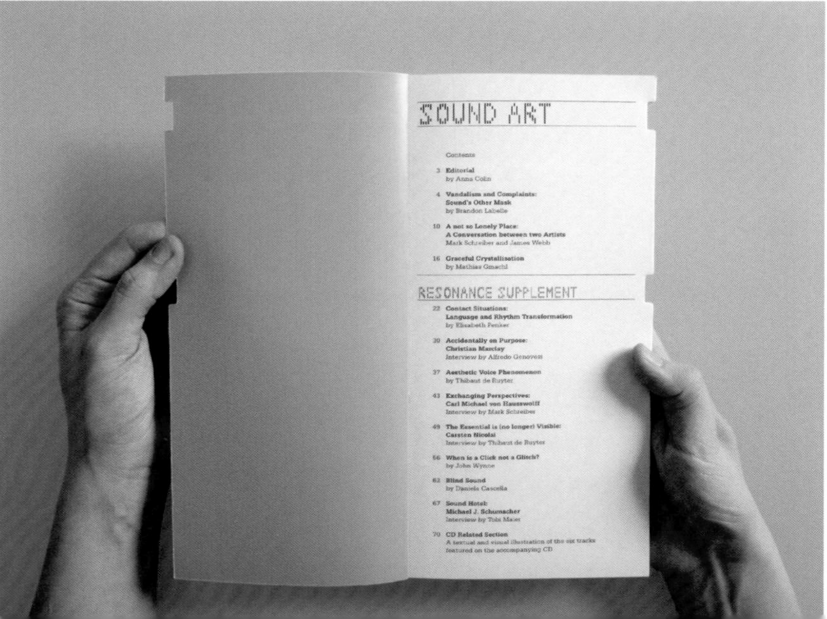

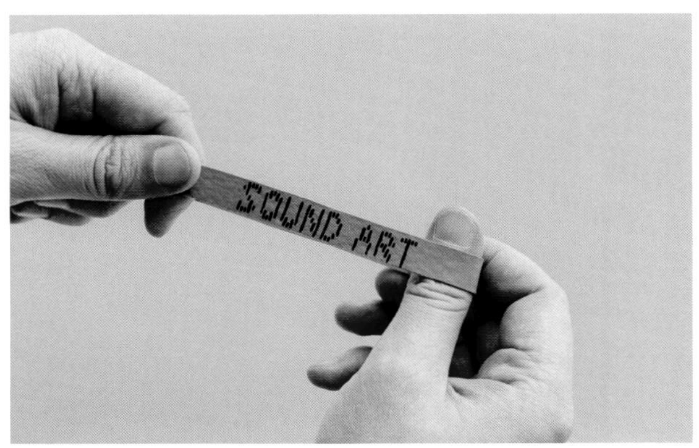
SOUND ART

RES
SUPPLEMENT

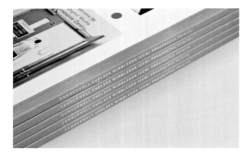

124

INVENTORY STUDIO

CLIENT | University of the Arts London (Camberwell, Chelsea and Wimbledon Colleges)

The Camberwell, Chelsea and Wimbledon Colleges of Art opened the CCW Progression Center in 2011, a center where the best post-graduate courses from each college are offered. They needed new printed material for its launch as a new institution, for which we used very vibrant colours that reflected the colours that each college is known for and a bold font, creating a striking visual identity. We designed the first catalogues and a set of invitations, banners and posters for the exhibitions at the end of the course of each of the institutions.

SHORT COURSES

2011 —2012

Short Courses in Art and Design
Camberwell, Chelsea & Wimbledon

2011–2012

E I

Quatre lletres: Eina!

N A

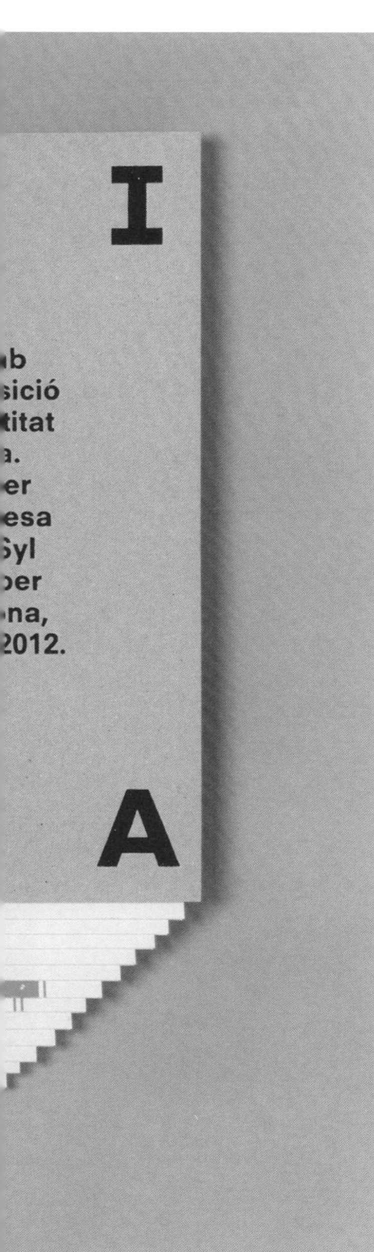

125

CLASE BCN

CLIENT | Eina

A proposal for solving how to produce a catalogue and an exhibition within a limited budget. It consisted of blocks of wood hanging from the wall, holding bound and printed sheets/posters so that visitors could see it as an exhibition and at the same time put together their own personalised catalogue which they took away rolled up in a specially made rubber band.

The "official" catalogue was made by using the same posters folded into 4 and bound together with hard covers stamped with the logo and with the book's title screen printed onto rubber bands.

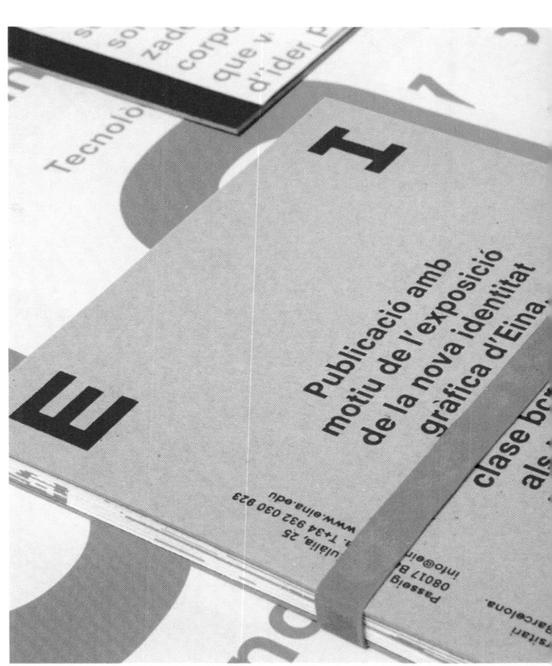

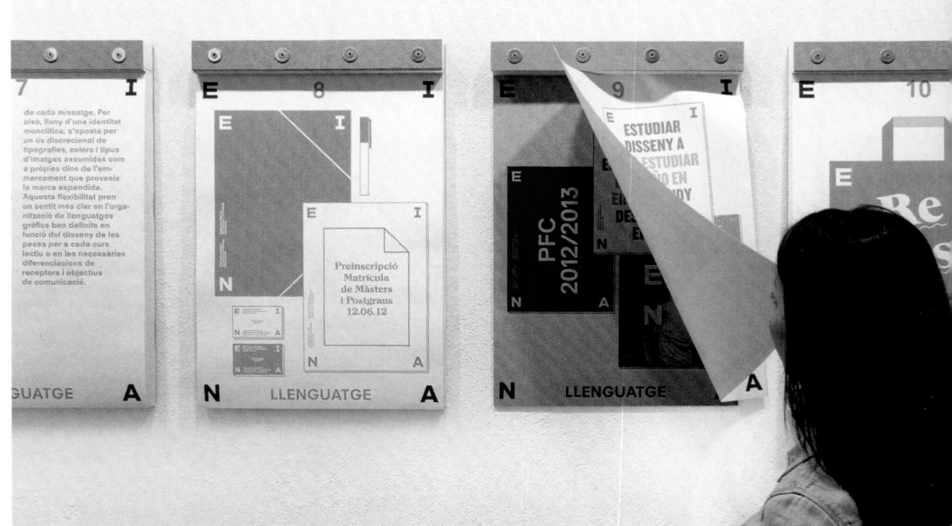

126

KOLEKTIV STUDIO

CLIENT | Regional Gallery of Fine Arts in Zlín

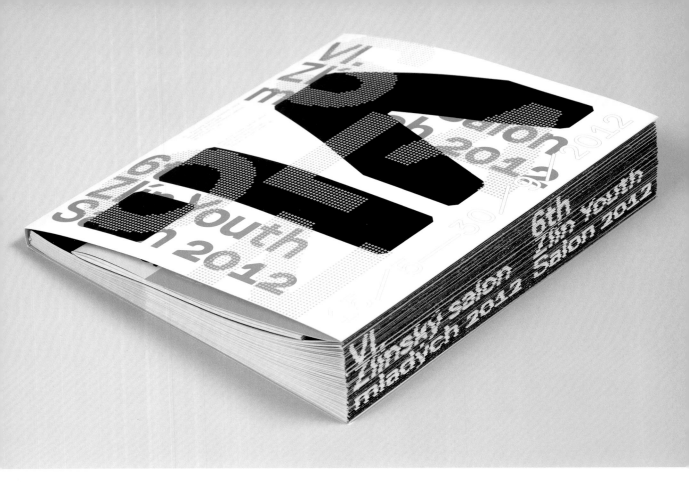

Catalogue for *VI. Zlín Youth Salon 2012. Zlín Youth Salon* is an exhibition of Czech and Slovak artists under 30 years of age which takes place regularly once every three years.

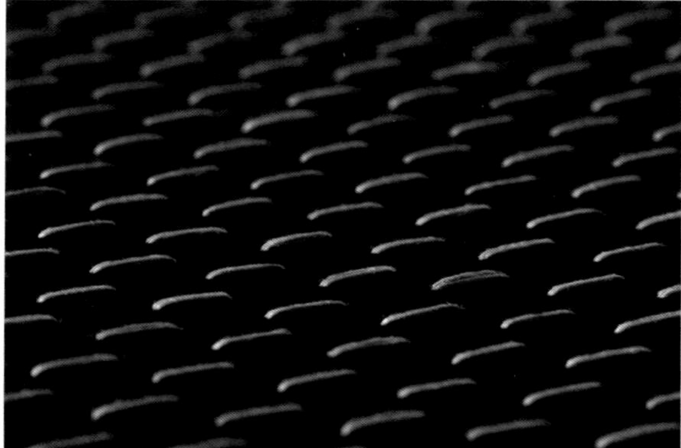

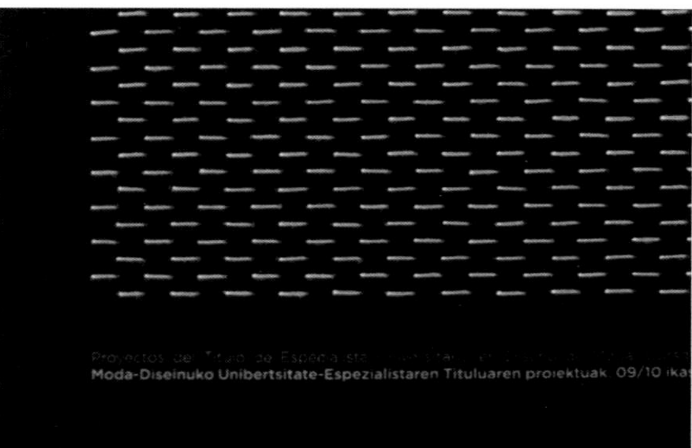

127

LA CAJA DE TIPOS

CLIENT | Universidad del País Vasco

Catalogue that brings together the final course projects from the students of the Title of University Specialist in Fashionable Design classes that are given at the Faculty of Fine Arts at the University of the Basque Country.

Due to the quantity of students and the disparity of styles in the projects, we preferred that the cover didn't show any of them to avoid favouring any project over the others.

For this reason, and as an act of allusion to the world of fashion, we decided to sew them with the colours of some of the various creations that are shown in the catalogue.

Janzkera'10
Moda-Diseinuko Unibertsitate-Espezialistaren Tituluaren proiektuak. 09/10 ikasturtea

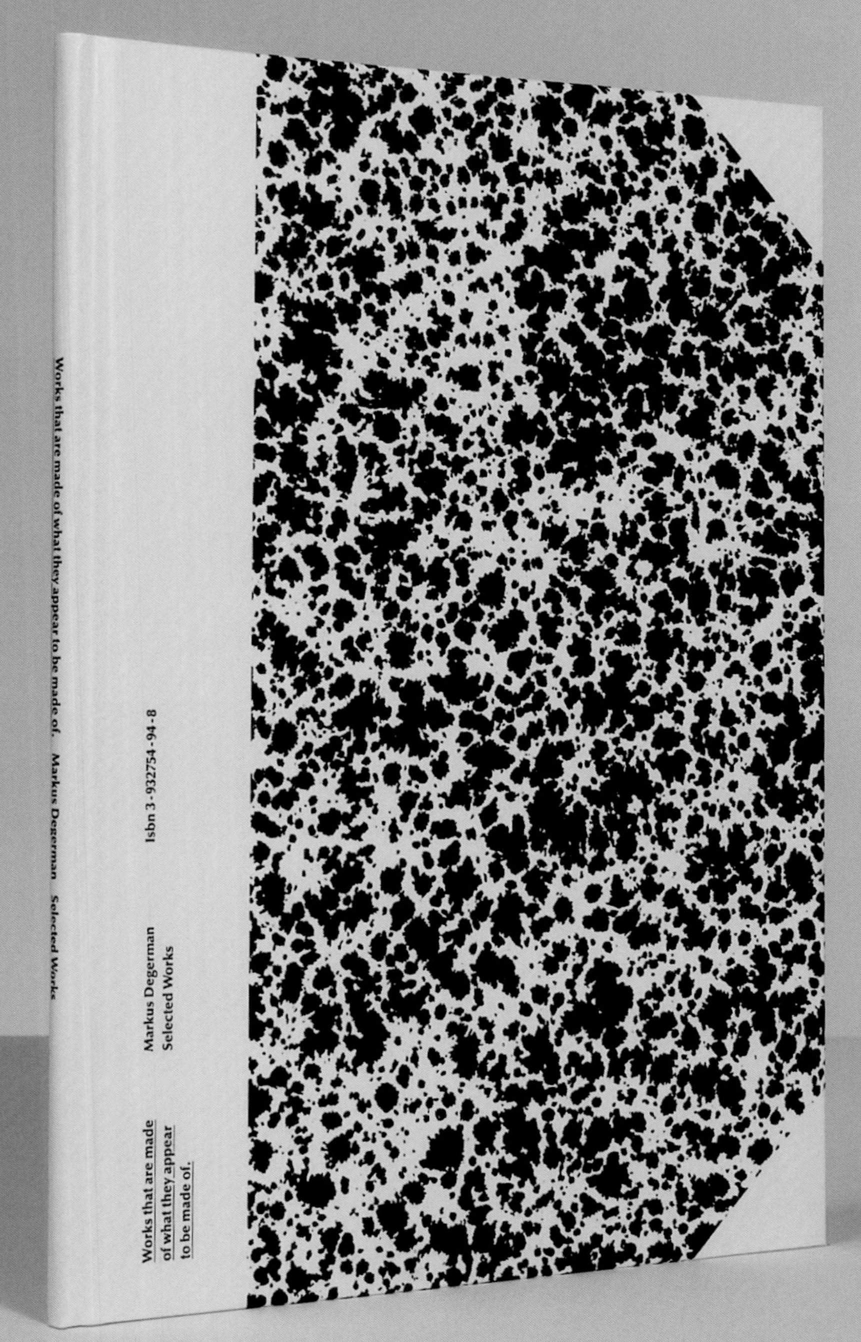
Works that are made of what they appear to be made of.
Markus Degerman
Selected Works
Works that are made
of what they appear
to be made of.
Markus Degerman
Selected Works
Isbn 3-932754-94-8

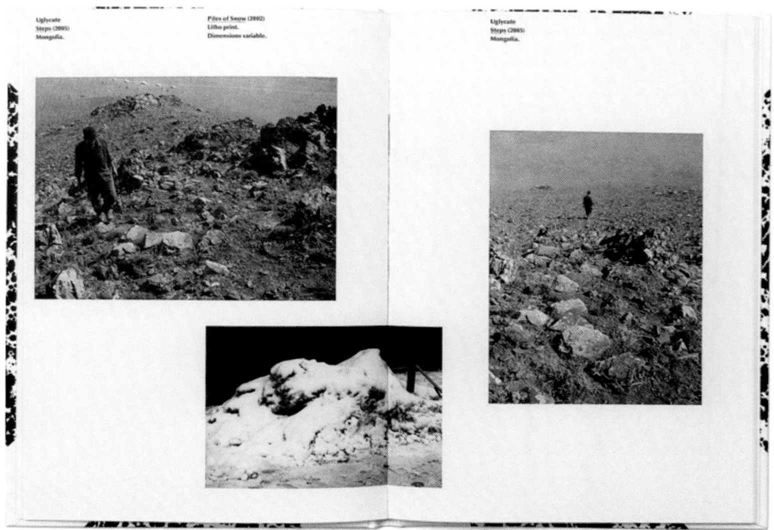

Uglycute
Steps (2005)
Mongolia.
Piles of Snow (2002)
Litho print.
Dimensions variable.
Uglycute
Steps (2005)
Mongolia.

128

RESEARCH AND DEVELOPMENT

CLIENT I Kunstlerhaus Bethanien

◆

Markus Degerman monograph *Works that are made of what they appear to be made of* was released on the occation of the exhibition *No matter how hard you work to bring things up, there is someone out there working just as hard, to bring them down* at Kunstlerhaus Bethanien, Berlin.

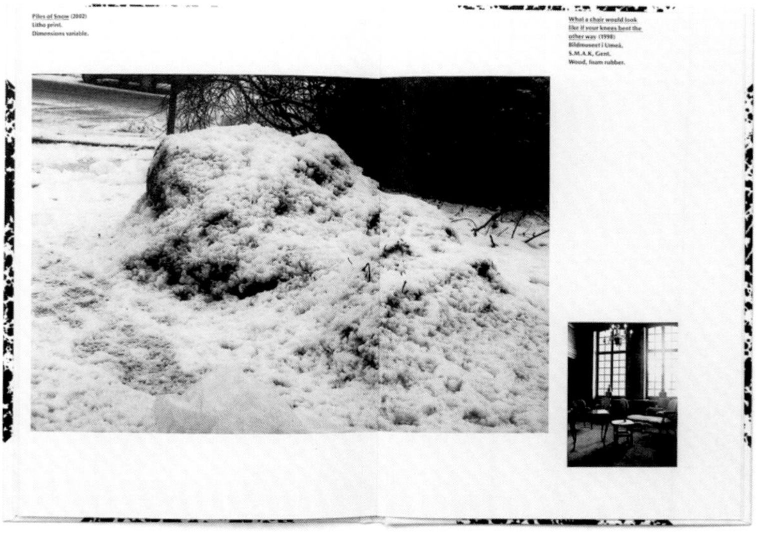

Piles of Snow (2002)
Litho print.
Dimensions variable.
What a chair would look
like if your knees bent the
other way (1998)
Bildmuseet i Umeå.
S.M.A.K, Gent.
Wood, foam rubber.

129

HOMEWORK

CLIENT | Danish Fashion Institute

Danish Fashion Institute is a network organisation to promote Danish fashion, created by and for the Danish fashion industry. Our purpose is to facilitate an extensive network that shall promote, market and drive Danish fashion forward. Danish Fashion Institute intends to position Danish fashion on the international fashion scene, to gain international recognition for our core design, quality, and aesthetic values. Danish Fashion Institute further wishes to contribute to innovation, an increase in export and to gain international interest in Danish Fashion.

130

KOLEKTIV STUDIO

CLIENT | Design Cabinet CZ in Prague

Catalogue for the Czech National Award for Student Design 2010. The catalogue has been consecrated by Mr. Petr Brzobohatý from Ecclesia Catholica sub utraque Bohemia.

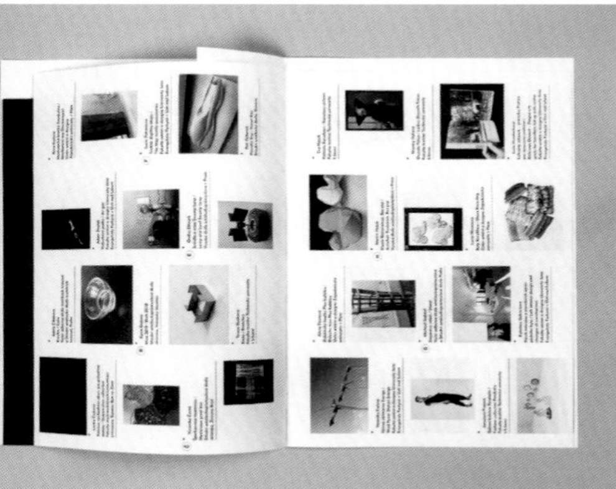

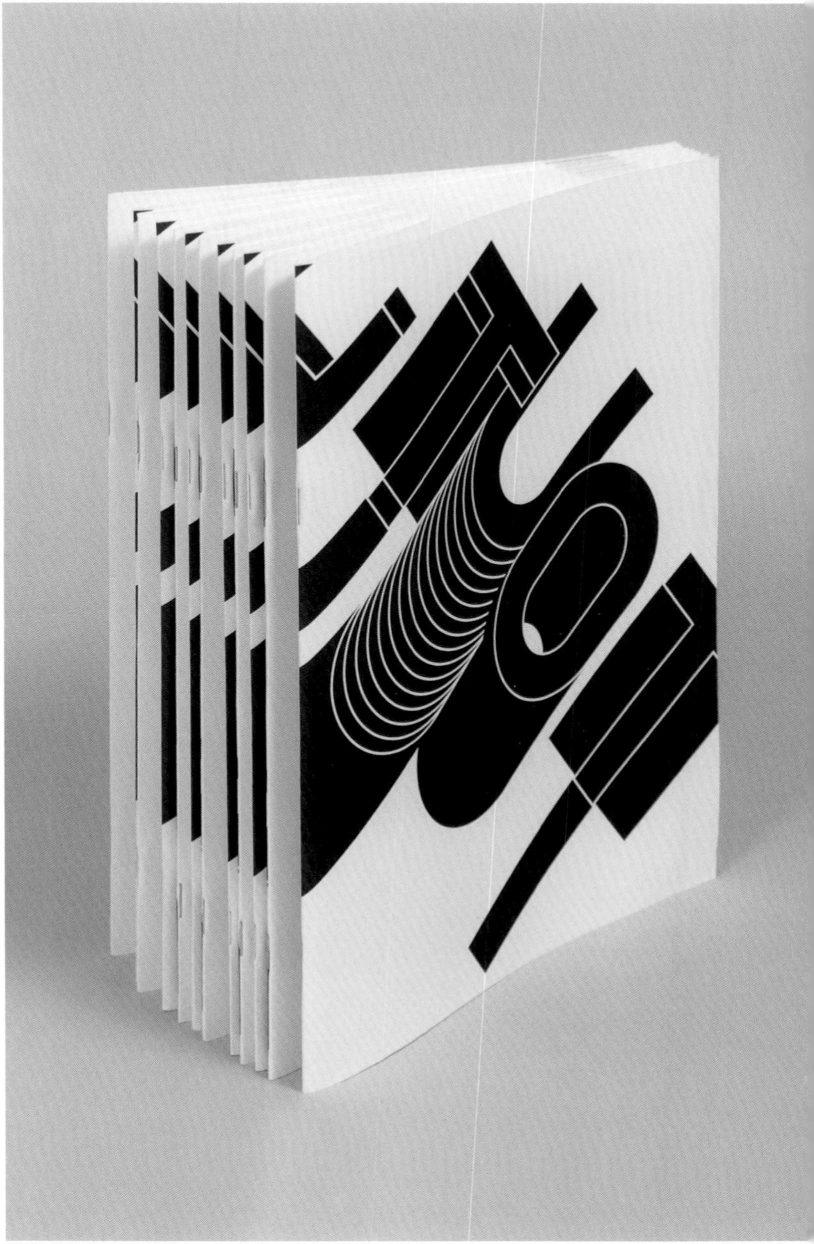

DÉSOLÉ

PLUS D'ESSENCE

L'INNOVATION ARCHITECTURALE
EN RÉPONSE À LA CRISE
PÉTROLIÈRE DE 1973

Giovanna Borasi
Mirko Zardini

Architectes, ingénieurs, artisans et penseurs ont consacré leur savoir-faire et leur inventivité à trouver des réponses aux problèmes que posait la crise pétrolière. Analyser leurs solutions, projets et expériences nous indique des voies à suivre par rapport aux enjeux actuels.

Centre Canadien d'Architecture
Corraini Edizioni

131

PITIS

CLIENT I Canadian Centre for Architecture & Corraini

Sorry out of gas:
This catalogue reports the contents of the exhibition *1973: Sorry Out of Gas*, curated by Mirko Zardini and Giovanna Borasi in 2008 at the Canadian Centre for Architecture in Montreal. The aim was to analyse the 1973 world energy crisis, the first meaningful event to demonstrate our inevitable dependence on energy resources and some of the possible solutions suggested by a few architects and engineers almost 35 years ago. Co-published by CCA and Corraini, the book has an insert illustrated by Harriet Russell, who is also the author of the handlettering on the cover. The book was published in two different editions, in English (*Sorry, Out of Gas*) and in French (*Désolé, Plus d'Essence*).

number ||||||||||

STUDIO

Client

Country

Descriptive text.

108

BILDI GRAFIKS

EADC - Generalitat de Catalunya
Spain

The catalogue of an exhibition of photography from 15 artists from different parts of the world. The typographic concept, given that the artists are from different places but found in the same space, starts with the informative panels found at airports; the challenge consisted in animating typography on support paper, and this was achieved by working with lenticular technology. The project won awards from Grand Laus, Red Dot Best of the Best, and was nominated by Deutschland Designpreis.

109

RAW COLOR

Onomatopee
The Netherlands

Onomatopee is a platform and publisher focusing on art projects reflecting on communication. They asked us to design a series of small books for the ongoing series "Nest", that spotlights emerging talent in art and design. Every publication represents one artist, who is also featured in an exhibition at the Onomatopee project space.
With this approach in mind we tried to translate this into a design, that creates a complete image as a series, but is at the same time able to highlight each artist's quality. Each booklet's cover is a folded oblique on the book block. It can be seen as a mismatching cover, in a way referring to the unadapted way of working of the featured artists. It exposes bits of the inside content of the book. This factor changes in colour and position during the series. The inside attempts a nice mixture of full colour and PMS printed pages. The work of the specific artist is enhanced by the text from different authors and a specific chosen lettertype.

110

FORMA & CO

Centre Cívic Can Felipa
Spain

Cultural agenda for the civic center Can Felipa.

111

RAW COLOR

Onomatopee
The Netherlands

The "Nest" series of 2011 is a follow up of the earlier series from 2010. Trying to keep a strong visual link with the earlier booklets we wanted to evolve their qualities into a new series. The booklets are based on a 8 page cover that is folded to the outside instead of to the inside. The outer flap is slanted cut, resulting in two colour surfaces and scattered typography. This factor changes in colour and position during the series.
The inside attempts a nice mixture of full colour and duotonal pages. The work of the specific artist is enhanced by the text from different authors and a specific chosen font type.
The ongoing series "Nest", spotlights emerging talent in art and design. Every publication represents one artist, who is also featured in an exhibition at the Onomatopee project space.

112

FIREBELLY DESIGN

TYPEFORCE 1 / The Annual Chicago Show of Emerging Typographic Allstars
United States of America

This small format book was created to honor and document the inaugural TYPEFORCE exhibition, which occurred in 2010. It features the 23 largely Chicago-based designers/artists who participated in the event, separated within the book by neon orange spreads containing everything from flaming pastry type to sign language. The cover is the result of an overhead photograph taken of a pyramid made of matching and increasingly larger layers of laser cut mat board messages.
Collaborators: Will Miller, Darren McPherson / Forward by Rick Valicenti / Design Assistance from Plural / Principle photography by Kyle LaMere / Sponsored by Unisource Paper, Graphic Arts Studio, Andrea Everman, and Domtar / Curated by Dawn Hancock of Firebelly Design & Ed Marszewski of Public Media Institute.

113

FIREBELLY DESIGN

TYPEFORCE 2 / The Annual Chicago Show of Emerging Typographic Allstars
United States of America

The second TYPEFORCE catalogue showcases the 25 artists involved in the TYPEFORCE 2 exhibition, which opened on February 11, 2011. This book requires a physical commitment from the reader, as a fresh copy can only be accessed by ripping a hand-affixed, perforated tear seal on the cover. Strips on the front cover serve as a table of contents, labeling the work of the artists inside, where colour guides the viewer: motivation in blue, experience in red, with substance denoted by full-color printing.
Collaborators: Will Miller, Darren McPherson, Nick Adam, Ohn Ho, Firebelly Design, and Co-Prosperity Sphere / Forward by Matthew Hoffman / Design Assistance from Plural / Sponsored by Firebelly Design, Graphic Arts Studio, Unisource Paper, Domtar, and I Shoot Rockstars / Curated by Dawn Hancock of Firebelly Design & Ed Marszewski of Public Media Institute.

114

TALLER DE COMUNICACIÓN GRÁFICA

Fundación Amparo and Credit Suisse
Mexico

Catalogue of the retrospective exhibition of the Mexican artist Betsabeé Romero at the Museo Amparo in the city of Puebla, Mexico. The show was also in Monterrey, Guadalajara, Mexico City and New York.
Interiors printed with 4 x 0 colours on 75g paper, with Japanese binding. Lining in 3mm cardboard bounded in boards with black flocking. The front and back of the lining are completely different and the flocking makes reference to a tire track intervened by the artist. Handsewn with dyed cotton thread.

115

NATIONAL FOREST DESIGN

Sixpack France
United States of America

The 160-page *Peyote Poem* catalogue National Forest created for Sixpack France featured location photography of the capsule collection we designed as well as flats of the entire line. Printed entirely on aged recycled paper, the shamanist book of sorts was meant to feel like an artifact lost and later found on a dusty shelf somewhere in the high desert.

116

DRAWSWORDS

KABK (Royal Academy of Art, The Hague)
The Netherlands

465-page catalogue containing all graduation projects of the students of the Royal Academy of Art in 2008-2009.
Instead of focusing on just the work the students produced during their graduation, we asked students about their future plans. These plans became the main design element - next to the images of their work - in the book.
We also asked the students to tag their work with predefined and self-defined keywords, which were then presented next to their work and also as clear, informative lists explaining how many times students from a certain course selected a specific tag or how many times a tag was selected in total amongst the 200 graduates. This information gave more insight in how students of specific courses think of their own work.
Designers: Mattijs de Wit, Rob van den Nieuwenhuizen.

117

NAKANO DESIGN OFFICE

Meguro Museum of Art, Tokyo
Japan

The retrospective exhibition of Kiyoo Kawamura, an artist from the Meiji period. For the cover, we used a combination of vermillion red and gold leaf referring to the bookbinding which Kawamura did by himself. For the body, we laid it out carefully so people can sense his delineations which are so sensitive but energetic at the same time.
Art Director and Designer: Takeo Nakano / Edit: Meguro Museum of Art, Tokyo.

118

TALLER DE COMUNICACIÓN GRÁFICA

Museo Nacional de Arte, Instituto Nacional de Bellas Artes, Fundación/colección Jumex
Mexico

Catalogue for the exhibition *The Practice of Everyday Life* at the National Art Museum (Munal) in Mexico City. The exhibition is a dialogue between Munal's collection and the contemporary art collection from the Jumex Foundation.
Interiors printed on 4 x 4 colours on coated 150g paper with the lining padded with 3mm cardboard with 2mm foam, printed with 5 x 0 colours and laminated with shine. Square folding. The front and back images refer to a piece from each one of the collections.

119

ENSERIO

Museu dels Sants d'Olot
Spain

Catalogue edited for the itinerant exhibition *Capgrossos, piques i berrugues. Figueres, Olot, Vic i els seus esparriots*, which brings together three traditional giant heads from three different cities with one characteristic in common: they come from the same mould. The catalogue is perforated and can be divided into three parts, an action which reinforces the concept of the exhibition.

120

CLASE BCN

Arts Santa Mònica

Spain

The catalogue for the exhibition *Claret Serrahima de Cap a Peus* is a book object composed of four chapters, each one created in a graphically independent way that corresponds to the four main concepts of the show: head, stomach, hands and feet. The four books that form the catalogue are held together by a cover/poster que recreates the environment that surrounds Claret Serrahima and his studio, clase bcn, with images of his work spaces and graphic references. A selection of more than 100 works created from 1980 to now.

121

TEAM 505

GSO-University of Applied Sciences, Nuremberg (Germany)

Germany

We made the exhibition catalogue and poster for the graduates of the design faculty of the GSO-University in Nuremberg, Germany. Edition of 500 catalogues.

122

TOUS

Tous

Spain

The Bliss lookbook shows the principal pieces of the SS 2013 collection from the brand Tous, with the Bliss inspiration: galactic floral.
Bliss is a state of complete happiness and well-being to which we wanted give a modern component (galactic) and a floral touch, which is represented in the majority of the pieces from the collection.
The lookbook perfectly represents this inspirational concept in all of its pages, with the cover being the culmination: a perfect combination of tradition (natural thread) and modernity (plastic and flourescent) with a strong artisanal component (embroidery).

123

MIND DESIGN

Resonance FM

United Kingdom

Catalogue, flyers, poster and press adverts for an exhibition on sound art in collaboration with Resonance FM. The exhibition took place in six different locations symbolised by the six speaker icons in the logo. The catalogue consists of a book and a CD held together by two rubber bands with punched slots on the side. In connection with the project a custom made font was designed which is inspired by volume scales on old stereo systems and expands when stretching the rubber bands.
Creative Director: Holger Jacobs / Designer: Cornelia Müller.

124

INVENTORY STUDIO

University of the Arts London (Camberwell, Chelsea and Wimbledon Colleges)

United Kingdom

The Camberwell, Chelsea and Wimbledon Colleges of Art opened the CCW Progression Center in 2011, a center where the best post-graduate courses from each college are offered. They needed new printed material for its launch as a new institution, for which we used very vibrant colours that reflected the colours that each college is known for and a bold font, creating a striking visual identity. We designed the first catalogues and a set of invitations, banners and posters for the exhibitions at the end of the course of each of the institutions.
Art Director: Inventory Studio / Designer: Alberto Hernández.

125

CLASE BCN

Eina

Spain

A proposal for solving how to produce a catalogue and an exhibition within a limited budget. It consisted of blocks of wood hanging from the wall, holding bound and printed sheets/posters so that visitors could see it as an exhibition and at the same time put together their own personalised catalogue which they took away rolled up in a specially made rubber band. The "official" catalogue was made by using the same posters folded into 4 and bound together with hard covers stamped with the logo and with the book's title screen printed onto rubber bands.

126

KOLEKTIV STUDIO

Regional Gallery of Fine Arts in Zlín

Czech Republic

Catalogue for *VI. Zlín Youth Salon 2012. Zlín Youth Salon* is an exhibition of Czech and Slovak artists under 30 years of age which takes place regularly once every three years.
Designers: Michal Krul, Lukáš Kijonka.

127

LA CAJA DE TIPOS

Universidad del País Vasco

Spain

Catalogue that brings together the final course projects from the students of the Title of University Specialist in Fashionable Design classes that are given at the Faculty of Fine Arts at the University of the Basque Country. Due to the quantity of students and the disparity of styles in the projects, we preferred that the cover didn't show any of them to avoid favouring any project over the others.
For this reason, and as an act of allusion to the world of fashion, we decided to sew them with the colours of some of the various creations that are shown in the catalogue.

128

RESEARCH AND DEVELOPMENT

Kunstlerhaus Bethanien

Sweden

Markus Degerman monograph *Works that are made of what they appear to be made of* was released on the occation of the exhibition *No matter how hard you work to bring things up, there is someone out there working just as hard, to bring them down* at Kunstlerhaus Bethanien, Berlin.

129

HOMEWORK

Danish Fashion Institute

Denmark

Danish Fashion Institute is a network organisation to promote Danish fashion, created by and for the Danish fashion industry. Our purpose is to facilitate an extensive network that shall promote, market and drive Danish fashion forward. Danish Fashion Institute intends to position Danish fashion on the international fashion scene, to gain international recognition for our core design, quality, and aesthetic values. Danish Fashion Institute further wishes to contribute to innovation, an increase in export and to gain international interest in Danish Fashion.

130

KOLEKTIV STUDIO

Design Cabinet CZ in Prague

Czech Republic

Catalogue for the Czech National Award for Student Design 2010. The catalogue has been consecrated by Mr. Petr Brzobohatý from Ecclesia Catholica sub utraque Bohemia.
Designer: Lukáš Kijonka.

131

PITIS

Canadian Centre for Architecture & Corraini

Italy

Sorry out of gas:
This catalogue reports the contents of the exhibition *1973: Sorry Out of Gas*, curated by Mirko Zardini and Giovanna Borasi in 2008 at the Canadian Centre for Architecture in Montreal. The aim was to analyse the 1973 world energy crisis, the first meaningful event to demonstrate our inevitable dependence on energy resources and some of the possible solutions suggested by a few architects and engineers almost 35 years ago. Co-published by CCA and Corraini, the book has an insert illustrated by Harriet Russell, who is also the author of the handlettering on the cover. The book was published in two different editions, in English (*Sorry, Out of Gas*) and in French (*Désolé, Plus d'Essence*).
Designer: Massimo Pitis.

FINAL DIRECTORY

STUDIO
number
studio website

A BEAUTIFUL DESIGN
022
www.abeautifuldesign.com.sg

ADRIANO ATTUS
048 / 074
www.adriano.attus.it

ALBERTO HERNÁNDEZ
014 / 124
www.hereigo.co.uk

ARIS ZENONE STUDIO
013
www.ariszenone.ch

BARBARA HENNEQUIN
089 / 091 / 094
www.barbarahennequin.nl

BELIEVE IN®
016 / 072 / 087
www.believein.co.uk

BILDI GRAFIKS
032 / 108
www.bildi.net

BRUKETA&ZINIC OM
009
www.bruketa-zinic.com

CLASE BCN
120 / 125
www.clasebcn.com

CODESIGN
006
www.codesign.in

CORALIE BICKFORD-SMITH
005 / 017
www.cb-smith.com

DAVIDELFIN
053
www.davidelfin.com

DRAWSWORDS
089 / 091 094 / 116
www.drawswords.com

DÚCTIL
008
www.ductilct.com

EDGAR BAK
027
www.edgarbak.info

ENSERIO
081 / 088 / 119
www.enserio.ws

ERIK OTSEA
035
www.elysianlandscapes.com

EVELIN KASIKOV
023
www.evelinkasikov.com

FABIEN BARON
054
www.baron-baron.com

FANAKALO
100
www.fanakalo.co.za

FEED
070
www.studiofeed.ca

MAI-BRITT AMSLER
082 / 101
www.maibrittamsler.dk

MARTA VELUDO
090
www.martaveludo.com

MATT DORFMAN
030 / 033
www.metalmother.com

MAX-O-MATIC
024 / 084 / 095
097 / 102
www.maxomatic.net

MIND DESIGN
123
www.minddesign.co.uk

NAKANO DESIGN OFFICE
020 / 036 / 117
www.nakano-design.com

NATIONAL FOREST DESIGN
115
www.nationalforest.com

NICOLA YEOMAN
065
www.nicolayeoman.com

NR2154
019 / 077 / 078
www.nr2154.com

PABLO ABAD
066
www.pabloabad.com

PAPERLUX
045 / 059
www.paperlux.com

PIERRE VANNI
047
www.pierrevanni.tumblr.com

PITIS
028 / 131
www.pitis.eu

PONTO
011 / 012
www.ponto.ws

POST PROJECTS
098
www.post-projects.com

RAW COLOR
001 / 109 / 111
www.rawcolor.nl

RESEARCH AND DEVELOPMENT
128
www.researchanddevelopment.se

RICARDO CAVOLO
076
www.ricardocavolo.com

RICARDO LEITE
090
www.rl85.com

ROC CANALS
037
www.photoroc.com

RODRIGO SÁNCHEZ
040 / 041 / 042
049 / 057 / 058
www.facebook.com/ColeccionMetropoli